236 Linden Avenue
Bellwood, Illinois

TRUE TALES OF THE GREAT LAKES

TRUE TALES OF
THE GREAT LAKES

By DWIGHT BOYER

~~~~~~

Illustrated with photographs and maps

DODD, MEAD & COMPANY

NEW YORK

ISBN 0-396-06372-1
Library of Congress Catalog Card Number: 79-158347

Printed in the United States of America
by The Cornwall Press, Inc., Cornwall, N. Y.

To my mother, Sue Boyer,
this book is affectionately dedicated

Acknowledgments

In retrospect one can only conclude, after reviewing their important and unique contributions, that a work of depth and understanding would be well-nigh impossible without the very special help and interest of grand people like Beryl H. Scott; Ritchie and Daphne With; Alex Walton; Frank A. Myers; Robert J. MacDonald; Milton J. Brown; Walter and Teddy Remick; Janet Coe Sanborn of the Cleveland Public Library and editor of *Inland Seas,* the esteemed quarterly of the Great Lakes Historical Society; and a dedicated trio from Port Dover, Ontario—Peggy Gamble Scruton, Verna Gamble and that delightful old patriarch of the family, George Gamble.

Nor would progress be easy without willing assistance from those of special knowledge such as Ernest H. Rankin, retired Executive Director of the Marquette County Historical Society; John A. Chisholm of the Muskegon *Chronicle;* the Reverend Edward J. Dowling, S.J.; Leslie D. Weston; the Reverend Alexander C. Meakin; James Marshall; Captain John Kelsner; Ross Mortimer and Frank Fauver of the Great Lakes Towing Company; William D. Carle III; the

Chicago Historical Society; Henry Steinbrenner; George M. Steinbrenner; Captain William M. Ward and Captain H. C. Inches, master mariner and recently retired curator of the Great Lakes Historical Society's marine museum, in Vermilion, Ohio.

Significant contributions, adding to the scope of the Great Lakes scene, past and present, also came from Robert Hartog; W. A. W. Catinus of Canada's Department of Transport; Dr. Julius F. Wolff, Jr.; Captain Junis Macksey; Captain Ernest Ridd; E. J. "Shine" Sundstrom of the *Sault Evening News;* W. H. Cranston; T. James Tully; Virginia Hawley of the Western Reserve Historical Society; John Grecol; Captain Ward White; Everett Mathews; Jack Brosco; the late Dr. John A. Bannister; Carolyn K. Blasius; Janice House Gerred; Mrs. L. J. Skuderin; Al McGinty of the United States Coast Guard; Ardath Danford of the Way Public Library, Perrysburg, Ohio; Captain Henry F. Wiersch; Elmer and Fred Yaxley; Elmer Misner; Robert A. Franklin; Bruce Pearce; Bill Lamb, Bill Ansley and Clayton Scofield, faithful keepers of Long Point Light; Ruth Knutsen, former chief of the *Plain Dealer* library, along with her successor, Grace Parch and her capable assistant, JoAnn Pallant.

Help, too, and greatly appreciated, came from Miss Flora Aker and the helpful staff of the Eva Brook Donly Museum, in Simcoe, Ontario; the Marine Historical Society of Detroit; Mrs. William H. Slack of the Lake County (Ohio) Historical Society; Rowland Macha of the Willoughby (Ohio) Public Library; Marion "Mike" Barber; Neil B. Myers; Bernice C. Sprenger, chief, Burton Historical Collection, Detroit Public Library; Ross Plaisted; W. H. Nicholson, librarian at the *Telegram,* Toronto, Ontario; Stephen A. Blossom, marine editor of the *Plain Dealer;* William H. Diehl; Stoddard White of the *Detroit News;* Fred S. Slocombe, chief, Nautical and Pilotage Division of Canada's Department of

Transport; William E. Kennedy, the United States Weather Bureau's port meteorological officer in Cleveland; Walter Vizneau; Captain Arthur W. Dana; Chan Harris of the Door County (Wisconsin) *Advocate;* naval architect Wilford G. Bartenfeld; James Collins; Tom Sords; Don Larick; Mrs. Lydia W. Searl; Fred Martin; John Greenwood; Cletus Schneider; Captain Ed K. Male; Captain Alfred C. Drouillard, Oliver T. Burnham and John A. Packard of the Lake Carriers' Association; the late Carroll Mitchell, long-time curator of the Fairport Harbor Historical Society's marine museum; and Bob Herrick and his old friend from the Bruce Peninsula, Archie Simpson.

And a very special tribute goes to my wife, Virginia, for her long hours spent in preparing the manuscript and to Vince Matteucci and Nicholas Dankovich, artist with the *Plain Dealer's Sunday Magazine,* for their unique and personal contributions of maps, sketches and drawings which skillfully augment the printed word.

Contents

⚓

The Enigma of "Tatey Bug" Burke

Of all Lake Superior's perplexing tales, none is more puzzling than the needless sinking of the *Arlington* and the bizarre behavior of her master, Frederick John "Tatey Bug" Burke. Why, as the leading character in a strange, early morning drama on the gale-lashed lake, he waved a poignant good-by from the rail of his foundering ship and chose to go down with her, rather than join his crew in the lifeboat, is as debatable today as it was then. His inexplicable decision is something only the captain could explain, and he, like the *Arlington,* lies over a hundred fathoms down, about ten miles southeast of Superior Shoal.

The nickname itself is worthy of attention and was the result, he once confided to a fellow shipmaster, of a frustrating speech impediment he had endured as a child, when his family called him "Teddy." By his own admission he had been unable to clearly pronounce his name. However he tried, and it must have been a traumatic experience, Teddy Burke always sounded like "Tatey Bug" to his listeners. While he eventually outgrew the speech impediment, he never lost the nickname. Tatey Bug it was, from one end of the lakes to the other, although its use seemed to cause him no embarrassment whatsoever.

Unlike the speech difficulty which left him with no more than a vestige of a stutter when he tried to talk too fast, he retained other very human characteristics which were peculiarly his through all of his fifty-two years. Big, florid and rough-talking, he was also erratic, stubborn, impulsive, moody and often intemperate. On the other hand he was extremely generous, fiercely loyal, and, because he did not overburden himself with details of discipline, always ran a "happy ship." Known the length of the lakes as a "heavy weather" sailor, as were many of the older generations of skippers, he was inclined to keep going when more cautious shipmasters were hauling for shelter. In spite of these strengths and frailties, shared by many of this earth's inhabitants, Tatey Bug Burke was, in a sincere tribute paid him by one of his early shipmates, "a hell of a sailor."

"He was an instinctive navigator," recalls Captain Ward White, who served under Burke as wheelsman, second mate and first mate. "In a heavy fog and when we weren't sure just where we were, he'd stick his head out of a pilothouse window, sniff a couple of times and then say, 'Ward, there's land nearby, drop the hook.' And, by golly, when it cleared, there it was. He raged, cussed and swore and would fire you at the drop of a hat. The funny thing was that he never meant it and never expected you to take him seriously. And he'd give you the shirt off his back."

This was the man, big, bluff and often irascible, who, at eight minutes after noon on April 30, 1940, maneuvered the *Arlington* from the Horn Elevator dock at Port Arthur, Ontario, with no more than the usual fuss and cussing as the lines were cast off and retrieved by the deckhands. At almost the same time another vessel, the 386-foot *Collingwood*, of Canada Steamship Lines, was taking her leave from another nearby grain elevator. The *Collingwood* was bound for Midland, Ontario, on Georgian Bay, the *Arlington*'s home port and Captain Burke's home town. The *Arlington*'s destination was the Great Lakes Elevator in Owen Sound, another Georgian Bay port. There was nothing unusual about either departure, both vessels being employed in the grain trade from the Canadian lakehead to a variety of ports where the good grain of Manitoba, Alberta and Saskatchewan was in demand by millers and processors. The bill of lading on Captain Burke's desk indicated that the *Arlington*'s cargo consisted of 51,466 bushels of No. 2 northern Manitoba hard wheat in hold No. 1, and 46,312 bushels of No. 1 northern hard wheat in hold No. 2. Altogether it gave her a draft of seventeen feet, two inches forward and seventeen feet, five inches aft. Chief engineer Fred Gilbert had also noted on his ledger that approximately 123 tons of coal remained in the ship's bunkers.

The year 1940 was the beginning of a new era in the career of Captain Burke. A sailor since he was fifteen, he devoted over a quarter century to learning his difficult trade. He had started out on the logging tugs of James Playfair's vastly diversified fleet of vessels, towing pulpwood rafts from lonely bays along Georgian Bay to mill towns. He had progressed rapidly, getting the most from his commands and learning to respect the deadly and often uncharted reefs and ledges of the area, finally being appointed master of a tug. Later he was promoted to the big bulk carriers, commanding, over the years, the *Glenlivet*, *Glenorchy* and *Gleniffer*. When part of the Playfair vessel properties was absorbed into the Canada Steamship Lines, he became skipper of the *James B. Eads* and later the *Ralph Budd*.

In the intervening years his two brothers, Captain Dave Burke and Captain Edward Burke, had founded their own marine business, the Burke Towing and Salvage Company.

It was a modest fleet for some time, consisting of two barges, *Allan No. 2* and *Salvus,* and a tug, the *Fanny Arnold.* The barges were mostly employed in hauling pulpwood. But in 1936 the brothers had purchased the *Arlington* to broaden their base of activities. She could carry grain in the spring and fall, the traditional "peak" seasons for the trade, shifting to pulpwood in the slack, midsummer season. They had suggested several times that brother Tatey Bug join them as skipper of the *Arlington,* but he, with over twenty-five years of service with the Playfair fleet, had been reluctant to cut the ties. Finally, however, during the winter of 1939-1940 he had consented. After the usual spring inspections by the shipping officials and underwriters he had taken the *Arlington* to Port Arthur for grain, returning in good time and with the ship's routine organized to his taste.

As was customary, jobs not being plentiful in the provinces, a ship's captain usually gave employment preference to his home-town people. Captain Burke was no exception. Many of the crew were from Midland and the immediate area. Two on the *Arlington* had never sailed before, and they were aboard because of the captain's enthusiasm for hockey. Francis Swales, only seventeen, was a star player on the Midland team, and Ted Brodeur was its nineteen-year-old goalie. During the winter Captain Burke had attended every home game and got to know them well. Since the ending of the hockey season coincided with the opening of the shipping season, he had offered them jobs as deck hands, the only positions open for beginners. Both had quickly accepted. Also from Midland were first mate Junis A. Macksey; wheelsmen Charles Paradis and Elmer Callum; chief engineer Gilbert; second engineer Lester Woods; oilers Arthur Noland and Jack Dempsey; and firemen Lester Hall and Dan Quesnelle. Second mate Arthur Ferris and watchman George Braithwaite were from nearby Penetanguishene. First cook Fred

Martel and second cook Maurice Ferry were also from the Georgian Bay area. The only exception was William Lee of Toronto, who doubled as watchman and wireless operator. This, then, was the crew commanded by Frederick John "Tatey Bug" Burke.

Born the *F. P. Jones* on the ways of the Detroit Ship Building Company in 1913 as hull No. 192, the vessel that was eventually to become the *Arlington* was sold in 1919. The new owners renamed her *Glencadam,* a name she carried well until 1925 when the Mathews Steamship Company bought her and renamed her *Arlington.* In 1936, when the Burke brothers bought her, it was decided to retain the same name. A typical canaller, she was 244 feet long and 43 feet of beam, just the right dimensions to negotiate the St. Lawrence River canals and trade into the smaller Georgian Bay ports. Gross tonnage was 1870, net tonnage 1117. She was twenty-seven years old in the spring of 1940, still a young lady by fresh-water standards, when the man who was to put his mark on her forever stomped aboard, succeeding Captain Roderick Graham.

Under cold but normal weather conditions the *Collingwood* and *Arlington,* having backed from their Port Arthur elevators at almost the same time, steamed past Fort William and the length of Thunder Bay before coming abreast of Thunder Cape Light and its bleak background, the forbidding silhouette of the Sleeping Giant, wreathed for the moment in errant snow flurries. By the time Trowbridge Island Light was abeam on the port side, the *Collingwood,* having somewhat more speed than the *Arlington's* ten and two-tenths miles per hour pace when loaded, forged ahead. Shortly thereafter exceedingly hazy visibility was encountered. The *Collingwood's* skipper, Captain Thomas J. Carson, a prudent man, checked his vessel down to let the *Arlington* take the lead. His reasoning was eminently sound—the little *Arling-*

ton had a direction finder. Although her owners were among the giants in the Canadian shipping industry with sixty-eight assorted bulk carriers, self-unloaders, package freighters and passenger vessels, they had not seen fit to lavish such luxury on the *Collingwood*. Since the next best thing to having a direction finder is to stay behind a vessel that does have one, Captain Carson was content to take station behind and a mile to port of the *Arlington*.

First mate Junis Macksey, a sailor for thirty-two years and a master in his own right, was sailing for the first time under Captain Burke. Ever mindful of the captain's reputation for an erratic disposition, he was, as the saying goes, playing his cards close to his vest. On watch when the *Arlington* left the shelter of Thunder Bay, Macksey found sea conditions somewhat contrary to the routine weather report received at the elevator—"fresh northeast wind with light snow and a moderate sea." There was, as a matter of fact, considerable more sea running on the open lake than the report had indicated. Accordingly, consistent with the *Arlington*'s low freeboard of three and one-half feet when loaded, he laid a course along the north shore. Here, in the lee of the bluff and rugged shoreline, vessel traffic would be protected from strong north or northeast winds. Traditionally the north shore course would be a curving route carrying the *Arlington* between the north shore and the Slate Islands before hauling to starboard for Otter Island Light. Still in the protected lee of the mainland, the *Arlington* could then steam all the way to Whitefish Bay in relatively calm waters. It was a longer route, of course, but an infinitely wiser one in doubtful weather.

Macksey had already given the wheelsman the course to the first reference point, Porphyry Point Light, when Captain Burke strode into the pilothouse and abruptly countermanded the order, gruffly telling the wheelsman to steer the direct course for Whitefish Point.

Somewhat miffed, Macksey commented: "You just think you're going to Whitefish."

At 5:28 P.M. that afternoon, as was noted routinely in the log, the *Arlington* was abreast of Passage Island Light, the common reference point for both upbound and downbound courses to and from the Canadian lakehead. The *Collingwood* was exactly ten minutes behind her.

At eight o'clock second mate Arthur Ferris checked the *Arlington's* hatches, finding all well in spite of seas that were boarding her consistently. He checked again at ten o'clock and drew the same conclusion, reporting on both occasions to Captain Burke, who had remained in his cabin since countermanding mate Macksey's north shore course. Both reports had brought only a gruff acknowledgment, nothing more.

Shortly after ten o'clock the wind approached gale proportions, building some truly significant seas. They were of such stature that even Captain Carson of the *Collingwood,* although his vessel had twelve feet of freeboard, eased up the speed of his vessel. At 12:30 A.M. he checked down to three-quarters speed, noting that the *Arlington* had also checked down.

Incongruously, at 11:30 P.M., one hour and a half after the weather had suddenly worsened, wireless operator William Lee had taken the routine weather report and had put a copy on Captain Burke's desk—a report that again read:

Lake Superior . . . fresh north-east to north winds; mostly cloudy with light snow falls or flurries; Thursday, fair and cool.

But whatever the report, it is doubtful if it would have altered Captain Burke's decision to avoid the sheltered north shore course. There is some question if, indeed, he would have taken time to read it. For Tatey Bug Burke was of the old school of skippers who had implicit faith in their own instinctive "weather sense" and who were distrustful of wireless and the messages it bore them. Operator Lee had frequently given the captain weather reports only to see them disregarded or thrown in the wastebasket. Thereafter he had been content to put them on the desk. Considering the outrageous discrepancies between the actual conditions existing that mad night on Lake Superior and those forecast by the responsible authorities, Captain Burke may have had every reason to scorn them.

Mate Macksey, who took over his pilothouse watch at 12:15 A.M. on May 1, was already aware that the wind had reached gale velocity. Captain Burke was still snug in his cabin and was obviously reluctant to leave it. Considering sea conditions and the punishment being absorbed by the *Arlington,* circumstances that would compel any conscientious master to remain on duty constantly, his actions were such as to later cause authorities to wonder if he was in complete control of his faculties. Subsequent actions on his part would later give ample support to those doubts. Whatever the case, those of the crew who were cognizant of the legends and foibles of Tatey Bug Burke had ample reason to recall them.

Considering the *Arlington*'s low freeboard, Macksey was particularly concerned about the hatches. They had been properly battened down before the vessel left Port Arthur and, as regulations dictated for the cargo and season, covered with tarpaulins and further protected by steel windbars or strongbacks to hold the tarpaulins firm and tight. But each sea was marching stridently over the *Arlington*'s deck—heavy, vindictive seas that could make a mockery of man's best efforts. Fifteen minutes after his watch began, Macksey turned the vessel before the wind in an attempt to inspect the hatch covers. Second mate Ferris had tried earlier and had almost been swept overboard. The change in the *Arlington*'s rolling and pitching apparently stirred Captain Burke into action. He stomped to the bridge in obvious displeasure and, before Macksey could even begin his inspection, turned the vessel once more on its course—a course that kept it continuously in the trough of the seas.

"We're never going to get anyplace going in the wrong direction," he grumbled. Once more he returned to the privacy of his cabin.

Aboard the *Collingwood,* even with its comparatively high freeboard, Captain Carson was taking no chances with his hatches. He had his searchlight directed on the deck constantly.

"Our decks were not awash, but the seas would occasionally surge over them," he later reported.

The punishment of the *Arlington's* hatches continued. Although the engine-room crew kept a full head of steam available, the forward speed was less than seven miles per hour. Macksey estimated that seas were now rolling over the deck, midships, at a height of ten feet. Between them he was certain he could see where the tarpaulins had been torn away and where strongbacks were bent or missing. Steel frames and bars on the deck had already been bent or washed away.

At 3:30 A.M. Macksey sent the watchman to call the captain. There was no response. Then the mate went below himself, hammered on the door and insisted that the captain take over the pilothouse so that he, Macksey, could try to effect repairs on the hatches. This time he heard some grumbling and the captain stirring about.

By the time Captain Burke reached the pilothouse, the tarpaulin on No. 5 hatch had been stripped off and others peeled back. The *Arlington* had also developed a five-degree list to port. From where he could safely survey the damage, Macksey found that not only had most of the tarpaulins been peeled off, but that No. 5 hatch had burst.

"Something will have to be done. The ship is going to sink," he said to Captain Burke.

The captain did not deign to answer, but he did have wheelsman Elmer Callum swing the ship once more before the sea, heading for the north shore.

If the *Arlington*'s troubles topside failed to get the proper attention of the man in charge, the reverse was true down in the realm of chief engineer Fred Gilbert, once he was apprised of the facts. Awakened by second engineer Lester Woods, just before 4:30 A.M., he was told that fireman Lester Hall was reporting cracking noises in the bulkhead between the fire hole and No. 2 hold with water leaking in and other noises that sounded like rivets snapping. Gilbert quickly detected the list to port and saw water rising in the ashpit. The bulkhead, obviously under intense pressure from water or swelling grain, continued to expel rivets and to bulge. A seam opened up and more water gushed in—more water, Gilbert knew, than could be handled by the ship's pumps.

"We're sinking," he called to Woods, at the same time heading for the ladder. Topside he grabbed the whistle cord, blew five short blasts to arouse the crew and once more went below to make sure all his men were ready to abandon ship. Most of the crew, without being told, had already concluded that the ship was done for. The list had quickly increased to thirty degrees and first mate Macksey, like engineer Gilbert, also blew a distress signal—several short blasts and four long ones. They were quickly noted and obviously expected by the *Collingwood*.

Unmindful of the storm, tumult and whistle blowing, hockey star Ted Brodeur was sleeping soundly when watchman George Braithwaite awakened him. "Get up, get up," he yelled. "She is sinking." Donning trousers and shoes, Brodeur bolted from his room and rushed topside. When he saw the *Collingwood* standing by 250 yards away, he returned for his wallet and watch.

Wireless operator Lee had already asked Captain Burke if he should send out an S O S but the captain only shook his head, mumbled, and nodded in the direction of the *Collingwood*.

Without waiting for a direct order to abandon ship, an order that obviously would not be forthcoming from her master, the crew automatically went about doing just that. Both lifeboats were aft, but the port boat, because of the heavy list and pounding of the seas, could not be launched. The engine room crew, under chief Gilbert, had already lowered the starboard boat by the time the forward crew fought their way aft. Even so, the seas were slamming it against the hull of the *Arlington*. Gilbert ordered the boat drawn around to the stern, in a more protected position.

Wheelsman Callum was the last to go aft. He had stayed on duty even though his presence in the pilothouse and at his post was a useless gesture. With the loss of steam when the fire hole flooded, the steering engine had ceased to function. When it was apparent that the *Arlington* was not long for this world, he had made a perilous journey aft through tossing hatch timbers and a Vesuvius of No. 1 hard wheat the seas were disgorging from No. 2 hold.

Tatey Bug Burke, silent and morose, stayed in the pilothouse.

Macksey, in charge of the lifeboat, asked the wheelsman where the captain was.

"He isn't coming," replied Callum.

Macksey then ordered the boat cast off.

At 3:34 A.M. Captain Carson had ordered his engine checked down to half speed but closed in on the *Arlington* when he noted that she had hauled around again, heading for the north shore. After the distress signals were heard, he brought the *Collingwood* in closer.

"It was just breaking day," Captain Carson recalled. "I was a quarter to a half mile from the *Arlington*. She looked

low in the water and I saw they were launching a boat over
the starboard side. She had gone into the trough of the seas
and looked to be in great distress. Then her stern settled
slowly, and when she got up to her No. 2 hatch, she simply
rolled over on her portside and went down."

The log of the *Collingwood* had the following entries:

At 5:15 A.M. steamer *Arlington* foundered, the crew leaving in
a boat.

At 5:30 A.M. crew of *Arlington* alongside in lifeboat, crew getting on board.

Supervising the job of helping the *Arlington*'s crew up
the rope ladder to the deck of the *Collingwood* was her first
mate, Raymond Palmer, who, like first mate Macksey, had
come on duty at 12:15 A.M. on that incredible morning when
Tatey Bug Burke went down with his ship.

The *Collingwood,* unlike the *Arlington,* was not only without a direction finder, but also without wireless. It wasn't
until she reached the locks at the Soo that Captain Carson,
his ship coated with ice, was able to wire Captains Dave and
Edward Burke that their ship had foundered, taking down
with her their beloved brother. Aware that the *Arlington*
had a home-town crew and that rumors would doubtless
spread like wildfire, Captain Carson emphasized that all
were well and safe aboard the *Collingwood.* Even so, and
despite a steady drizzle, a crowd estimated at seven hundred
awaited as the *Collingwood* made her berth at Midland,
burgee and ensign at half mast.

It was a strange mixture of joy and sadness which greeted the
Collingwood [reported the *Midland Free Press Herald*].

On the docks crowded the families of the survivors. Some of
them were in tears, while others were almost hysterical with joy.
Captain Carson of the *Collingwood* was the first man to leave
his boat after she docked. He was a close friend of Captain

Burke and as he walked across the dock to greet the lost captain's brothers, tears streamed down his face and he was sobbing audibly.

Crew members of the *Arlington* were instructed not to discuss the matter until after the preliminary inquiry, scheduled to begin the next day at Midland Town Hall under the jurisdiction of Captain Fred S. Slocombe, supervising examiner of masters and mates.

The verbal acounts of Captain Carson, the *Arlington*'s crew and further expert testimony by various official inspectors and surveyors did nothing to unravel the mystery of Tatey Bug Burke's peculiar passing from this world. Rather it seemed to confuse the issue, largely because personal impressions of the *Arlington*'s crew members varied to the extreme. Press coverage noted that on only one other occasion within memory of the experienced seamen present had a Great Lakes shipmaster deliberately chosen to go down with his ship. That was in 1903 when Captain William Morris of the *William F. Sauber* took the final plunge with his vessel, also in Lake Superior. Opinion as to whether Captain Burke went to his doom by design or accident was about evenly divided. Also, his actions and decisions, or perhaps a lack of them, from the time the *Arlington* left her Port Arthur dock until she rolled over and sank were subject to debate, again depending upon who was watching, and when.

Mr. G. P. Campbell, representing the Department of Transport, and G. R. Mackensie, in the interests of the cargo insurers, got some oddly conflicting testimony, all of it sincerely and honestly given.

The two newest members of the *Arlington*'s crew, and perhaps the least qualified by experience to judge the actions of their captain, were hockey players Francis Swales and Ted Brodeur, both of whom put the mantle of heroism on the broad shoulders of the burly captain.

"He stuck in the wheelhouse guiding the ship while the rest of us took to the lifeboat," said Swales.

"There was ample time for the master to have made his way aft," testified first mate Macksey. "He had lots of time. He served no useful purpose in the wheelhouse, for we had no steam to steer her by."

Young Brodeur made an even more dramatic episode of the captain's last moments, recalling a courtly gesture which likened him to an old warrior sadly leaving the battlefield with a valedictory salute to his men. "The captain ordered us to the boat while he stood at the wheelhouse rail. When we were fifty yards from the ship, he took off his cap, waved to us and then walked into his cabin and closed the door."

Strangely, no other member of the crew recalled hearing the captain ordering his men to the boat or in any way directing its launching. The move to the lifeboat was a spontaneous one by men who knew their vessel was about to founder. It was pointed out, from wheelsman Callum's account, that the captain did not leave the pilothouse, which was at the bow of the vessel. The lifeboat was aft at the very stern where first mate Macksey and chief engineer Gilbert supervised its launching.

Chief engineer Gilbert also caught a brief glimpse of the captain after the boat had been cast off. "He was at his office door on the starboard side, braced against the door frame with one hand on the knob and looking inside," reported Gilbert. "I hollered at him once, but I apparently couldn't make him hear."

Watchman George Braithwaite also saw the captain, probably a second or two before Gilbert. "I saw the captain last when I was in the lifeboat. I saw him come down the steps from the wheelhouse just as we were dropping astern. As he came down to the bottom step, he took a bad fall but got right up. He was hanging on there. I saw him wave one hand.

Then he went to his rooms. We were only fifty feet from the *Arlington* when she went under."

Probably as a result of conflicting testimony, Captain Edward Burke, brother of the *Arlington*'s lost skipper, made a statement to the press reiterating his belief that his brother was trapped when he went down with the ship. It was his opinion that when members of the crew saw their captain wave from the door of his cabin, he was probably giving an order. "He always made a habit," said Burke, "of waving his arms while issuing orders. He was a big, bluff, good-natured seaman without a reason in the world to go down with his ship. He did what any other captain would do—he waited until all his men were off the boat. He had no life belt and naturally would try to get one before leaving. We have no doubt he must have been injured in some fashion that left him unable to leave the boat before it sank."

"There were lifebuoys on the starboard side of the pilothouse which Captain Burke could have reached," testified W. L. MacKenzie, Midland steamship inspector.

Hanging over the heads of all, above and beyond the fate of the *Arlington* and her curious master, was concern for the fate of Canada's mother nation, Great Britain, at war with Germany since the previous September. On May 10, as the Germans invaded Belgium, the Netherlands and Luxemburg, the court of inquiry was recessed so all could hear Prime Minister Neville Chamberlain's radio speech of resignation.

When the inquiry resumed, Captain Carson of the *Collingwood* took the witness chair, sadly explaining that he could give no reason for Captain Burke's refusal to leave his ship.

Non-sailors made much of the theory that Captain Burke had obviously remained true to the old tradition that masters always go down with their ship.

Mate Macksey was quite vehement in scorning such yarns.

"Nonsense," he snapped. "I've been on the lakes all my life and that story about going down with your boat being a tradition of the lakes is a lot of poppycock."

Although the primary cause of the *Arlington*'s foundering was never in doubt—overwhelming seas that destroyed the watertight integrity of her hatches—the investigators were duty-bound to examine other aspects of the vessel's seaworthiness in search, perhaps, of contributing causes. Such deliberations in the past had yielded information suggesting changes or improvements for safer operations. The *Arlington,* the present case in point, had foundered in a gale that had claimed no other ships. It was the frank and considered opinion of Midland's many experienced seamen that the loss was due in no part to any shortcomings of the vessel. Obviously, then, the blame fell on her stubborn skipper. It was he who stayed in his cabin, not only refusing to ascertain her true condition as the seas sledge-hammered her vital hatches, but preventing others from doing so. Had he concurred in turning the ship before the wind, first mate Macksey could have made his examination of the hatches and perhaps may have effected temporary repairs. Although none were called as official witnesses to so state, it was the consensus among these veteran seamen that a more prudent master would never have permitted his men or his ship to be where the *Arlington* was, but rather safe in the quieter waters along the north shore, snugly at anchor. With a great shaking of heads and clucking of tongues, they concluded that Tatey Bug, for reasons known only to him, was "not himself" that night.

Referring to the general conditions of the *Arlington,* Captain Edward Burke testified that the vessel was in excellent condition when she left Midland. He further added that the *Arlington* had been on the Collingwood drydock on June 16, 1939, for general repairs and inspection, and again in

August of that year following a grounding at Collins Inlet, at which time $11,426 were spent for repairs.

First mate Macksey told the court that on the single previous trip that season (his first on the *Arlington*) the ship had loaded 97,200 bushels of grain and had arrived safely at Owen Sound without a pound of wet cargo.

"I supervised the loading and trimming of the grain at Port Arthur," said Macksey. "She had a little more grain in hold No. 1 than in No. 2, but No. 1 Northern is heavier than No. 2 Northern, so we would put more in the No. 2 forward. The hatch covers were in good condition. There were two tarpaulins on each hatch and they were all well fastened."

"The *Arlington* often carried cargoes of this size before," explained Captain Edward Burke. "Such a cargo wouldn't put her down to her load line. She'd be all full aft and slightly light forward."

Henry W. Morris, surveyor for the American Bureau of Shipping, gave evidence that he had surveyed the vessel on the sixteenth day of April, 1940, finding her in good condition, with only the usual, minor hull indentations. Pursuant to his survey a certificate was approved but had not been issued at the time of the disaster.

On April 20th, only twelve days before the *Arlington* foundered, she was again inspected, this time by William L. MacKenzie, a steamship inspector for twenty years, who had inspected the *Arlington* each year since 1922. His duty was to inspect the hull, the boiler and the equipment. Finding all in order, he issued the proper documents.

Based on this evidence the court found that the requirements of the Canada Shipping Act of 1934 and regulations thereunder were complied with in regard to hull, machinery and equipment.

Inspector MacKenzie noted that a life line was aboard at the time of inspection, and brackets to which to hook it. At the time of the inspection the life line was not in place, nor, according to the evidence given, was it in place at the time of the disaster. The life line is a steel cable suspended the length of the hatch deck, between the forward and aft structures. Its purpose is to assist crewmen in passing from one end of the vessel to the other when sea conditions would make such a journey extremely hazardous without the life line. In official language the regulation states:

> Gangways, life lines or other satisfactory means shall be provided for the protection of the crew in getting to and from their quarters.

Much talk was bandied about during recesses, to the effect that while a life line might not have helped in making repairs to the stripped hatch covers, it would have permitted earlier discovery of the damage before the port list developed. It was glumly agreed, though, that in the prevailing state of the captain's disposition, judging from all the evidence given, that a life line would not have saved the *Arlington*.

It was time, too, as the Midland phase of the inquiry ended and the proceedings moved on to Toronto, for old-timers to recall the legends and tales of Tatey Bug Burke and his career, most of which still make good listening wherever old sailors gather to yarn. Some of the more penetrating judgments of the captain come from those who sailed with him, particularly on that last long voyage. One of them is Charles Paradis, wheelsman on the captain's watch. Like first mate Macksey, it was his first season on the *Arlington*. Now retired, he still lives in Midland.

"Yes, he had a reputation of being a 'heavy weather' sailor," recalls Paradis. "But you must remember that he got that reputation while sailing the large boats with plenty of freeboard, not a little canaller like the *Arlington*. The *Collingwood*, for example, had much freeboard, and she was near us in the same gale without suffering damage. It just didn't work out on the *Arlington* when we only had between three and four feet of freeboard when we were loaded."

One news commentator had advanced his interpretation of the captain's passing to the unspoken tradition that when he loses his third ship, the master always chooses to stay with her, going knowingly to his death. Since this was the third vessel to be lost under his command, it followed, according to the learned commentator, that Captain Burke had remained faithful to this grisly tradition.

This sparked a brisk reply from the Port Arthur *News-Chronicle*:

> It is a far-fetched explanation and one which need not be believed. There is no such tradition . . . it is an unwarranted reflection on both Captain Burke's courage and intelligence to indicate that he deliberately went to his death because it was number three in a series of accidents.

The accidents referred to concerned two of Captain Burke's earlier commands, a wooden vessel (probably one of the lumber raft tugs) which caught fire, burned to the water line and sank off Point au Baril, in Georgian Bay. The second was the loss of the big steel freighter *Glenorchy,* one of the Playfair vessels, in an almost stem-on collision with the American steamer *Leonard B. Miller*. It happened in a pea-soup fog off Harbor Beach, Lake Huron, sixteen years before the *Arlington* went down. In neither instance was any blame placed upon Captain Burke. In the *Glenorchy* sinking he proved to be a man of great courage, exhibiting such concern for his crew that two of them owed their lives to him. One was Captain Ward White, who earlier in this tale commented on Tatey Bug's instinctive navigation and idiosyncrasies. Like wheelsman Paradis he, too, is retired but still lives in Midland.

A wheelsman on the *Glenorchy* at the time, White was off duty and in his portside fo'c'sle room when the *Miller* struck, crushing both his room and the one forward of it, where an off-duty watchman was sleeping. Burke sensed immediately that his ship was mortally holed and blew the abandon ship signal on the whistle. Then, as the two vessels lay temporarily locked together, the *Glenorchy* sinking fast, he counted heads as his men jumped across to the deck of the *Miller*. All were accounted for but two—White and the watchman. Again, sensing what had happened, Captain Burke grabbed a fire ax and hurried below. White was already trying to fight his way out of his collapsed room with another ax but was almost buried in wood, steel, furniture and piping, the door hopelessly jammed. The watchman, injured, was in even more desperate straits. Swinging his ax with great effect, Captain Burke freed White and both of them then pulled the watchman from the entangled debris. Seconds later they helped him across the gap between the vessels, the captain being the last man to leave his stricken ship—and none too soon, for in seven minutes from the time of impact the fog-shrouded *Glenorchy*, loaded with grain, rolled over and went down. Thanks to Captain Burke, Ward White lived to become a shipmaster himself, later commanding such vessels as the *Guardian*, *Glenbogie* and *Alexander Holly*.

The startling contrast between the alert, brave, efficient and compassionate man who was master of the *Glenorchy*, and the mumbling, stupefied and seemingly unconcerned skipper of the *Arlington* was astounding. The clear, crisp and efficient orders he issued seconds after the *Glenorchy* was rammed were the result of experience and instinct. What had happened to Tatey Bug Burke in sixteen years? When the *Arlington* had been fighting for her life, he had remained in his cabin during the hours when critical decisions had to be made. When he had finally appeared in the pilothouse, it had been too late. Questions put to him went unanswered or resulted in indecisive mumbles. This was the man, a sailor for thirty-seven years, who seemed completely unaware of conditions as they existed when even the novice seamen aboard knew instinctively that the *Arlington* was going to sink and went about their preparations to abandon ship without counsel or help from her master.

The final, almost ludicrous act in the tragic scene was almost a parody on the behavior of a shipmaster. The only witness to it was William Lee, the young wireless operator. According to Lee, long after both chief engineer Gilbert and first mate Macksey had blown distress signals on the *Arlington*'s stentorian steam whistle with what steam was left, Captain Burke, belatedly giving voice to his thoughts, had stood outside the pilothouse and bawled into the shrieking gale at the vessel still 250 yards away, "*Collingwood,* stand by."

"They were his last words," Lee had testified.

Chief engineer Gilbert, a ten-year employee of the Burke brothers, with five of them on the *Arlington,* apparently had little faith in the flight-of-fancy statement by the news commentator that the third disaster is the last. Already the survivor of three sinkings, he was not about to make the fourth his final one. Once he had personally viewed the water pouring in the ruptured bulkhead, he had gone swiftly and efficiently about the task of rounding up his men and preparing a lifeboat for launching.

The published report of the official investigation into the foundering of the S.S. *Arlington,* which concluded at Osgoode Hall, Toronto, at 12:20 P.M. on the twentieth day of May, 1940, while covering the known facts thoroughly, could do little to explain the strange behavior of Captain Burke. But it did make some pointed suggestions for new regulations to prevent similar situations from developing.

The marine field is a highly complicated one and obviously the delving into matters relating to it is for qualified experts. The counsel for such investigative panels are all men representing legal firms that specialize in the field. They are assisted, as assessors or surveyors, by men who have had a close personal relationship with the shipping industry most of their lives, often as captains or chief engineers. In the inquiry on the case of the *Arlington,* F. H. Barlow, District Judge in Admiralty of the Exchequer Court of Canada, for the Ontario Admiralty District, was appointed Commissioner of the formal investigation into the circumstances attending the foundering. Assisting him were assessors Henry W. King and Francis J. Davis, the latter gentleman the retired master of the *Keewatin,* a famous Canadian Pacific Railroad passenger ship, a man of vast experience. Counsel for the various interests were G. P. Campbell for the Department of Transport, Frank Wilkinson for the Burke Towing & Salvage Company, and for the cargo interests, G. Russell McKenzie assisted by Carl Essery of Detroit. They listened well to all the testimony given by the men of the *Arlington,* Captain Carson of the *Collingwood* and the surveyors representing the cargo and hull insurers and the government's Department of Transport.

Above all, and far beyond the realm of the average citizen not conversant with the peculiarities and intricacies of operating, managing and navigating steamships, these experts are aware of the awesome responsibilities of command, of the factors that jell into the making of a decision, and the variances that can sometimes alter or change those decisions. They do not condone faulty judgment, they merely understand it, and by that very understanding are likely to deal leniently with one whose judgment has been found in error.

Testimony had disclosed that, while a life line was aboard and brackets to which to hook same had been present and in good order, the life line had not been operative at the

time of the disaster. Thus, because there was no means of
communication between the engine room and the navigating
bridge (there was no telephone system) , chief engineer Gilbert was unable to apprise Captain Burke of the desperate
situation aft resulting from the failure of the bulkhead between the fire hole and the No. 2 cargo hold. While mildly
censuring engineer Gilbert for not making the facts known
to the master, at the same time admitting that this was
something he could not have accomplished without risk of
life, the report strongly recommended that the laws henceforth require a telephone connection between the engine
room and the navigating bridge. Further, that the life line
be in place and operative when a vessel departs her port, the
fact to be noted in the ship's log. The report, in a way of
making amends, did say that Gilbert and second engineer
Lester Woods were deserving of favorable comment on the
seamanlike manner in which they performed their duties
with respect to saving the after end crew, the chief engineer
for arousing all his men and the second engineer and fireman for not leaving their posts until the water had put out
the fire and they could no longer be of any assistance.

Point No. 7 in the report was a commendation for Captain Carson and the crew of the *Collingwood,* a reward for
the "seamanlike manner in which the *Collingwood* was
handled and which resulted in the saving of all those in the
lifeboat." "If they had not so maneuvered the *Collingwood*
as to keep the lifeboat in her lee," the report went on, "it is
questionable whether all those in the lifeboat could have
been saved. Captain Carson is to be most highly commended."

First mate Macksey, while mildly chided in official terms
for not reporting back to his commander the state of affairs at
the hatches after the captain had belatedly turned the vessel
before the wind, was commended "for the seamanlike manner

in which he and the crew lowered the lifeboat in a most perilous sea."

As to Captain Burke, the court exhibited the customary kindness accorded a skipper who has gone down with his ship and consequently not on hand to defend his judgment or actions.

In its marine column on the afternoon of May 1, twelve hours after the *Arlington* had perished, the Port Arthur *News-Chronicle* noted that:

> A 50-mile-an-hour gale, driving snow, sleet and rain before it, swept across Northern Lake Superior and the Thunder Bay District last night, holding temperatures below the freezing point and driving lake vessels into shore-line shelters.

Among those at anchor and hugging the protective north shore, as caution would have dictated, were many vessels larger than the *Arlington*—vessels whose masters had prudently decided to wait out the blow and be damned to the delay. Captain Burke's decision to take the shorter but infinitely more dangerous course in view of the weather was not directly questioned.

On the question as to whether the *Arlington* had been navigated with proper care and caution considering the weather when first mate Macksey turned her before the wind and after Captain Burke turned her again on course, Commissioner Barlow ruled:

> On the evidence and considering what my assessors tell me I am of the opinion that it would have been good judgment on the part of the Master to have put the vessel head to wind and reduce speed. In this respect she was not properly navigated.

Another question for the opinion of the court asked: "Was the loss of the S.S. *Arlington* caused or contributed to by the wrongful act or default of any person or persons, and, if so, of whom?"

The answer, carefully phrased in the report, cast no aspersion upon the missing master:

After a most careful consideration of the evidence it appears that the Master did not realize the dangerous situation and did not spend as much time on the bridge as would have been advisable under the circumstances. The Master, however, lost his life and is not here to make any explanation. Under the circumstances I do not feel that he should be further censured. The course that was taken by the vessel was the usual course and even if it might be suggested that an error in judgment was made in continuing on this course after the wind developed into a gale, yet such an error in judgment is not something for which the Master should be blamed.

Not as the result of a direct question during testimony but probably cognizant of the riddle still unanswered, the court made the following observation:

There has been much speculation, and on the evidence it must be speculation, as to why the Master was lost. The wheelsman was aware that all was not well with the vessel. As a result of which after telling the Master that he was going below and asking him if he was coming, to which he received no reply, he went down to find that the lifeboat was being launched. When it is remembered that the Master had no knowledge of the conditions which had developed in the engine room and did not realize that the vessel was helpless until such time as he rang for full speed ahead and failed to get a response except the ringing off by the second engineer on the ship's chadburn [telegraph], it is quite evident to me that the Master did not realize the seriousness of the situation. . . . I cannot help but think that the Master, in holding up his hand to those in the lifeboat, not realizing how serious the situation was, intended that they should wait for him while he went into his cabin to secure a lifebelt and perhaps the ship's papers or personal effects. The evidence shows that the list of the vessel was such that the Master easily could have slipped or been thrown into the lower corner of his cabin and being a heavy man would have found it next to impossible to climb out. There is no evidence to suggest that he intended to go down with the ship and it must be found that in returning to his room for the purpose of saving the ship's papers and other effects he became trapped and went down with the vessel. The evidence shows that the vessel listed very rapidly after the Master went into his room and went down almost immediately.

The court and its people were obviously being very kind to Tatey Bug Burke. But the repeated statement that the captain had not realized the seriousness of the situation brought expressions of disbelief not only from members of the crew, but from others who had spent their years in ships. The travesty of a commander standing outside the wheelhouse in a raging gale, seeing the ship's hatches open to the sea, the after end already well down in the water, the crew taking to a lifeboat and a thirty-degree list to the vessel not being aware of the seriousness of the situation? It was a statement that defied all reasonable considerations. Still, a harsh censuring would not have brought Captain Burke back to the realm of the living, nor would it have brought about a reincarnation of the *Arlington* or her cargo. All were gone for eternity.

Perhaps in its benign pronouncement of absolution the court felt that a man who had gracefully borne the name of "Tatey Bug" for so many years had already suffered enough.

2

Who Speaks for the "Little Feller"?

On what everybody had hoped would be a delightfully sunny day, the morning of Saturday, July 24, 1915, began with light, steady rain and a somber sky in the Chicago area. Over to the west, however, the overcast was slowly lightening, giving promise of better things to come.

At six o'clock, throughout the city and its sprawling suburbs of Cicero and Hawthorne, several thousand households were already astir for a very special reason. For the nine thousand employees of the Western Electric Company it was the "big" day of the year; the date of the long-awaited, grand-and-glorious Hawthorne Club picnic and excursion boat jaunt to Michigan City, Indiana—a full day of fun and games at the largest resort in the midwest. It was the fifth such annual frolic sponsored by the seven-year-old club, each bigger and livelier than the last.

The Hawthorne Club was originally formed as an educational organization for the employees, the members arranging dinners, organizing theatricals, sponsoring baseball teams and initiating night classes for its many Polish and Bohemian workers experiencing language barriers. It was, by Company standards, an almost instant success, and its mushrooming influence soon became a significant if somewhat insidious factor in the daily lives of those employed at the big plant.

The club's own little newspaper, the *Jubilator*, in a pink "sporting extra," had trumpeted the cause of the picnic most insistently.

> Are you all set and ready for the big event?
> A long time ago Jonah took a trip on a whale.
> There is no Jonah about this but it will be a
> Whale of a Success. Get your tickets early . . .
> . . . Adults 75¢ . . . children under five free!
> . . . Children between 5 and 12 . . . half fare!

And in another *Jubilator* "extra":

For instance:
Have you fixed it up with the wife?
Have you arranged for plenty of sandwiches and cake and bananas and other fixin's for the kids?
Have you . . . what! . . . . . You're single?
Well then,
Have you asked the young lady to save the date for you?
Have you determined to help your department win that parade prize?
Have you fixed the alarm clock to wake you in time for the first boat, so you won't miss anything?
Have you bought your ticket? 75¢ at the works . . . 75¢

Energetic sub-committees had made pretentious plans for the day—baseball games, tug o' wars, sack races, balloon-blowing contests, foot races, pie-eating events, canoe races and free lemonade. The paramount event was to be the big parade, complete with the band, departmental floats and last of all, a pageant depicting the great telephone achievement of the decade—the linking of New York and San Francisco by long-distance wires. It was a matter of special pride for Chicagoans, for it was at the Western Electric plant that the

equipment had been manufactured. Advance billing had indicated a crowd so large that the Michigan City officials had
granted permission for the parade to extend beyond the con-
fines of the park, down Franklin Street. Yes, largely because
of the aggressiveness of the plant ticket sellers (some employees called it coercion) the 1915 gala picnic gave every
promise of topping them all.

The ticket selling campaign had been so successful, with
7300 tickets bought and paid for, that on the night before
the excursion the Hawthorne Club's top officials, president
Holmes, vice-president F. J. Sheriden and secretary J. P.
Krivanek looked doubtfully at each other, each with the
same unanswered question: "Have we got enough boats?"

Weeks earlier Charles J. Malmros, chairman of the club's
picnic committee, had entered into a contract with W. K.
Greenbaum, general manager of the Michigan City–based
Indiana Transportation Company, for five lake passenger
steamers to accommodate the expected crowd. Greenbaum's
company, affiliated with the resort, owned no vessels, merely
chartered them for such happy occasions.

The *Jubilator* had already announced the sailing times of
the steamers, all of which were to be moored along the Chicago River in the area of the Clark Street bridge: *Eastland,*
7:30 A.M.; *Theodore Roosevelt,* 8:00 A.M.; *Petoskey,* 8:30
A.M.; *Racine,* 10:00 A.M. and the *Rochester* at 2:30 P.M.

"And don't," urged the blatant *Jubilator,* "wait for the
last boat."

The warning was needless. The tempo of the pre-picnic
excitement had inspired an epidemic of early preparations.
Most workers apparently wanted to get to the scene of the
festivities as early as possible.

The enthusiasm generated by the outpouring of Western
Electric people was almost as if, subconsciously, they knew
some time might elapse before such an event could again be

held. The flames of war had already engulfed much of Europe, and incidents at sea threatened to involve the United States. On May 7 the *Lusitania* had been torpedoed with a loss of 1198 lives, 124 of them Americans. Eighteen days later the U.S. ship *Nebraskan* was attacked, but the Germans had quickly expressed a willingness to make reparations. On July 16, Uncle Sam began to flex his muscles, demonstrating the mobility of the nation's sea forces by sending battleships through the Panama Canal for the first time. On July 21, President Wilson dispatched his "Third *Lusitania* note" to Germany, warning that further violations of U.S. rights would be regarded as "deliberately unfriendly." But the horrors of war were still a long way from Chicago. In the very heartland of the country, today was still just another rainy Saturday morning, the beginning of the gala day of the year, if you believed the *Jubilator*.

Although she was afraid of water and boats, eighteen-year-old Agnes Kasperski wanted to attend the outing. She and her close friend Stella Michaski, both employed in the same department of the plant, had talked of it for weeks, planning to enter the "single ladies race." Sharing the burden of their picnic basket, they left the Kasperski home in time to catch the first boat.

Not far away Barbara Lukens was studying a mirror, giving final approval to the new dress she had made for the occasion. The task had taken the better part of a month, but both Barbara and her husband William agreed that it was time well spent. A relative was to stay with the four children while the pair joined the celebrants at Michigan City. They left the house shortly before six-thirty that morning.

Little Martha Behnke, daughter of the Julius Behnkes and three years old, was too young to grasp the full significance of the new day, but the hectic preparations and holiday atmosphere told her there was something very special about getting up so early. She was cradled in her father's arms, her mother carrying the picnic hamper, when they boarded the streetcar for downtown.

Willie Novotny was seven years old and had a new suit for the occasion, a brown checked affair with two pairs of matching knickers. Somehow it made him feel as old as his sister Mamie, eight. Their parents, James and Agnes Novotny, had been telling both of the wonders to be seen and experienced on the boat and at the resort. The youngsters were big-eyed with excitement as the family walked to the streetcar stop.

For Mike Javanco the day had begun much earlier, and for him it was just another working day. He had hitched his horse to his wagon at 3:00 A.M., and shortly thereafter departed for the market district, on the fringe of the downtown area. Mike peddled vegetables for a living, selling them on a neighborhood route that had produced many warm friends and satisfied customers.

He purchased his vegetables wholesale at the markets, retailing them house-to-house after a modest mark-up to insure a fair return for his time and labors. As the horse clip-clopped over the Clark Street bridge, the empty wagon making quite a clatter, he noticed the sheer white bulk of the *Eastland,* only an hour home from a moonlight excursion, moored near the bridge. Wisps of steam rose from her deck machinery, empty beer barrels were being rolled out a gangway, and a noisy group with a dray was unloading ice for her cold chests. Mike, with little time for the frivolity the preparations suggested, was unimpressed.

Both Captain Harry Pedersen and chief engineer Joseph M. Erickson had retired in anticipation of an arduous day. The *Eastland* was scheduled to leave at 7:30 A.M., disembark the factory excursionists at Michigan City and hurry on to St. Joseph, Michigan, for a regularly scheduled stop. She would then return to Michigan City to bring home the tired Western Electric people and whatever passengers had been taken on at St. Joseph.

The vanguard of what was to be the *Eastland*'s human cargo began arriving long before the ship was ready to receive them. Supplies were being loaded through a starboard gangway and crew members were sweeping up debris left from the moonlight ride and hosing down the decks. Cartons of bagged peanuts were carried aboard and popcorn machines on deck were ready for a brisk trade. The early arrivals, their number swelling by the moment, were patient. The light rain continued and the sky was still overcast. Still they came, legions of them trooping down from the streetcar stops and most of them freighted down with obviously well-stocked baskets, boxes and hampers. The mood was festive and good fellowship reigned.

Upon returning from the moonlight excursion, Captain Pedersen had backed his twin-screw ship alongside the dock just west of the Clark Street bridge. Ballast was then pumped out to bring the starboard gangways up to the level of the dock where the morning excursionists would board. When the service and supply people had finished their tasks, all but one gangway was closed, that through which the Western Electric workers would make their way aboard. But already some far back in the crowd had concluded that the *Eastland* would be too crowded for comfort and began to head for the *Theodore Roosevelt,* moored on the east side of the bridge. Scheduled to depart one-half hour later than the *Eastland,* she had already taken aboard several hundred people. Nearby was the *Petoskey,* not due to sail until 8:30 A.M. but already accepting passengers.

At 6:30 A.M. deputy collector of customs, Robert H. McCreary, in charge of the loading, stationed two of his men, Luman A. Lobdell and Hurdus G. Oakley, at the single

boarding gangway and signaled for operations to begin. Lobdell and Oakley clicked their little hand counters as the passengers streamed by, hurrying to get the choice seats near the
rails. The *Eastland* was licensed to carry 2500 people, excluding her crew. The previous year, 1914, and up until less
than a month before the present charter, the number had
been limited to 2183, but the federal steamboat inspector at
Grand Haven, Michigan, Robert Reid, had recently seen fit,
after pleadings by the steamer's owners, to raise the figure.

Mr. McCreary's men, however, had an unusual method of
calculating the numbers of people hurrying aboard, one
which strangely coincided with the ticket price arrangement
between the Indiana Transportation Company and Mr.
Malmros of the Hawthorne Club's picnic committee. Children under five, admitted free and usually carried aboard by
their parents, were not counted at all. Half-fare children between five and twelve went up the gangway in pairs, but
each pair was counted as one adult. Others not subject to
count were concessionaries, their assistants and members of
an orchestra.

At about 6:53 A.M. enough people had found their places
on the portside, the side offering the choice view of the river
and its changing scenes, to cause the ship to list slightly in
that direction. Chief engineer Erickson, noting the list on his
plumb-bob type inclinometer, immediately opened the valve
on the No. 2 ballast tank on the starboard side and also
cranked open the starboard sea cock for about five minutes.
He was assisted by the ship's gauge tender, John Elbert, a
Titanic survivor. The sea cocks, one port, one starboard, admitted free water into the hold for quick ballast low in the
hull, where it was most needed. The list was soon corrected,
or actually overcorrected, for the ship then listed slightly to
starboard. At 7:05 A.M. Captain Pedersen, having earlier ordered the engine room to "stand by" on the telegraph,

phoned engineer Erickson to "limber up" the engines. Erickson started the propeller shafts turning slowly, the starboard screw working astern, the port screw ahead. Meanwhile the listing condition had been erratic, changing several times from side to side, but at 7:16 A.M., with a slight list to port developing and persisting, the valve on the No. 3 starboard ballast tank was opened. On the upper deck a little mandolin and fiddle orchestra was playing a selection of popular ragtime numbers. Over on the *Theodore Roosevelt* a brass band was giving an enthusiastic rendition of "I'm on My Way to Dear Old Dublin Bay."

Along the upper port rail of the *Eastland*, Barbara Lukens, clutching her new dress to prevent it from snagging on rough places on the bench, thought the tilting of the deck was great fun.

Agnes Kasperski and her chum Stella Michaski had also found places along the upper port rail, fortunately near a refreshment stand where lemonade and soft drinks were already being handed out by a harried attendant. The Behnkes were not among the earliest arrivals and had to be content with places along the starboard rail. Little Martha, perched on her father's shoulder, was entranced by the dockside commotion. Also among the last to board were the Novotnys, and the congestion was so great that they had to be content with a spot away from the rail and on the lower deck.

Although the *Eastland* normally operated as economically as possible, dispensing with assistance when it could be avoided, Captain Pedersen had ordered a tug to help him away from the dock and tow the ship beyond the State Street bridge, which was on a sharp turn in the river. The tug *Kenosha* of the Great Lakes Towing Company responded and was ready for her work, the towline attached but still not taut.

At 7:18 the ship had straightened up somewhat, actually

heeling slightly to starboard, but shortly regained her slight
list to port, where she stayed steady for about two minutes.
The engines were stopped but ballast was still being pumped
into the two starboard tanks. At 7:23 the *Eastland* listed
sharply to port again. Engineer Erickson sent men up to the
main deck to ask the passengers to move to the starboard side.
A few complied.

Joseph R. Lind, assistant harbormaster, had joined harbormaster Adam F. Weckler as the *Eastland* was about to cast
off her lines. He called his superior's attention to the growing list to port. "Yes," agreed Weckler, "it's a shame to send
a boat out with that big a load."

Along the curb lane of the Clark Street bridge Mike Javanco, his wagon piled high with crated vegetables, was returning from market. Not familiar with any aspect of ships
or their handling, he was instinctively alarmed at the sight
of the *Eastland* leaning far over toward the river channel.
Standing up and cupping his hands, he yelled to the crowd
of young men on the bow, "Get off, de boat's turning over."

He was answered by a chorus of jeers and a shout by one
loud-mouthed lout, "G'wan, dago; you're crazy."

Captain Pedersen had already stationed the second mate
at the stern lines, ready to cast them off on signal. The tug
crew, under Captain John H. O'Meara, was impatiently
awaiting the signal from the *Eastland*'s whistle. On the dock
harbormaster Weckler kept shouting, "Are you ready, Captain?" Captain Pedersen had indeed been ready, but the unexpected list had given him pause. It had given many of the
crew more than pause, for before the passengers became
aware of any impending danger or could do anything about
it, many of the *Eastland*'s crew clambered over the rail
and jumped for the dock. Then, suddenly, as though the spectacle of his men abandoning ship had released a mental bloc,

the captain shouted from the starboard bridge wing, "Open the inside doors and let the people off!"

But it was too late! At 7:23, with the words of warning barely out of her master's mouth, the *Eastland* increased her list to port—25—30—35 degrees and still going over. By this time tons of water were pouring in open ports and the three big open gangway doors on the river side. Passengers, furniture, picnic hampers, benches, refreshment stands, popcorn machines, barrels of lemonade and boxes of candy slid into piles on the portside amid a dreadful, overpowering volume of yelling and screaming. Over she went until she was flat on her portside on the river bottom. Only about eight feet of her white starboard side remained above water, giving her the appearance of a great stranded whale.

Over on the *Theodore Roosevelt* where the crowd had gathered five deep at the rails to watch the *Eastland* depart, the officers were faced with incipient panic. Women fainted by the dozen, others were shrieking hysterically. Men foolishly went about throwing overboard anything that would float, although this could only be a symbolic gesture of help to the hundreds of bobbing heads around the capsized ship. The *Roosevelt*'s officers sternly quieted the men and ordered everybody to the lower deck, where most of the sights were obliterated but not the horrifying sounds. Many bolted out the gangway and rushed across the bridge to assist in the rescue work.

A few hundred people, most of them from the upper deck, had managed to clamber over the *Eastland*'s starboard rail to find safety on the slippery plates of the exposed side. But the waters around the ship were teeming with men, women and children fighting frantically for their lives, shouting, thrashing and clutching at anything afloat, even their fellow victims. So fierce was the struggle for survival that some of those pulled to safety had their clothes stripped off by the clawing of others seeking to stay afloat another precious moment. Above all the cataclysmic scene there was a great and dreadful wailing sound as the cries and pleas of the drowning blended in a terrible symphony with the moans and apprehensive shrieks of those who stood helplessly on the dock or watched in disbelief and torment from the other excursion vessels. Already the mortal remains of those who had quickly lost their fight for survival were beginning to drift slowly down the river in a modest current.

What little help could be forthcoming quickly was a spontaneous reaction. The lineman on the tug *Kenosha* had severed the towline with a single stroke of an ax when the *Eastland* started over. Now its captain, realizing that the tug's powerful propeller would do more harm than good in the maelstrom of thrashing humanity, quickly backed his vessel against the now horizontal bow of the stricken steamer, letting his bow swing over to the dock, thus forming an impromptu bridge over which many of those passengers who had gained the upper side of the *Eastland* got ashore without even getting their feet wet. Ironically, the single lifeboat that drifted away from the wreck was picked up with one passenger, a red-haired boy of six whom someone had apparently rescued and hoisted over the side.

Directly across the river from the *Eastland*'s dock was the big Reid-Murdoch & Co. warehouse. The bloodcurdling cries that came welling out of the ship as it rolled over brought quick action. Momentarily petrified by the sight that first met their eyes, the workmen quickly began throwing boxes, crates and lumber into the river, anything that could support a human being. One of the Chicago Fire Department's fireboats, stationed only a stone's throw from the site, responded at once. Other tugs, police boats, Coast Guard craft, private yachts and ship supply launches converged upon the appalling scene. From inside the compartments on the exposed portion of the *Eastland's* hull could be heard terrified shouts and muffled moaning. Those still dazed and standing safe above them could feel and hear the frenzied pounding of many fists against the under side of the hull plates. But for those who had been sitting or standing in the center of the ship or on the portside there would be no more shouting or pounding. For them it was all over. Lifeboats lowered from the *Roosevelt* made their way to the foundered *Eastland,* passing and ignoring dozens of bodies. There were still lives to be saved; the dead could wait.

The Lukenses, Barbara and William, were still at the upper port rail when the steamer began her fatal roll. William, sensing the coming disaster, threw their bench into the river and somehow, in the mad crush of falling chairs and fellow passengers, both had managed to reach it. It seemed so unreal, being there in the river and watching a streetcar cross the Clark Street bridge, that Barbara's only reaction to the dunking were words that proved to be her last—"Oh, my dress, my dress." A second later another victim, fighting for a grip on the bench, pushed her away and she was gone.

For Agnes Kasperski her dread of water was a dream come true. Plunging free of the rail as the ship toppled, she came to the surface and was reaching for her friend Stella Michaski when an icebox from the refreshment stand crashed down upon them.

The Behnkes, at the starboard rail, had clung grimly for life for the few seconds it had taken the *Eastland* to capsize. They were wet but still above water and hanging to the rail when helping hands reached down from above. Little Martha, still clinging to her father's shoulder, was handed up and passed along the human chain that stretched over the *Kenosha's* deck to the dock. Moments later the parents gained the safety of the ship's exposed starboard side.

The Novotnys—James, Agnes, Mamie and Willie—had

been unable to find a place at the rail and had contented themselves with a bench midway between the port and starboard sides. The final and sudden list of the *Eastland* made them just four pieces of the gigantic jigsaw puzzle of people, chairs, benches, picnic baskets, tables, refreshment counters and ship's gear that piled up on the portside and was quickly submerged.

The words of the rude rebuff his warning had received from those on the *Eastland*'s bow were still ringing in his ears when Mike Javanco saw the ship go over with hundreds of people spilling off her upper deck. Abandoning his wagon, he ran across the bridge and to the dock to join in the rescue work. Mike Javanco was one of many heroes that day.

Considering that it was an era before the instant mass communication wonders of radio and television, word of the calamity spread with remarkable speed. Once the gravity of the situation was known, every Chicago hospital rushed ambulances, doctors, nurses and resuscitating devices and first-aid equipment to the dock. Dr. Thomas A. Carter, head police surgeon, was early on the scene, followed closely by Dr. E. W. Ryerson of Henrotin Hospital. Together they organized squads of doctors and nurses. Dr. Joseph Springer quickly examined the victims as they were brought out of the *Eastland*, a shaking of his head meaning that it was too late, a brisk nod indicating that the resuscitators might here save a life. When it appeared that space would not permit more stretchers or workers, the doors of the big Reid-Murdoch warehouse were thrown open, the building to serve as a temporary hospital and morgue. Many of those obviously beyond help were taken to the *Theodore Roosevelt,* there to lie in long lines on the decks so recently trod by a joyful and expectant crowd of Western Electric workers. At the warehouse Doctors W. A. Evans, John B. Murphy, John F. Golden and J. R. Pennington were soon joined by a Red

Cross team of nurses with Doctors M. K. Little and J. S. Soldini. The teams of police were bringing in victims at the rate of two a minute. Above the tramp of feet, the murmur of voices and the muted swishing sounds of the resuscitators came only an occasional cry of triumph as eyelids fluttered and chests heaved.

Among those who quickly responded to the emergency was N. W. LeVally, manager of the Oxweld Acetylene Company, who brought as many men as he could muster and all the supplies they could carry. Rescuers on the exposed side of the ship pointed to places where they could hear shouting and hammering from those still trapped below. One of the cutting torch men was J. H. Rista, who had scarcely begun his work when he was rudely shoved aside by Captain Pedersen and ordered to stop. Rista heatedly refused and it took rough talk by several of the workers to keep the captain and first mate Dell Fisher from further interfering with the rescue work.

"After I got rid of Pedersen," Rista later told newsmen, "we took forty people, all alive, out of that hole he had tried to stop me from cutting."

Elsewhere more holes were being torched in the hull, some yielding dazed survivors, others only the dead and a growing collection of picnic baskets and hampers, derby hats, thermos bottles, pocketbooks and garments shredded in the fierce battle for life. Divers, all who could be quickly located, disappeared through the holes to locate more victims and in their grisly searching found many.

Strangely, not one member of the *Eastland*'s crew of sixty was lost. Captain Pedersen and first mate Fisher, after the hole-cutting episode and further incidents of interference, were placed under arrest by Herman Schuettler, first deputy superintendent of police. On the way to Schuettler's city hall office where they were to be questioned by Coroner Peter

Hoffman and Charles Center Case, assistant state's attorney, they were assaulted by a mob. Despite an escort of twenty policemen, one man broke through the cordon and struck Captain Pedersen before being himself felled by a nightstick.

All day, as the news spread, morbidly curious Chicagoans wended their way to the scene, the crowd growing by the minute. By late afternoon they were there by the thousands, perched on bridge girders, all along the river docks and standing six deep on the roof of commercial buildings. Long before dark, anticipating an all-night ordeal, workers of the Commonwealth Edison Company had ringed the area with powerful temporary lights. Still the crowd grew although the proportions of the tragedy kept them relatively quiet, their senses dulled by the enormity of the disaster. Each still form lifted from the hull served as a reminder of how quickly joy can turn to grief.

For most of the observers there existed an ironic, completely incongruous atmosphere to the whole grim spectacle. It was simply inconceivable that here, on a mild summer morning, in the very shadows of skyscrapers and where elevated trains and streetcars roared by within a few hundred feet, a prosaic excursion boat, still lashed to its dock, could precipitate a disaster of such epic proportions. Even less believable was the fact that thousands had looked on in mute helplessness, witnessing a catastrophic event whose ramifications in loss of life and family tragedies could as yet only be an extremely morbid guess.

The recovery task now better organized, arrangements were made to turn the big Second Regiment Armory, at Curtis Street and Washington Boulevard, into a temporary morgue, transferring there the silent victims from the decks of the *Theodore Roosevelt* and the Reid-Murdoch warehouse. At the armory sober officials from the coroner's office attached a numbered tag to each body. Others noted the sex, approxi-

mate age and description of clothing on records with du-
plicate numbers. One of the first to be identified was eighteen-
year-old Anna Quaine whose father, policeman John Quaine,
had been detailed to help in the work at the armory. The
long lines of still forms grew as the hours passed—one hundred, two hundred, three hundred, four hundred, five hundred. And still the police and mortuary vehicles continued
their shuttle from the dock warehouse and the dock alongside the foundered *Eastland,* which looked by this time like
a tin toy boat awash in a gutter.

At 11:00 P.M. that tragic Saturday night the crowds of idle
curious, most of whom had no reason to be there, had grown
to such proportions that those seeking news of loved ones
had difficulty gaining admittance to the armory. Coroner
Hoffman, almost distraught with the enormity of the task
that had suddenly become his responsibility, mounted a
stepladder outside the main entrance to make a dramatic
appeal.

"In the name of God," he implored, "I ask you to go
away and let those seeking relatives and friends come in and
identify their dead."

Based on the number of bodies recovered and tagged at
that hour, five hundred and twenty-six, and the known fact
that many more were probably still entombed in the hulk,
the Chicago *Tribune,* in its Sunday morning edition, estimated the probable loss and proclaimed:

919 Bodies Recovered . . . Total *Eastland* Victims May Reach
1,200!

Somebody made a big mistake! One of the big mistakes of history . . .

"Somebody made a big mistake," thundered State's Attorney
Maclay Hoyne.

"Somebody made a big mistake," echoed District Attorney Charles F. Clyne.

"A big mistake was made by the officers," intimated Captain Ira Mansfield and William Nicholas, the local steamboat inspectors.

The discrepancy in the total loss of life emblazoned on the newspaper's front page and the number of victims at the armory was the result of some inevitable duplication in count, taken at the *Eastland*'s dock, the Reid-Murdoch warehouse and on the decks of the *Theodore Roosevelt*. The paper further stated that the toll might possibly be as high as 1800, the figure depending upon how many had escaped the ship without reporting the fact.

Reporters on the scene, looking for authoritative sources of information, quickly seized upon the words of wisdom from John V. Elbert, the *Titanic* survivor who was on duty with chief engineer Erickson when the *Eastland* took her fatal list. Elbert was quoted as calmly saying that the capsizing was the result of most of the passengers rushing to the portside of the *Eastland* to watch a launch passing by.

This was quickly challenged by a bystander—one who had, by sheer luck, escaped a watery tomb on the vessel. He was C. B. Hadley who, with two companions, had found themselves in a part of the deck used as a smoker.

"It would have been impossible," said the bitter Hadley. "People were packed aboard too closely to budge. We found the companionways between stairway and promenade so crowded we had to squeeze through. From my observation I should say there were about 3500 passengers aboard. Every part of the boat was crowded to standing capacity."

In that same Sunday morning issue the *Tribune* expanded its "mistake" pronouncement—"Somebody made a big mistake . . . what will take rank as one of the big mistakes of history . . . and the placid, shallow, narrow, utilitarian Chicago River folded to its bosom perhaps as many human beings as ever were caught in any ocean tragedy of modern times."

But perhaps the most pertinent item to appear on that frightful page on a warm Sunday morning in July of 1915 was a small but prophetic paragraph referred to in newspaper terminology as a "sidebar."

According to steamship men the amount of damages the relatives of the persons who lost their lives on the *Eastland* can recover is only to the extent of the value of the hull. It was estimated to be worth $10,000.

The steamship men were simply pointing out that however fearful the toll, admiralty law limited damages to the value of the surviving wreckage. It was an insidious law, energetically sustained and supported by shipping interests for years, and one that obviously deprived survivors of disasters, or their families, from compensation no matter what the circumstances, how qualified the officers in charge of a stricken ship had proven to be, or, for that matter, how negligent had been the owners and managers. But it was the law.

"Punish the guilty," was the cry of city, state and federal authorities who immediately began separate investigations. State's Attorney Maclay Hoyne indicated that his inquiry might reveal "an incredible story of human avarice and graft." District Attorney Charles F. Clyne was instructed by Federal Judge Kenesaw Mountain Landis (later Commissioner of Baseball) to invoke the full force of federal law to ferret out the facts and fix the liability. The federal law, unlike the civil admiralty law which dealt most leniently in regards to monetary compensation, had drastic provisions against corruption or criminal negligence on the part of boat owners, their officers and public officials, including steamboat inspectors, in instances of disasters that resulted in loss of life. The penalty was $10,000 fine or imprisonment for ten years, or both. Punishment for similar offenses under the state law called for a $5,000 fine and/or three years' imprisonment.

The official indignation was enthusiastically supported by Victor A. Olander, secretary of the Lake Seamen's Union, who charged that the federal inspection service was worse than a farce. Mr. Hoyne, with evidence supplied by Mr. Olander, pointed out that the United States inspection bureau had full warning of the dangerous conditions of lake excursion boats a full year before the dreadful calamity that had befallen the *Eastland.*

In the wake of the fist-shaking and righteous desk thumping, Coroner Hoffman ordered the arrest of every official of the Indiana Transportation Company. Chief of Police Charles C. Healey, with Captain Pedersen and first mate Fisher already in custody, ordered further arrests of the *Eastland*'s crew, from chief engineer Erickson to the mess boys—twenty-nine in all.

Ironically, at the time Mr. Greenbaum was entering into contract with Mr. Malmros of the Hawthorne Club's picnic committee, operators of most of the Great Lakes passenger and excursion fleets were still congratulating themselves on obtaining important concessions and changes in the recently passed LaFollette Law, which originally sought to require vessel operators to supply more lifeboats and increase the crews on their boats. Albert W. Goodrich of the Goodrich fleet, A. A. Shantz of the Detroit and Cleveland Navigation Company, and Thomas F. Newman of the Cleveland and Buffalo Transit Company had all appeared before congressional committees, contending that if they were required to carry lifeboat capacity for every person aboard, every passenger vessel on the Great Lakes would stay tied up at the docks. To many this sounded like a threat rather than a simple statement of fact. Under consideration for twenty-two years, the law had been proposed by the various seamen's unions, who pointed out that the crowded boats often operated literally with skeleton crews of experienced seamen and that, in emergencies, the passengers would be the ultimate losers.

A case in point, relative to the *Eastland,* was dramatized by Dr. Fred D. Farr, one of the rescue physicians who was photographed aboard the ship, pointing to a topside compartment of one hundred life preservers—unused because the compartment was padlocked and remained so while the *Eastland*'s crew fled the ship unscathed and while hundreds of passengers floundered about in the river. Later it took workmen with crowbars to pry loose the padlocks and staples that held the door closed.

"What were they saving them for?" questioned Dr. Farr.

By Monday all but fourteen of the dead at the armory and various undertaking establishments had been identified. The known toll at this time was eight hundred and ten, with more thought to be deep in the overturned hull. As the number at the armory had dwindled, there developed a heart-tugging mystery. Still unidentified was a small boy, obviously dressed in his Sunday best, as the picnic occasion merited. On the tag he was "No. 396"—no more, no less.

"Who is little No. 396?" the newspapers asked. "Who is the 'little feller'?"

Coroner Hoffman suspected that the lad remained unnamed because his parents were still included among the unidentified or were perhaps still in the *Eastland*'s submerged rooms or passages.

The small, quiet form of the "little feller" had a curious psychological effect on Chicagoans. To them the single, lonely, unclaimed victim symbolized the enormity of the catastrophe, the fickle forces of adversity and a fate which, but for the grace of God, could have been theirs.

"Who is the little feller?" everybody asked.

In the wake of frequent vengeful promises by the prosecuting authorities to punish the guilty—inspectors, owners and crew—and the certainty that the red tape of legal procedures would be further complicated by the defense of the politically powerful vessel operators, one paper returned some semblance of perspective to the scene by asking: "Who speaks for the little feller?"

Eight days later a pair of youngsters, brought to a mortuary where the little feller had been moved, pointed to him and said, "That's him—that's Willie!" The two were playmates of Willie Novotny—Walter and Willie Cech. But an uncle from another city did not agree with the identification.

"But we been livin' right next door to him," protested the Cech brothers. "We was at his birthday party when he turned seven. Get Willie's grandmother—she's all that's left next door. She'll tell you."

Willie's grandmother, who had already buried her daughter, son-in-law and eight-year-old Mamie, was Agnes Martnek, obviously in a state of shock, distraught and plagued with a language barrier. Unaccountably she had failed to notify authorities that there was still another Novotny missing.

Brought to the mortuary in tears, she was carrying a small bundle. Opened by a policeman, it revealed a small pair of brown knickerbockers, never worn.

"If it's Willie, he's got on pants like these," she haltingly explained. "It was a new suit he went to the picnic in, and two pairs of pants came with it. These are the other pair."

No. 396 was indeed Willie Novotny.

For the tragedy-plagued Plamondon family one might say their predilection for mass disaster was predictable, almost ordained by fate. First to feel the brush of death was young Charlotte Plamondon. Charlotte was in box A in Chicago's spanking new but shamefully overcrowded Iroquois Theater that fateful day of December 30, 1903, when the scenery caught fire and precipitated a conflagration and panic that killed 602 people. Miraculously rescued but in a state of collapse, she was prostrated for weeks.

When Captain Walther Schwieger of the German submarine *U-20* unleased a torpedo at the *Lusitania* off the Head of Kinsale, Ireland, on May 7, 1915, it had, as the saying goes, "the Plamondon name on it." Charlotte's parents, Mr. and Mrs. Charles A. Plamondon, were among the 1198 lost, 124 of them Americans.

Now again, just over two months later, there were nine Plamondons aboard the overcrowded *Eastland*, apparently with no premonition of calamity. Only eight came home that night. Susie C. Plamondon had been the latest victim of the family with a curious affinity for wholesale tragedy.

The Behnkes, when they handed little three-year-old Martha up to the arms of a helpful stranger, expected to join her in safety as soon as they had wended their way over the steel plates of the *Eastland* and across the temporary bridge formed by the tug *Kenosha*. But little Martha and the stranger had both been swallowed up in the mass of hysterical humanity. Nor could the kind people who had been part of the human chain recall what had happened to her. Panic-stricken, they appealed to the Chicago *Tribune* for help. The *Tribune,* true to its credo as being the "World's Greatest Newspaper," ran a story. "Missing," the story began, "Martha Behnke, aged three. Please return to Mr. and Mrs. Julius Behnke, 3816 South Lincoln Street, or call YArds 5419 and Mrs. Behnke will send Mr. Behnke for the child."

The reunion was prompt and tearful.

For Edward Bartlett and LeRoy Bennett who began their

long association as enemies and soon became fast friends, the end had come quickly and mercifully on the lower deck. Twenty years earlier, as strangers, they had faced each other in a long and bloody prize fight in George Kerwin's saloon. Both fought to utter exhaustion, collapsing in each other's arms. They had walked out of the saloon as admiring friends and were as close as brothers thereafter. Bartlett was not a member of the *Eastland*'s crew, but tended bar for a concessionaire. Bennett was his trusted assistant. When divers found them, they were again clasped in each other's arms, just as at the end of that savage fight at Kerwin's saloon. But this time it was an embrace of death.

The long lines of victims were still growing in the Second Regiment Armory when charges were being fired at the Western Electric Company in general and the Hawthorne Club in particular—charges intimating that the club was not the happy and benevolent organization outsiders considered it to be, but an insidious and malignant agent of management and a source of bitter resentment among those who feared not to comply with its demands.

Sobbing with uncontrolled grief and raising his fists to the Almighty as he stood over the bodies of his daughters Agnes and Anna, Anthony Thies charged that his girls, both employees of department No. 2311, had been forced to buy tickets and go to the picnic. "They forced them to go," he yelled. "I begged them to stay at home, but Anna told me she would lose her job if she didn't go. She said the foreman of her department, a Mr. Patterson, had warned her that unless she and Agnes went, their names would be scratched from the payroll."

Speaking for another cold form, that of Agnes Kasperski, the girl who was afraid of the water, was her uncle, County Commissioner Thomas Kasperski.

"Agnes' fear of the water had been conquered by her fear of losing her job," Kasperski said flatly.

Numbers of survivors came forward to report that they bought tickets only because they thought they would lose their jobs if they did not do so. Many of them said that the foremen of their departments hinted strongly that they would be expected to go. Others asserted that employees who did not accompany the excursionists the year before were subsequently laid off without apparent reason.

"I was working for the Western Electric Company last year and did not go to the picnic," volunteered Frank Baubies. "Shortly afterward I was laid off and I was never able to learn why. Several other employees whom I knew had similar experiences."

Peter Frisina, white and trembling, identified the body of his wife Anna, nineteen years old. He dropped weakly into a chair and told his story.

"Oh, if I hadn't taken tickets, even if it cost me my job," he moaned. "The employees of the Western Electric Company held two big parades on the company's ground just last week. The foremen of the various departments talked to those working under them and told them the plan for the excursion.

" 'We'll all have a great time,' they said. 'Everybody will be happy. It will be the biggest thing we've ever done. The factory's going to close down and everybody's going. We will arrange it so you can each take your wife or best girl and two or three friends. Tickets for the trip will cost you only 75¢ each.'

"The foremen themselves distribute the tickets," Frisina continued. "I was in the japanning department. I got tickets for my wife and myself. The foreman's name was John Jensen. We got the impression that our jobs were no good unless we went along. Some of us didn't want to go, but we finally decided to because we didn't want to be fired."

Other unhappy ticket holders complained that departmental Booster Clubs parroted the words and wishes of the
foremen, putting undue pressure on employees to support
and attend dinners, banquets, concerts, social events and
especially the big picnic at Michigan City.

Among the first documents seized by State's Attorney
Hoyne was the contract between the Hawthorne Club's Mr.
Malmros and the Indiana Transportation Company—one
which gave every incentive for the "hard sell" ticket campaign
among the workers. It provided for a substantial rebate for
the club, to be subtracted from the adult ticket charges, on
a sliding scale basis, 42½ cents on 2500 or more tickets, 45
cents if more than 3500 were sold and a 50 cents rebate on
sales beyond 4100.

Coroner Peter Hoffman, in planning his inquest, retained
the services of W. J. Wood, a naval architect held in high
respect by marine people. He was to remain on the scene as
the ship was raised, assuring that no evidence would be lost
or destroyed. He was then to submit his expert testimony on
the reason or reasons for the capsizing. Mr. Wood knew the
Eastland as few men did, having been hired by the original
owners to study and correct obvious faults shortly after the
275-foot vessel was launched at the Jenks Shipbuilding Company at Port Huron, Michigan. One of the first problems
was the ship's deplorable habit of shedding her propeller
blades, due, the shipyard workers said, to her extra-power-
ful engines. This was corrected by using one-piece propellers
rather than those with detachable blades that could be removed from the hub in case of damage. This did nothing to
alter her stability, or lack of it. The *Eastland* was a "tender"
ship from the day she slid down the ways, and her reputation
as a difficult vessel to manage became legend all over the
lakes.

The owners commissioned Mr. Wood to rectify her nasty
characteristics but failed to produce a copy of her architec-

tural "lines" and allocated him only $12,000 for the job—$2000 for experimenting and $10,000 to remedy her ills.

Mr. Wood was a Scotsman who had received his training in the famous shipyards along the Clyde, wherein, it was said, labored the most skilled shipwrights in the world.

With a native burr as broad as a Glasgow dock, he once described to a colleague the events on the day he gave the *Eastland* the all-revealing "S" test. This involved steaming full ahead with ballast tanks empty, then turning the wheel "hard over" to starboard, followed shortly thereafter by a "hard over" to port, reversing the curve. Said Wood: "I thocht the domned shep wad tak the turrns on herrrr side lak a skipping stane."

With the money available, all Wood could do to improve the *Eastland*'s behavior was to remove the staterooms from the hurricane or top deck and relocate her heavy engines. He also recommended that the ballast compartments be kept full whenever possible.

Another Chicago naval architect, John Devereaux York, came forth with documentary proof that he had warned the authorities two years earlier of the precarious condition. The proof was a curt letter he had dictated on August 3, 1913:

> U.S. Harbormaster
> Port of Chicago
> Dear Sir:
> You are aware of the condition of the S.S. *Eastland,* and unless structural defects are remedied to prevent listing . . . there may be a serious accident.
>
> Architect
> John Devereaux York

"It was a crime to issue a certificate for the *Eastland*," reiterated York. "That vessel shouldn't be permitted in a millpond. I wrote the note to the harbormaster not long after I

Photo courtesy Rev. Edward J. Dowling, S.J.

Above: The *Arlington* in her usual midsummer role, carrying pulp-wood from Georgian Bay. Inset, Captain Junis Macksey. *Below:* The *Eastland* in her heyday, decks crowded with happy excursionists.

Photo from the author's collection

Above: Moments after the *Eastland* rolled over, survivors stand on the hull or cling to it as rescue craft converge. *Below:* Excursionists on the *Theodore Roosevelt* watched in stunned disbelief as the *Eastland* rolled over at a neighboring dock in the Chicago River.

Left: His face registering the horror of the moment, a Chicago fireman carries the body of a child from the overturned hull of the *Eastland. Right:* Diver and firemen recover the body of a young lady, a victim of the *Eastland* disaster.

Above: Crowds gather at the Clark Street bridge, only a few feet from the *Eastland. Below:* Long lines of *Eastland* victims in Chicago's Second Regiment Armory.

Photo courtesy Peggy Gamble Scruton

Above: A rare photo of the Long Point Lifesaving Station and crew in early years. *Below:* The U.S.S. *Wilmette,* the naval training ship that was once the *Eastland.*

Photo from the author's collection

Above: Long Point in winter is utter desolation, the light and its keeper's homes deserted. *Below:* Bones of an old schooner, high and dry on Long Point.

Photo from the Robert J. MacDonald collection

Photo from the author's collection

The ill-fated *Sevona* after being lengthened. Inset, Captain Donald Sutherland McDonald, her brave commander.

Typical of the cells on the *Success* was No. 22. Here dwelt James Lovelace, one of the famous "Six Men of Dorset."

Above: The *Success* drew good crowds wherever she went on her Great Lakes tour. *Below:* Early victim of the "Big Blow" was the wooden steamer *Louisiana,* ashore and burned at Washington Harbor, Lake Michigan.

Above: The *L. C. Waldo* before her meeting with Gull Rock, Lake Superior. *Below:* The *Leafield,* lost with all hands off Angus Island, Lake Superior.

Above: The *Paliki*, only vessel of the four purchased abroad by F. H. Clergue to escape the curse of Lake Superior's islands. *Below:* The unlucky *Monkshaven*, wrecked on Pie Island, Lake Superior.

Photo courtesy Dr. Richard J. Wright

Above: The *Monkshaven* in happier days, loading railroad iron at the Algoma mill. *Below:* The *Henry B. Smith,* lost with all hands on Lake Superior.

Photo from the Milton J. Brown collection

Photo from the Milton J. Brown collection

Above: Dancing Chauncey Ney's command, the *John A. McGean*, lost with all hands on Lake Huron. *Below:* The *Howard M. Hanna Jr.* was wrecked on Port Austin Reef, Lake Huron.

Photo from the Milton J. Brown collection

Above: The *Charles S. Price,* the "mystery ship" found floating upside down in Lake Huron, all hands lost. *Below:* The *Wexford,* lost on Lake Huron with her entire crew.

The *Hydrus (Above)* and the *Argus (Below)* were lost on Lake Huron with all hands.

Photo courtesy Mrs. Merle Gerred

Above: Four years before she vanished on Lake Huron, the *Isaac M. Scott* rammed and sunk the *John B. Cowle* in Whitefish Bay. Here is the *Scott* after the collision. *Below:* Lost on Lake Huron, the *Isaac M. Scott* took all hands with her.

Photo from the Milton J. Brown collection

Photo from the Milton J. Brown collection

Above: The *Regina,* lost with all hands on Lake Huron. *Below:* A Long Point victim of 1913, the steamer *C. W. Elphicke.*

Photo by W. A. Gordon

had taken a trip on the *Eastland*. She listed badly. In trying to make the harbor, it was like steering a log of wood. She wouldn't obey the helm. The rudder, of course, is merely a continuance of the keel, and the rudder is not much good if there is no keel. The *Eastland* has no keel. It was built entirely for economy. The idea was to save coal by keeping the hull as much out of the water as possible. The draft was cut in two. To insure stability, sixty percent of the hull, measuring from the keel to superstructure, should have been under water. The actual figure for the *Eastland* was thirty percent!"

"Punish the guilty," was the insistent cry that went up from official sources, and the "guilty" in their estimation were the officers of the ship, her owners and the federal steamboat inspectors.

"The federal steamboat inspection is rotten," declared Mr. Hoyne.

"Worse than a farce," agreed Victor Olander of the Lake Seamen's Union. "They had full warning more than a year ago."

Coroner Hoffman announced that he had ordered the arrest of every official of the Indiana Transportation Company. The true owner of the *Eastland* was the St. Joseph and Chicago Steamship Company, and one by one its officials were subpoenaed and ordered to appear before the investigating bodies.

Evidence, if it could be termed that, began to pile up. Many people, some of them one-time passengers, crewman or former officers of the *Eastland*, volunteered their experiences or propounded theories to newspaper reporters in cities all along the lakes.

In Minneapolis, Fred W. Beecher, a former officer, said that the big ship was doomed from the beginning in sailors' eyes, and that it had twice before barely escaped the fate it finally met—once in Chicago and once at Grand Haven,

Michigan. Said Beecher: "Each time its intake pipes were not large enough to take in necessary ballast quick enough."

Captain Merwin S. Thompson, skipper of the *Eastland* from 1911 to 1913, when she sailed out of Cleveland to Cedar Point, recalled that "it was necessary to watch her ballast below the water line very closely."

Another former commander of the ship, Captain Claud Evans, said that in his opinion the accident was caused by the water ballast being removed so the *Eastland* could dock in shallow water.

Someone produced an item that had appeared in the "Around the Great Lakes" column of the *Marine Review,* back in 1904, a full eleven years before the *Eastland* surrendered to the Chicago River, and when she was only one year old:

> The senseless crowding of passengers on the shady side of the steamer *Eastland* on her return trip from South Haven to Chicago on Sunday night caused a temporary panic on the boat. The steamer lacked her customary water ballast and the crowding to starboard gave the vessel a bad list. Strange to say, while the cause of it was perfectly apparent, the crowd refused to move until the fire hose was turned on them. This proved effective and the weights were properly distributed thereafter. But some of the women on board insisted on wearing life preservers until the boat reached her dock.

John Canning, a dining room steward, reported that the *Eastland* had listed badly for an hour while coming from St. Joseph the previous Tuesday night. He also declared that the men on the vessel were so accustomed to a slight list that no one paid much attention to it. As to the morning of the tragedy: "It was only when the dishes began to crash to the floor and it was difficult to keep one's feet that we began to be frightened. I was alone in the mess hall. I could not get the door open on account of the water pouring in against it.

Everyone on the boat has known for a long time that something was wrong that caused the occasional listing, but what
it was no one seemed to know."

Even Chicago's mayor, William Hale Thompson, rushing
home by train from San Francisco where he was honored on
"Illinois Day" at the Panama-Pacific Exposition, had his say
about the *Eastland*. Interviewed in Omaha, Nebraska, by
reporters, Thompson said: "The *Eastland* was built for speed
and should never have been chartered to carry a heavy load
of passengers."

Mayor Thompson further remarked that he had declined
to be a passenger on the *Eastland* after his first ride on the
steamer because he was afraid it would capsize.

"Who," the papers continued to remind officialdom,
"speaks for the little feller?"

In its early years the ill-fated steamer had operated out of
Chicago, steaming mostly between that city and South Haven,
Michigan. Listing on frequent occasions was apparently the
only difficulty that came to the attention of anyone but her
officers.

In 1907 the vessel was sold to Cleveland interests, many of
them city officials in the administration of Mayor Tom L.
Johnson, who operated the ship under the banner of the
Eastland Navigation Company. As strictly an excursion craft
she ran daily to Cedar Point, returning in time for a moonlight cruise. A twin screw steamer with impressive, ocean-
type lines and substantially faster than her chief competitor,
the side-wheel steamer *Goodtime*, the *Eastland* was a popular
ship. The *Goodtime*'s daily summer schedule called for her
to depart her dock fifteen minutes before the *Eastland,*
which usually passed her about the time they were abreast
of Lorain, Ohio. The *Eastland* boasted a calliope on the top
deck, between her twin funnels. On such occasions it was
frequently the wont of the orchestra's piano player to un-

limber the calliope in a loud and mocking version of "The Girl I Left Behind Me."

Although she carried thousands of passengers without a fatality over a period of years while based in Cleveland, the *Eastland* was involved in so many minor incidents, most of them associated with docking and maneuvering, that her reputation as a "crank" persisted. High out of the water and thus easily influenced by winds, she had numerous brushes with piers and docks. At one time during her Cleveland tenure rumors of her instability were so rampant as to cause the Eastland Navigation Company to offer publicly a five-thousand-dollar reward to anyone who could reveal the source of such scurrilous gossip. The company was sure the rumors originated and were propagated in the offices of their competitors. Proving it was another matter.

Despite her busy schedule the *Eastland* was not a money-making vessel in Cleveland. The facts of life in the excursion business included long winter lay-ups but continual maintenance. In service she burned five tons of coal per hour and required a competent crew, somewhat difficult to recruit on a short-season basis. The fact that she was owned by persons prominent in local politics was another adverse factor. Political favors came easily in the form of guest passes, especially on the moonlight cruises. Fully half of her human cargo on these occasions consisted of constituents of the councilmen and public officials then in power at city hall. At the end of the 1914 season the owners were still encumbered with $130,000 in outstanding bonds, held by the Depositors' Savings and Trust Company, the bank headed by the mayor himself, Tom L. Johnson.

Coincidental with the grim financial picture in Cleveland, another sort of crisis was developing in St. Joseph, Michigan, and its close neighbor, Benton Harbor. The two cities, along with Grand Haven, South Haven and other communities on the east shore of Lake Michigan, were heavily dependent upon the lake steamers from an economic standpoint. All were in the great fruit belt famous for apples, peaches and cherries, but all were equally involved in the lucrative tourist and summer resort business. The east shore of the lake, the beneficiary of the lake-cooled pervailing westerly breezes, was exceedingly popular with affluent Chicago and Milwaukee people fed up with the heat and humidity of their cities. The many hotels, cottages, rooming houses and other family accommodations, with their associated food and beverage services, constituted a major source of income. In the heat of summer all who could afford the luxury beat a retreat from the big cities to take up weekend or summer residence along the east shore or the pleasant little communities lining the banks of the lake or streams that fed it. St. Joseph was no exception. But prosperity continued only as long as the major ports continued to provide the fast and economical service to the heat sufferers. The crisis in St. Joseph developed as the result of a decision of the Graham & Morton line, after the death of E. A. Graham, to discontinue service to St. Joseph specifically, building new docks midway between the neighboring cities. Graham's son-in-law, William H. Hull, then undertook to save the summer resort by organizing the St. Joseph and Chicago Steamship Company to service the port directly. He issued stock for $100,000, mostly taken up by wealthy local fruitgrowers, and set out for Cleveland, hoping to buy the *Eastland,* since it was general knowledge that the ship had proven to be a financial embarrassment there and "was available." What's more, the *Eastland* was ideally suited for the dual role of the Lake Michigan excursion vessels. The end of the tourist season happily coincided with the beginning of the fruit harvesting season, the boats then put to work carrying vast tonnages of fresh picked but perishable fruit quickly to the Chicago markets.

Mr. Hull's proposals at Cleveland aroused the interest of the Eastland Navigation Company, but the financial consideration was thought too little although the asking price was less than half the original building costs of $325,000. The Cleveland organization wanted $150,000 for the vessel—$50,000 more than Mr. Hull was prepared to offer, even though he recognized that the figure requested was a "whale of a bargain."

Returning to St. Joseph, Hull and others organized a mass meeting of citizens, raising another $25,000. The St. Joseph Development Company, subsidized for the development of the city, purchased $10,000 worth of stock and various individuals made up the difference. Walter C. Steele, a prosperous fruitgrower and farmer, contributed the greatest personal investment and as a result was named secretary and treasurer of the new steamship company, duties which were to carry him into strange realms, far beyond the relatively simple complexities of fruit farming.

Cook County coroner Peter Hoffman, whose inquiry into the *Eastland* disaster was the first of several investigations, had some very pertinent questions for Mr. Steele.

Q. "What is your occupation?"
A. "I till the soil."
Q. "What are your duties as secretary and treasurer?"
A. "Signing my name to a block of bank checks."
Q. "Who owned the principal stock of the company?"
A. "I did."
Q. "Then you were the angel of the corporation?"
A. "Yes, sir, I was the angel. I put in the most money."
Q. "Why did you buy the boat?"
A. "I thought it was a bargain."
Q. "How much did you pay?"
A. "It cost us $150,000."
Q. "How much did it cost to build the boat?"

A. "The original cost to build the boat was about $325,000."
Q. "Didn't you think it queer that a boat which cost so much should be offered for sale at such a ridiculously low price?"
A. "Yes, sir, I thought it somewhat odd."
Q. "Has the company made any money since it bought the *Eastland?*"
A. "No, sir; in fact, we have lost some money."

Mr. Steele's answers to subsequent questions proved only that his answer to the first one was absolutely honest—he was a tiller of the soil, not a steamboat man. He did not know who insured the ship or what was covered; he knew nothing about the circumstances of hiring the officers or crew; was unfamiliar with any of the steamship company's bylaws, how many men were required to staff the steamer, their salaries or, specifically, their duties.

Q. "You don't know much about the business, do you?"
A. "I know nothing about the practical end."

Before leaving the stand, Mr. Steele did confirm that the company's stockholders at the moment were himself, Mrs. E. A. Graham, Mr. and Mrs. George T. Hull and William Hull. A Mr. Arnold was president.

Martin Flatow, excursion agent for the *Eastland,* under questioning confirmed that children between five and twelve went aboard two on a ticket.

Q. "Have you ever seen a larger crowd on the *Eastland* than there was on this particular morning?"
A. "No."
Q. "When you came to the conclusion she was going over, what did you do?"
A. "As soon as I saw she was going over, I jumped from the fender of the boat to the dock."

Harbormaster Weckler gave important testimony regarding events after his arrival at the dock at ten minutes after seven.

"At that time the boat was listing to port," recalled Weckler. "I called up to Captain Pedersen and told him to trim his boat, shouting that I would not give him the bridge until the boat was righted. I never saw the boat loaded as heavily as it was Saturday morning, and I have seen her depart many a time."

Q. "What, in your opinion, was the cause of the listing?"

A. "There was no water in the ballast tanks. There is no doubt it had been pumped dry during the night and the captain seemed unable to take water fast enough to trim the boat before it went over. He should have been able to trim it in from three to six minutes."

Q. "Did you ever observe the *Eastland* to be a 'cranky' boat?"

A. "A boat that is difficult to handle under all circumstances is known as a 'cranky' boat and I have noticed the *Eastland* 'cranky' constantly."

Q. "Observing all these conditions, do you think the boat was overloaded?"

A. "Well, I don't think the *Eastland* should have been allowed to carry more than 1200 passengers. The *Eastland* did not have enough draft and stability to carry a larger load. Only last Tuesday I talked to Captain Pedersen and told him his boat needed trimming and was constantly 'on her ears' as we say along the river. After his arrest I heard Captain Pedersen say he tried for seventeen minutes to trim the boat. He insisted he could not get water fast enough."

Q. "Who, in your opinion, is responsible for this disaster?"

A. "It is a hard question to answer. If I had been the captain, I would never have allowed that number of passengers to board."

Q. "How long do you suppose the captain would have held his job if he had refused to accept the number of passengers which the government allows?"

A. "I don't think he would have been given an opportunity to make an explanation."

Q. "Did you know that three tons of concrete had recently been used beneath the dance hall floor?"

A. "I did not know that. How was it used?"

Q. "You say that the boat should have been trimmed in from three to six minutes. Yet the captain has said that he tried for seventeen minutes to trim his boat. How is that?"

A. "There must have been something the matter either with the pumps or the intake or outlet valves. I don't think the captain realized there was much danger until she took the plunge. Then I heard him yell to the passengers: 'Get off the best way you can.' "

L. C. Wheeler, assistant division superintendent of the Department of Justice of the United States, then read for the record the temporary inspection certificate issued June 4, 1913, by United States inspectors at Cleveland. That certificate allowed the *Eastland* to carry 2000 passengers and its validity was not to exceed one year. A later temporary certification was then read, dated June 15, 1915, issued at Grand Haven and valid for one year. This certification, signed by Robert Reid, inspector of hulls, and Charles C. Eckliff, inspector of boilers, allowed the *Eastland* to carry 2253 people, including the crew.

Deputy coroner Kennedy then produced still a third certificate, issued on July 2, 1915, twenty-two days before the disaster, giving the owners of the boat permission to carry 2570 passengers and crew. It was issued by inspectors Reid and Eckliff, at the request of Captain Pedersen.

Mr. Hoyne called attention to the fact that the date of the certificate was one day previous to a letter written by Mr. Greenbaum to the Western Electric picnic committee, agreeing to take the employees of the company on the excursion trip.

"I am not arguing a case," Hoyne told the coroner's jury, "but I want you to see the proximity of the two dates."

Earlier, while being questioned by reporters, Captain Pedersen had explained the certification process.

"Robert Reid, federal inspector of hulls at Grand Haven, pronounced the *Eastland* safe for passengers on May 7, 1915," said the captain. "I believe it was in the latter part of June that I went to Reid and got a new certificate from him increasing the capacity to 2500, excluding the crew."

"On whose request did you see Mr. Reid and obtain the certificate for the increase of the passenger capacity?" he was asked.

"On the orders of the officials of the steamship company," the captain replied. "I had been told in advance I would get what I was after."

Mr. Reid acknowledged that the passenger capacity figure had been raised as the result of a telephone request he had received from William H. Hull, the company's vice-president. Accordingly he had, upon assurance from Mr. Hull that additional life rafts would be provided, issued the new certificate.

"Isn't it rather unusual," Reid was asked, "to issue a license the day before a written application is received?"

"I had the greatest confidence in Mr. Hull," replied Reid.

Poor Mr. Reid had been under unmerciful fire from the moment the *Eastland* rolled over. Shortly after the disaster a Chicago paper made the startling discovery that steamboat inspectors lived pretty much like other people, did not endure monastic lives and were actually known to be on friendly terms with many people, including steamboat owners. Mr. Reid, it found, and somehow deplored, was a boyhood friend of George T. Arnold, president of the St. Joseph and Chicago Steamship Company, and was also acquainted with Mr. Hull and Mrs. Graham, stockholders. The paper was under the impression it had hit pay dirt when it also unearthed the astounding fact that chief engineer Joseph M.

Erickson, the man in charge of ballasting the vessel, was inspector Reid's son-in-law.

"Inspector's son-in-law got 'fat' job on the *Eastland*," said the headline.

This inspired the obvious question at the coroner's inquest.

"Did you ever recommend anybody for a position on the *Eastland?*"

"I never did," replied Reid.

Mr. Erickson's presence on the *Eastland,* as other questioning developed, was actually the result of Mrs. Erickson's influence with old friends in St. Joseph, some of whom were financially interested in the ship or close to people who were. Since a ship's engineer is "home" only when his ship is in port or during the winter lay-up, one location is as good as another.

"Why did Mrs. Erickson want her husband on the *Eastland?*" Reid was asked.

"So that he could live in St. Joe, where she went to live."

While the paper's terminology of the chief engineer's position as a "fat" job was not one to win friends among any who had shared the burden of responsibilities incumbent to the title, it was generally agreed that improper ballasting, with perhaps contributory causes, had spelled doom to the *Eastland.*

The blame could not be put entirely upon Mr. Erickson, who was doing his best to put the vessel on an even keel. Nor was the engineer one of the crew who abandoned ship when capsizing was imminent.

Mr. Elbert, the loquacious gauge man, told newspapermen that Mr. Erickson had probably averted a boiler explosion by ordering the injectors of the boilers filled.

"Had there been not enough water in the boilers, the onrush of cold water from the river would have caused a certain explosion," explained Elbert. "The chief engineer did all in his power to save it. He stayed in the engine room until the rush of water from the side made him stand in it up to his neck."

The usual rapport between shipmaster and owners certainly did not exist between Captain Pedersen and the officers of the steamship line, or, if it ever had, the time-honored relationship exploded into nothingness when vice-president Hull placed the blame for the tragedy entirely on the captain.

Mr. Hull, who refused to make the charge personally, had Charles E. Kremer, considered to be Chicago's foremost admiralty proctor, issue a formal statement placing all the responsibility on Captain Pedersen.

Kremer, in reviewing the history of the boat, asserted it had carried as many as 3300 passengers on many trips, that altogether one million passengers had ridden on the ship, and not a soul had perished until that dreadful Saturday of July twenty-fourth.

"Water ballast," Kremer said, "is the answer to the tragedy. The captain was to blame for failing properly to scatter his load over the decks and failing to watch the water ballast tanks. It was up to the captain to size up and distribute his cargo, whether human beings or pig iron. The captain is an autocrat. He could throw the President of the United States off his boat if he tried to boss the job. The captain can't personally do everything, but he can give orders. I cannot imagine any reason in the world why the ship should not have been ballasted that day."

Ill and in jail, Captain Pedersen fired back, bitter about the eroding authority of a shipmaster, especially one employed by the St. Joseph and Chicago Steamship Company.

"The master of a ship nowadays does not possess the powers he did years ago," said Pedersen. "It formerly was the custom for the captain to be in absolute control of his boat and the business carried on by the vessel. Now the captain has nothing to say about the freight, passengers, crew or sailing. The only man I had power to employ was my first mate. Officials hired the engineer, and practically everything else was handled from the main office. The responsibility is not mine. I often noticed the boat list, but it was never anything serious and I believed the engineer knew his duties and business. I had certain duties to perform and my power was limited to those. I carried out orders to the best of my ability."

State's Attorney Hoyne, rubbing his hands in evident satisfaction, confided to the press: "The captain has come through. He isn't going to be made the goat."

And still that insistent, demanding question posed by the press in the midst of official verbiage: "Who speaks for the little feller?"

An examination of the *Eastland*'s past passenger-carrying certifications proved only that inspectors displayed a wide variance in judgment as to the safety limit. Captain Ira B. Mansfield, a Chicago inspector, had issued over a period of years permits for 2800, 2907 and, on one occasion, a permit for 3000.

"How do you determine the number of passengers that can be carried in safety?" Captain Mansfield was asked.

"It depends first on the life-saving equipment," he replied.

"Is it true that you simply measure the deck area and authorize a passenger every square foot?"

"No, we fix the limit to prevent overcrowding."

Naval architect Wood was critical of methods the inspectors used to determine the capacity of a passenger or excursion ship, terming the new certificate issued to the *Eastland* as "irregular."

"The number of passengers a steam passenger ship may carry is calculated not alone on the basis of the amount of life-preserving apparatus aboard, but also upon the amount of deck space. The certificate allowing the increase in the number of passengers to be carried was presumably granted because four life rafts had been added to the ship's life-saving equipment. These life rafts did not increase the deck space, and if the vessel could carry only a few more than 2000 passengers before the addition of the rafts, it could carry no more afterward. Nine square feet per passenger must be allowed, according to law, and the addition of life rafts should not have been allowed to alter this rule."

Mr. Greenbaum, the Indiana Transportation Company's man in Chicago and charter party in arranging the excursion with the Hawthorne Club's appointed committee, was also in very hot water. Assistant State's Attorney Duval, in a dramatic gesture, charged: "That at a time when men, women and children were dying in the water, Greenbaum was counting tickets, overlooking the scene, in the effort to protect himself against charges of overloading the ship."

Ironically, a full year before the disaster, in his annual report, William L. Bodine, the quiet and efficient superintendent of compulsory education for Chicago's board of education, predicted just such a fate as befell the *Eastland*'s happy excursionists:

> Our investigation shows that the average lake excursion boat is frequently crowded to the rails on weekend trips and holidays . . . many women and children will someday pay the tragic penalty of overcrowded boats and lack of adequate life saving facilities. I recommend that the lake excursion of the vacation schools be abandoned. It is only a question of time when there will be a disaster on one of these excursion boats that will stagger Chicago.

The toll of the *Eastland*'s capsizing fortunately did not reach the 1200 figure the *Tribune* had originally anticipated. Altogether 812 bodies were recovered and identified. Others

who died later as a result of injuries brought the total to
835 people. Twenty-two entire families were wiped out. By
any standards it was a calamity of enormous proportions. In
Cornish, New Hampshire, where he was taking a short vacation, President Woodrow Wilson, appalled by the news
accounts and alarmed by early charges of negligence upon
the part of the steamboat inspectors, quickly assured Chicago
officials that he was aware of the tragedy and its ramifications
by making public the text of his wire to the Department of
Commerce, calling for "a searching investigation to determine if any violations of the steamship inspection laws were
involved." "Begin the investigations with all possible haste,"
concluded the President.

His feathers ruffled by the intensity of the criticism in
Chicago and doubtless alarmed at the President's promise of
a thorough airing of one of his departments, Secretary of
Commerce William C. Redfield interrupted the San Francisco
vacation of General George Uhler, supervising general of
the steamboat inspection service, sending him to Chicago
forthwith. From Washington he also dispatched acting supervising inspector, Dickerson N. Hoover. Shortly thereafter,
piqued at the continuing outcry, Redfield also departed for
Chicago.

"A big joke," warned Victor Olander, the Lake Seamen's
Union secretary. "The United States inspection service is
directly responsible for this disaster. Now they are either
here or are on their way here, for what? To investigate their
own service and their own officials? The inspection service
has been an open scandal with seamen for years. Now is the
time to inspect the inspectors and here are the men who
should be investigated—George Uhler, the ten supervising
inspectors and particularly investigate Charles H. Westcott,
of Detroit, the inspector for the Eighth District. If he didn't
know that the *Eastland* was an unsafe boat, then he is unfit

to be an inspector. If he did know and permitted the boat to go on in its unsafe condition, then he should by all means be investigated."

"There has been a cheerful good-fellowship between the inspectors and the boat owners in fixing the capacity," roared Mr. Hoyne. "The only basis has been guesswork and influence."

Miffed, Secretary of Commerce Redfield issued a statement challenging Mr. Olander to present his charges under oath and to justify his complaints by facts.

Mr. Olander, it transpired, had been a thorn in the side of Secretary Redfield for a long time, being the author of numerous inspired communications citing instances of laxity on the part of local inspectors in particular and the inspection service in general. The contents of the letters and resultant inaction on the part of the service now became a daily theme in the Chicago papers where Olander's charges, old and new, received exposure that deeply embarrassed both Mr. Redfield and General Uhler.

Olander detailed how one sincere inspector at Duluth, Captain Monaghan, appalled at the great losses in the November storm of 1905, had tried to force some changes in the hatch systems on Great Lakes bulk vessels. He was overruled by Uhler, according to Olander, on a mere technicality. Then, after the 1913 storm claimed twelve vessels with all hands, Captain Monaghan had again taken the matter up with his superiors, who advised him to wait a few days. "Shortly afterward," charged Olander, "he was told to 'drop it.' And since 1905 thirty-one vessels have gone down on the Great Lakes with every person on board."

Stout substantiation for Olander's unremitting requests for changes in the inspection service came from E. L. Nockels, secretary of the Chicago Federation of Labor. Slightly more than a year before the *Eastland* tragedy Nockels wrote Assistant Secretary of Commerce Sweet that he had proof that "inspectors of the steamboat inspection service have taken orders from the shipowners."

He also reminded Mr. Redfield's assistant that up until four or five days before it sank on September 9, 1910, the steamer *Pere Marquette* had been carrying large excursions out of Chicago daily. "Fortunately," he continued, "when it sank there were only sixty-one people on board, practically all members of the crew, but twenty-seven were drowned. The United States inspectors who investigated the case reported that they were unable to determine what caused the sinking although they had earlier certified it seaworthy."

Nockels further asserted that the inspectors were doing the bidding of the shipowners by not requiring a full and experienced crew, naming as examples the steamers *Christopher Columbus, Racine, Iowa, Alabama, City of Grand Rapids,* and *Carolina.*

A typical Olander-to-Redfield missive was the result of a trip the union official took on the *Christopher Columbus* on August 8, 1914. "I noted that every one of the eight large gangways are in such condition that not one of them can be closed quickly in the event of an accident."

"Prove it," was in essence the challenge of Redfield, who again stoutly defended his inspectors.

Olander did prove it by badgering two of the Chicago inspectors to accompany him to the *Christopher Columbus* one night. In triumph he reported to Redfield on the incident: "It took about one hour partially to secure the gangways while the vessel was lying at its dock and where the services of every member of its deck crew were available!"

Although still maintaining that his inspectors were above reproof, Mr. Redfield belatedly did initiate an investigation but, strangely, it began in Atlantic and Gulf ports where two supervising inspectors and eight inspectors were dismissed.

The investigation had not reached the Great Lakes district when the *Eastland* calamity brought a swarm of critics down upon his head.

Although Mr. Redfield was supposedly an astute politician and as such given credit for being able to judge the public, its temper, moods, whims and wishes, he showed little knowledge of these important attributes upon his arrival in Chicago. The very first night, almost as though the *Eastland* affair was incidental to his political duties, he was the guest of honor at a dinner given at the Indian Hill Golf Club by Rush C. Butler, A. W. Shaw and Cornelius Lynde. Members of the federal trade commission were also guests.

Despite headline warnings of "self-inquiry" tactics, the secretary almost immediately announced that this was exactly what was about to take place. He appointed Frank W. VanPatten and William A. Collins, steamboat inspectors at Milwaukee, to conduct the inquiry with the assistance of the commanding officers of the steamboat inspection service, naming in particular General Uhler, the supervising inspector, and Albert L. Thurman, solicitor for the department of commerce. Redfield himself was to be chairman of the inquiry board.

Obviously shaken by the protesting cries of "whitewash" by the press and local law-enforcement officials, he quickly modified the proposed inquiry board by appointing as additional members Harry A. Wheeler, vice-president of the Union Trust Company; Marvin B. Pool, vice-president of Butler Brothers; and an engineer from the staff of the Western Electric Company, unnamed at the moment. None of the appointed gentlemen could be expected to know starboard from port, fore from aft or a propeller steamer from a side-wheeler.

He explained the added starters as an honest effort "to give the people of this city an opportunity for a part in this inquiry."

"Who speaks for the little feller?" thundered the news-papers.

But Mr. Redfield was really just beginning to feel the heat of public wrath as the inquiry began, and it soon became ob-vious to observers that the inspectors were not going to suf-fer as a result.

One politically prominent Chicagoan protested in the *Tribune:* "I don't believe President Wilson understands what this man has been doing. To come out here while we were mourning over our dead and tell us that everything was all right, that no one was to blame and that his inspec-tion service was above reproach. . . . I am in favor of recall-ing the coroner's jury and making a special report on this man Redfield to the President!"

Attorney Charles A. Churan wrote the President: "I sub-mit that Mr. Redfield has forfeited his usefulness to the government. . . ."

The board of directors of the Women's City Club adopted resolutions protesting against the Redfield investigation and requesting the President to appoint two United States naval engineers and two private naval engineers, augmented by Chicago citizens, to constitute a board of inquiry in which "the public might have confidence."

Assistant corporation counsel Max M. Korshak was quoted prominently in the *Tribune* as saying: "One is surprised at the boldness of the attempt so soon after the death of in-nocent men, women and children to give a clean bill of health to persons responsible for the disaster."

Shown Korshak's statement, Redfield shrugged and said: "I am uninterested. People are so previous."

But thereafter Mr. Redfield maintained an aggrieved at-titude, turning most of the questioning over to solicitor Thurman.

In the matter of investigations, however, Mr. Redfield and his hand-picked board were only part of a small army of men trying to find out exactly what had happened and who was guilty. On Wednesday, July 28, no less than six inquiries were under way or about to begin. State's Attorney Hoyne's grand jury had already subpoenaed over one hundred witnesses. Coroner Hoffman's jury had already swung into action and United States District Attorney Clyne was competing for interest and witnesses at the same time. The Harbor and Wharves Committee of the city council announced procedural hearings to begin at once, and the state public utilities commission was insisting that it had jurisdiction as an investigative body. Meanwhile, Captain Pedersen and thirty-seven of his crew, from chief engineer Erickson and first mate Delbert Fisher to porters and firemen, were languishing in various city jails, waiting to be called as witnesses. The steamboat inspectors and officials of the steamship company were permitted to stay at hotels, under observation by police officers.

Where to start? Mr. Hoyne had long since dispatched an investigator, A. H. Payne, to Grand Haven, there to seize and impound the inspection records of the *Eastland*. Others dashed to the offices of the steamship company in St. Joseph, there to impound more data—passenger statistics, revenue figures and correspondence between Mr. Greenbaum and Mr. Hull relative to the availability of the steamer for the Western Electric picnic.

Back in Chicago a donnybrook developed over possession of evidence seized on the vessel itself. Hoyne called upon Chief of Police Charles C. Healey to surrender documents taken from the ship by police. He was told that the police had no documents save one inconsequential bit of paper. Hoyne was told by coroner Hoffman, however, that the police did have very important evidence. Hoyne then angrily called the chief by telephone only to be informed that he was too late, that the evidence had already been impounded by Mr.

Clyne. Highly vexed, Hoyne issued a blistering statement calling for harmony on the part of all investigators. He was joined by coroner Hoffman in declaring that the government and the city police were opposing the state's attorney and the coroner, seriously impeding the exposure of facts. "If necessary," roared Hoyne in righteous wrath, "and in event there is any attempt made to interfere with the progress of the coroner's inquest into this disaster—that is, with reference to withholding evidence—I will go before the grand jury and make a request for the issuance of a subpoena duces tecum to produce such evidence."

The evidence in question originally seized by police was an order carried by Captain Pedersen, issued to him in 1913 or 1914 by the heads of the steamship company, that 2200 be the limit of the number of passengers carried on that boat at any one time; the certificate of inspection issued at Cleveland in June, 1914, by M. W. Phillips, federal inspector, fixing the limit as 2000 exclusive of the crew of seventy; the charts of the boat, the boat's license, the engineer's license and other papers that might prove of value in fixing the blame for the accident.

Federal Judge Landis, meanwhile, strengthened the government's hand by ordering the hulk of the *Eastland* seized by United States Marshal John J. Bradley. This was done to give the government complete jurisdiction over the boat and to prevent state or local authorities from tampering with it or removing such parts as might become important evidence in the prosecution of the grand jury hearing. Under orders from Mr. Clyne, workmen began sealing up all openings and posting notices of seizure in conspicuous places on the hull.

Mr. Hoyne, thoroughly enraged by Secretary Redfield's condescending attitude and fearful that inspectors Robert Reid and Charles Eckliff, along with officials of the steamship company, would escape guilt and punishment in the inquiry being conducted by the inspection service, prepared his own indictments and subpoenas, these to be held in abeyance and enforced should the proceeding turn out to be what he suspected—a "whitewash."

Hoyne's wrath had been aroused one day by Redfield's bumptious statement that the state lacked jurisdiction. This had sent the state's attorney and his assistants to poring over statutes, ordinances and court opinions far into the night. Morning found Mr. Hoyne waxing triumphant. They had found a court opinion in the case of Cummings versus the City of Chicago where the court had overruled the federal government in a dispute over building a dock on the Calumet River, allowing the city concurrent jurisdiction. Hoyne then announced that his office had complete jurisdiction in the *Eastland* case so far as it affected anybody who was on the boat that fateful Saturday morning.

"Also," snapped Hoyne, "the police power of the city, which extends three miles into the lake, is a charter ordinance."

If the physical evidence seized by police was the subject of heated jurisdictional disagreement, it was no less distressing than the squabbles over the human element involved. Hoyne had early ordered the arrest of steamship company officials Hull and Steele, Captain Pedersen, chief engineer Erickson, Walter Greenbaum and Grand Haven inspectors Reid and Eckliff. Mr. Clyne had done likewise, only sooner. Greenbaum and Steele were able to obtain bonds. Secretary Redfield kept the two inspectors from the indignity of the cells by assuming personal responsibility for their appearance when needed. Captain Pedersen and chief engineer Erickson remained in the poky although several lake captains tried vainly to arrange for their release.

Dispatches from St. Joseph shortly after news of the disaster became known there reported that the shock of the affair had left Mr. Hull, vice-president and general manager of the steamship company, prostrate with grief, a nervous wreck.

"Physicians and nurses who are attending him refuse to allow anyone except near relatives in his room," the news story revealed.

But only the next day, upon receiving a federal subpoena, Mr. Hull underwent a remarkable recovery, departing for Chicago with considerable alacrity. The federal subpoena, issued by Judge Landis, turned out to be the instrument that kept him out of jail.

On Wednesday night Mr. Hoyne learned that Hull was in conference with his lawyers, Charles E. Kremer and James J. Barbour, in the Insurance Exchange Building. Deputy sheriff Peonki, having specific orders to arrest Hull, made his way with all promptness to Kremer's office. Attorneys Kremer and Barbour, however, claiming to be outraged by the procedure, refused to allow the deputy to serve the state mittimus on their client. Apprised of the state of siege in the law office, Assistant District Attorney Joseph B. Fleming sent special agent Frank Cantwell to escort Hull to the Federal Building. The lawyers and deputy sheriff Peonki trooped along behind them, apearing forthwith before Judge Landis. Fleming and Kremer called the court's attention to the fact that Mr. Hull had come to Chicago as a government witness.

"This man is here in response to a federal grand jury subpoena and must not be molested," Judge Landis ruled. Pointing to deputy Peonki, he continued: "I can't permit you to dart out of a dark alley and nail him. The law is plain. Go tell them to look up their law. Tell them also, if they say anything to you, that I did it."

This led to another heated conference at the office of sheriff Traeger with the sheriff, chief deputy Peters, coroner Hoffman and attorneys Joseph Graber and Patrick O'Donnell trying to decide whether or not to defy Judge Landis and arrest Hull. The sheriff and the coroner were for making the arrest without further delay. The matter was decided after a phone call to Mr. Hoyne, his first knowledge of Judge Landis' ruling.

"Do not arrest him," Hoyne sighed. "Follow Judge Landis' ruling. I will take all the responsibility."

The coroner's jury, as expected, promptly indicted William Hull, Captain Pedersen, chief engineer Erickson, inspectors Robert Reid and Charles Eckliff along with Walter Greenbaum, charging them with criminal negligence and manslaughter. District Attorney Clyne was also successful in having George T. Arnold, president of the steamship company, named among those he intended to try for manslaughter, naming all of them in three indictments returned by the grand jury.

When the wrangling and desk thumping had subsided, possibly because of sheer exhaustion of official vocal cords, some degree of sanity returned to the scene. Those named in the indictment who had not previously been allowed bail were finally permitted to post bond and walk from their cells, free men for the time being. Although the breach between the ship's officers and the steamship company officials had widened into an awesome chasm of no return, all concerned beat a hasty retreat to their Michigan homes.

The immediate economic result of the *Eastland* affair and the unanswered question still posed—stability, overcrowding and the qualifications of the inspectors—had the effect of bringing lake travel out of Chicago to a complete halt. The boats of four companies, Graham & Morton Transportation Company, South Haven Steamship Company, the Goodrich Transit Company and the Northern Michigan Transportation Company lay idle at their docks, decks unsullied by the feet of paying passengers. Upkeep and overhead, meanwhile, were reaching ruinous proportions. Desperately, the officials of each company issued public statements welcoming full and complete inspection by "competent persons." Each used the exact term, indicating that there had been a free exchange of views and a meeting of minds. "Competent persons" obviously did not mean the existing steamboat inspection service.

Renewed confidence in the steamers, particularly the Goodrich Transit Company's *Christopher Columbus,* was achieved by a masterful bit of public relations work. This particular vessel, the only whaleback passenger steamer in history, had an enviable record as to safety and stability. The trouble was that her unusual construction made her *look* top-heavy, thus subjecting her to unfounded and very damaging rumors.

The Goodrich people knew that only a dramatic display of her unusual stability would quiet the ugly implications and planned a convincing demonstration to prove their point. With a barrage of advance publicity they invited as many people as cared to test their courage to board the vessel for a unique voyage, adding five hundred tons of sandbags to approximate a full passenger complement. Then, with all the sandbags, newsmen, city officials and a hired band all on the starboard side, the *Christopher Columbus* toured the harbor, her big whistle booming and the band giving out with rousing airs. Even with this tremendous off-center load she listed but a few degrees. Ironically, it was August 24, exactly a month from the day when the *Eastland* lay over on her side like a tired horse. Within a few days the *Christopher Columbus* was again doing capacity business. Boats of the other lines also found renewed patronage, and by early fall all were almost back to normal operations.

In official circles things were still at sixes and sevens. State's Attorney Hoyne and District Attorney Clyne were still calling down anathemas upon the heads of Mr. Redfield, the inspectors, the ship's officers, the officials of the steamship company and upon each other.

The St. Joseph and Chicago Steamship Company, just a

couple of days after the disaster, had asked for bids to raise and right the vessel. The winner of the contract on a no-cure, no-pay basis was the Great Lakes Towing Company. In due course of time the big wrecking tug *Favorite,* with divers and assorted ancillary gear, arrived and tied up near the tomblike hull. From Cleveland the company sent two big pontoons, specially designed for such projects. The task, under wrecking master Alex Cunning and closely observed by United States Marshal Bradley, began on August 4, and on August 16 the *Eastland,* upright and pumped out, was moored to a nearby dock, still under guard.

On the very next day, August 17, when the St. Joseph and Chicago Steamship Company began its limitation of liability proceedings, the steamer was conveyed to a Trustee appointed by the Court. Shortly thereafter a monition was issued requiring all persons having claims against the *Eastland* or her owners, arising out of the disaster, to file such claims by December. And there were plenty, literally hundreds—filed by administrators of estates of people who lost their lives or had suffered personal injuries or property loss. Others included firms or individuals that had performed services for the ship or had supplied her with her needs—repairs, fuel, groceries, paint or the scores of items a vessel requires and must receive as a matter of course.

And now, at last, there was somebody to speak for the "little feller," attorney James F. Bishop, administrator for the estate of the Novotnys. But Willie Novotny's voice was small, for Mr. Bishop also represented the estates of Susie C. Plamondon, Anna Frisina, Agnes Kasperski, Stella Michaski, Barbara Lukens, Anna Quaine and two hundred and twenty-six other victims.

On December 15, the Trustee of the Court sold the *Eastland* at public auction under direction of the United States Marshal's office to Edward A. Evers, whose $46,000 bid was highest. The limitation of liability proceedings initiated by the owners in August brought back the words of many wise and experienced marine men who said the morning after the disaster:

> . . . the amount of damages the relatives of the persons who lost their lives on the *Eastland* can recover is only to the extent of the value of the hull. . . .

Forty-six thousand dollars to be shared by nearly a thousand claimants?

It transpired that the haughty Secretary of Commerce, Mr. Redfield, had the last laugh on the subject of jurisdiction, leaving both Mr. Hoyne and Mr. Clyne red-faced and chagrined. Of those previously held, all but Mr. Greenbaum were legal residents of Michigan and as such entitled to the protection of the federal courts in that state. District Attorney Clyne sought to have them removed to the northern district of Illinois for trial, an action the defendants fought bitterly before District Judge C. W. Sessions, in the District Court of the United States for the Western District of Michigan, Southern Division. The reasoning was based on the obvious argument that the hysteria and hatred engendered by statements of Mr. Hoyne and Mr. Clyne and headlined in the public press precluded a fair trial if, indeed, they were guilty of any crime against the United States or the state of Illinois. If so, the state and District Attorney Clyne had to show reasonable proof of wrongdoing. The six defendants were aided and represented by distinguished counsel including Clarence Darrow, Senator James Barbour and John D. Black, later president of the Illinois and Chicago Bar Associations.

It was the great Darrow's task to defend Captain Pedersen. Much had been made of the *Eastland*'s chronic instability, and although experts had unsuccessfully attempted to correct her deplorable characteristics, it was somehow assumed that Captain Pedersen should have been able to do something about it.

The prosecution put upon the witness stand a university professor who described in lengthy detail the factors that go into designing a ship and the attendant labors in building it, from the laying of the keel to applying the last coat of paint. When this self-admitted authority on ship construction was turned over to Darrow for cross-examination, the local attorneys associated with him insisted that he break down the damaging testimony. "No, no," replied Darrow, "I shall build him up." Then, with his unmatched talent for assimilating technical information, he led the professor through the mechanics of shipbuilding from the beginning of time, plying him with complex and technical questions for days on end. Not only the professor, but the judge and other witnesses were exhausted and outraged at him for so inconsiderately wasting their time. When the professor had completed his lengthy testimony, much of which was far beyond the listeners, Darrow asked simply:

"Professor, is there anyone else in the world beside yourself who knows everything there is to know about ship construction?"

"Only one other man," replied the professor without a trace of false modesty. "He lives in Scotland."

"Then," demanded Darow, "if there are only two men on the face of the globe who know everything there is to know about ships, how could it be possible that the poor captain of a lake steamer could know what was wrong with the *Eastland?*"

On February 18, 1916, Judge Sessions released his eight-page decision, of which the last paragraph is most pertinent:

The dead can not be restored to life. The sorrows of the living can not be lessened by claiming other victims. The majesty of the law can not be upheld and vindicated by forcing men from their homes to stand trial among strangers upon accusations which there is barely a scintilla of proof to sustain. The evidence in this matter wholly fails to establish probable cause for believing any of these defendants guilty of any crime charged in the indictments. The application for a warrant of removal will be denied.

Gleefully, Mr. Redfield reported to his Washington superior, the Speaker of the House:

> As this was the only action in which the local inspectors at Grand Haven, Mich., Messrs. Reid and Eckliff, were concerned, the result of the judge's decision is to exonerate them fully. These officers have therefore been restored to duty, rank and pay.

While Mr. Clyne was unsuccessfully petitioning for the return of the defendants to Illinois, the Chicago and Cook County authorities had strangely lost their ardor for prosecution. Divers, in raising the *Eastland,* had found several submerged pilings and a mass of concrete on the bottom of the river. A new theory was then advanced by marine men, and one that could obviously be exploited by the defense—that the ship had capsized because it could not possibly be ballasted properly if its bottom had rested on the submerged objects. In this event either the city or county, or both, could possibly be held liable, not the ship's owners or its officers. It was a theory that neither the city nor the county authorities wished to pursue.

The *Eastland,* meanwhile, had ceased to exist as such. Edward A. Evers, the successful bidder at the public auction, sold the vessel to the United States Government for conversion into a gunboat for the training of Naval Reservists. Radically cut down, altered and renamed U.S.S. *Wilmette,* she steamed 150,000 miles on the Great Lakes, giving thousands of sun-tanned midwestern farm boys their first taste of rolling decks. One of them was the great Ernie Pyle, who later recalled his service aboard her in one of his syndicated newspaper columns:

> We sailed on the *USS Wilmette,* formerly known as the *Eastland.* It was the ship that turned over in the Chicago River in 1915 and drowned eight hundred twelve people. When it was raised, the Navy bought it and painted it gray and filled it full of innocent farm boys who wanted to be sailors. It was still in sinking condition, I assure you. It constantly shied to the right, and once in a while felt as though it wanted to lie down in the water.

Over the years she became as familiar to Chicagoans as the Wrigley Building. As the U.S.S. *Wilmette,* however, she was still haunted by those rumors of the past and recollections of that terrible rainy Saturday morning on the Chicago River, none of which inspired a feeling of security among the trainees. But rather early in her career as a training facility the *Wilmette* did what no other Great Lakes vessel had ever done—she sank a submarine!

The confrontation between the *Wilmette* and the *UC-97* took place long after the Armistice and thirty miles north of Chicago. It was decidedly a one-sided affair. The *UC-97,* with seven Allied ships to her credit, was a war prize turned over to the United States for exhibition purposes. Entering the lakes via the St. Lawrence and its modest canals, she was shown at many ports, ending up with a two-year stay at the Navy Pier in Chicago. In accordance with the Treaty of Versailles the understanding was that on or before July 30, 1921, she was to be destroyed and sunk in not less than fifty fathoms of water. On June 7 of that year she was towed to a designated spot, there to become a target for the *Wilmette* and another training ship, the U.S.S. *Hawk.* Selected for the task of sinking her with the *Wilmette*'s biggest gun were Gunner's Mate J. O. Sabin, who fired the first American shell in World War I, and Gunner's Mate A. F. Anderson, the man who fired the first American torpedo of the conflict. Out of the thirteen shells fired, ten found their mark and in ten minutes the *UC-97* took her last long dive.

Although the *Eastland* was no more, her name was still frequently on the court dockets by virtue of a great multiplicity of civil claims against her former owners—claims still valid and subject to litigation. Decisions and appeals made their tortuous way through the courts, comprising a volume of legal proceedings almost without precedent in respect to time consumed and work involved. The complete legal record of the *Eastland* affair would—does in fact—fill shelves in law libraries. World War I, already under way in Europe when the *Eastland* rolled over, burst upon the immediate horizon and dragged on until 1918. The post-war prosperity years of the 1920s were succeeded by the grim realities of the Great Depression. And by now the papers had ceased to ask who was speaking for the little feller. Claimants, witnesses, attorneys, technical experts and judges passed on and were succeeded by others. And still the matter of the *Eastland* remained on the dockets.

An interesting legal point was raised early in the proceedings when the Great Lakes Towing Company prayed for payment of its $34,500 fee, the agreed figure of the salvage contract. This action triggered a barrage of objections by other claimants. The hull of the *Eastland,* lying on its side in the river, was worth practically nothing. Only after it had been raised and pumped out did the hull become worth the $46,-000 paid for it at public auction. Therefore, the towing company reasoned and petitioned, since its services provided the $46,000 through faithful performance of its contract, it should be treated as a preferred lien claimant and promptly paid. This petition the District Court denied, a decision the towing company fought and carried on to higher courts.

Five and one-half years later the towing company was awarded the contract price plus interest and legal fees, payable by the St. Joseph and Chicago Steamship Company.

But this was only one of many, many cases that kept attorneys gainfully employed over an incredible span of time, and all because, back on the morning of July 24, 1915, "somebody made a big mistake."

In 1946 the U.S.S. *Wilmette,* nee *Eastland,* was offered for sale, as scrap, by the Government. Potential buyers ranged her hull, tapping her plates and gauging her ribs in estimating the yield in tons of good melting stock. In the end the successful bidder judged her to be worth $2500 and in due time his workers attacked her with their burning torches. Pound by pound and ton by ton they reduced her to fragments. Finally, forty-three years after she had made her troublesome and cranky debut in the cool waters at Port Huron, the *Eastland* was no more.

But the end for the army of still-hopeful claimants had come long ago, in August of 1935, to be specific, when the final court decision in the ship's long wake of trouble and travail was announced:

"In Chicago," the teletypes in newspaper offices clicked out, "the United States Circuit Court of Appeals today upheld a District Court ruling that the St. Joseph-Chicago Steamship Company, former owners of the steamer *Eastland,* which sank in the Chicago River on July 24, 1915, is not liable for the 835 deaths in the disaster."

"The Court held (as predicted on the day after the disaster) that the company was liable only to the extent of the salvage value of the vessel; that the boat was seaworthy; that the operators had taken proper precautions and that the responsibility was traced to an engineer who neglected to fill the ballast tanks properly."

Finally, twenty years after he had marched so happily over the *Eastland*'s gangway, there was no point in anyone speaking up again for "the little feller."

⚓

3

Wind, Wrecks, Whisky and Abigail Becker

Wherever geographical characteristics and the malevolent whims of nature have conspired to spawn death traps for Great Lakes ships, none was more feared for the better part of two centuries than Lake Erie's Long Point. Shorn of some of their specific elements but none of their deadliness, it was held as much in awe and dread as those nightmares of the salt water mariner—insidious Sable Island, southeast of Nova Scotia; wreck-strewn Cape Hatteras; or those twin devils of the English Channel, the hell's brew of rock and tide called the Minkies, and the clutching Goodwin Sands.

Hooking down from the Canadian shore and the flat to-bacco lands of Norfolk County, then bearing almost due east, Long Point juts twenty-two miles out into Lake Erie. And like a diabolical scythe blade it has gathered in an incredible harvest of brigs, barks, schooners, barges, scows and steamers. Its sandy beaches and offshore bars still entomb the hulks of scores of vessels, while the shifting sands of the Point itself have long since hidden the graves of sailors who found it their last port of call. The long south shore whose approaches have always been guarded by a phalanx of deadly and restless bars, has spelled doom to dozens of sailing vessels and early steamers sore beset by the dreadful southwest gales that sweep the length of the lake, unchecked until they meet that low, saberlike agent of destruction that is the peninsula of Long Point. Around the hook, on the north side, where even the big steamers of today take thankful shelter in Long Point Bay when the southwest gales roar, the seductive serenity of a safe anchorage can change to danger and destruction when the winds shift to east or northeast. For here, too, shifting sandbars lurk offshore and always, the worst of all, Bluff Bar awaits to claim the unwary, much as it did the steamer *Siberia* which, to the delight of thousands of gulls, blew off her hatches and spewed out her big cargo of barley when she foundered one wild October day in 1905.

Long Point has an excellent lighthouse, fog signal and radio beacon and while the wonders of radar, ship-to-shore radiotelephone and automatic direction finders have helped rob it of its sting, a strange paradox exists. Long Point has seemingly been bypassed by civilization as it is known today, remaining as remote and wild as it was two centuries ago. Its history, beyond that of the ships and men it has claimed, is laced with true tales of murder, piracy, ship looting, smuggling and poaching. At one time its heavily timbered swales were energetically harvested by commercial lumbermen. Their wilderness camps drew a lot of rough characters and inspired the inevitable saloons to furnish drink and relaxation. Weekly brawls, cuttings and bloody confrontations between men of rival camps kept constables and police inspectors busy. In shacks near the dreadful south shore lived the nefarious brigands and outlaws whose occupation was plundering vessels that came ashore, pirating the cargoes and looting the bodies of the unfortunate sailors. One wretch was observed stripping the body of a drowned captain of his watch and a large sum of money, but fear kept the witness silent for years. Tales of vanished riches and buried loot

abound, and the treasures have been sought by generations
of mainlanders.

Early in the 1800s a canal-like dike was dug across the
landward end of Long Point, where the peninsula narrowed
to a scant few hundred feet. Vessels bound for, or out of,
north shore ports and drawing less than nine feet of water
were thus able to avoid the long trip around the Point. This,
technically, made Long Point an island. Beyond the "Old
Cut," as it was called, the peninsula thrusts its form in that
deadly sweeping curve to the east. The inner bay along the
north shore is fringed with immense bogs and interlaced
with countless inlets, literally a mecca for ducks, geese and
waterfowl of all species. The land varies from one to three
miles in width, in places marked by a pronounced succession
of sand ridges with small, placid lakes and moors between
them. The ridges are covered, for the most part, with a jungle
of red cedar, balsam and pine, often interlaced with vines
growing with tropical profusion. Weirdly contoured sand-
hills, shaped by years of gales, are dotted with dense thickets
of juniper bushes and small trees, strangely contorted by the
same gales. Intermittently, gloomy forests and stagnant ponds
break the monotony of sand and scrub growth. Deer abound
and stare at intruders, curious and fearless. Local history
has endowed the Point's wilderness and shore with many
place names, some known only to those whose fathers and
grandfathers haunted the bogs or forests in search of game
or fished the bays and inlets of the north shore—Squire's
Ridge, Thoroughfare Point, Courtright Ridge, Allan Ridge,
Pottohawk Point, Big Rice Bay and countless others.

On the south shore and running its full length are the
beaches, sometimes wide but often narrow and obstructed
by fallen trees, that have taken the greatest toll in ships. The
beachcomber, finding them strewn with an incredible array
of flotsam and litter, often comes upon evidence of a long-
ago disaster in the form of a rotted spar, a shattered keelson,

a twisted sternpost or the jutting ribs of a once-sturdy ship. Above them, hidden by scrub growth and now obliterated, are the graves of many unknown seamen. Wind and sand have long since destroyed the crude headboards that marked the graves, and they are gone forever. One of them indicated the last resting place of William Wilson, wheelsman on the car ferry *Marquette & Bessemer No. 2,* lost somewhere off the Point in December of 1909. Wilson was identified by the serial number of the fine watch he carried and was buried by lightkeeper S. B. Cook. Few of the many who wandered ashore were known. Being sailors, they were a restless lot by nature and in the shifting sands they found their Vahalla.

Long Point remains virtually a wilderness today because of the peculiar circumstances that prevailed in the 1860s and would not be likely to occur again. Unable to stem the tide of violence and lawlessness that prevailed on the Point, and probably happy to be relieved of the responsibility of law enforcement, the provincial authorities looked kindly upon the proposal of a wealthy group, some of them Americans, that the Point be sold to them for maintenance as a private game preserve, to be kept as a primeval hunting and fishing area open only to members and their guests. The new owners, under the name of the Long Point Company, immediately took steps to evict a small army of squatters, most of them trappers, game hunters and fishermen. This policy, pursued adamantly and with vigor, caused much bitterness among those who had long considered the Point their private and sacrosanct preserve. As time went on, mainland sportsmen claimed that the Company annually extended its water boundaries to include much good duck hunting territory that rightfully belonged to the public. They therefore disregarded directives and warnings with such enthusiasm that, despite a force of keepers employed by the Company, the duck population was largely depleted and the deer herd in great danger of annihilation. In desperation the Company hired a detective, John Allan, whose job was to ferret out the most prolific poachers by joining forces and mingling with them. One morning he went out alone on a hunt, absent-mindedly leaving his credentials among his belongings in a small cabin he occupied outside the property. Apparently the cabin had visitors in his absence and his secret was discovered, for the following day he was found shot through the head. A dead deer lay beside him, but the shell in his gun had not been fired nor were there any powder burns on his person. A long investigation by the authorities was conducted, but the mystery of detective Allan's death was never solved. He is remembered today by Allan Ridge, one of those name places known locally, but not on any map or chart. The Long Point Company still owns and rules most of Long Point. The only other privately held area on the Point and relatively modest in size compared to the Company's holdings, is the Anderson property.

But while Long Point continued to claim a tragic annual toll in ships, one man's misfortune was another man's happy windfall when its wrecks lavished their cargoes upon the mainlanders, many of whom put these bonanzas from the sea to good use. There are buildings standing today along the Ontario shore built largely from timbers yielded by the Point's wrecks and later made snug by subsequent disasters that brought forth shingles, nails, hardware, stoves and coal. In the villages and farms along the lakes the lot of the settlers was one of frugality, hard work and subsistence with the bare necessities. Whatever else came their way was looked upon as a favorable visitation from providence. Thus, all along Lake Erie a shipwreck usually meant more than an exciting interlude, for the rewards of beachcombing often eased the rigors of a Spartan existence. A November storm of 1838 put twenty-five vessels ashore along Lake Erie and over a wide geographical area. The brig *Manhattan* "went on" at Point Abino with general merchandise, her broken hull disgorging tallow, potatoes, tin household utensils, farm tools, shoes, saddles, soap, patent medicine, spirits and dry goods, all of which was put to good use. Bolts of calico and gingham were drying on farm fences for weeks. Over on the south shore the steamer *New England* was aground seven miles below Fairport. In their haste to lighten ship before the seas could finish her, the crew threw overboard five hundred barrels of flour and six tons of butter, thus assuring Fairport residents of buttered biscuits for months to come. Later the steamer *Odd Fellow,* laden with chestnuts, was wrecked on a reef east of Gravelly Bay and the roasting of chestnuts by the fireside provided much pleasure and camaraderie along the Ontario shore that winter. The steamer *Henry Clay* founded off the Point in 1851 and for days the beaches were dotted with her cargo of baled wool—a supply that kept mainland spinning wheels whirling for years.

But always it was Long Point itself, that time-proven provider of the unexpected but welcome gifts from the sea, that most frequently yielded the conglomerate lading of its hapless victims. Before the *Henry Clay* there was the schooner *America* with a load of salt and after her the *Sarah J. Eason,* loaded with cheese which thrifty householders stockpiled in cool cellars. Then came the *New Haven,* heavy with railroad iron, much of it put to good use in farm and village forges before the spring plowing.

Lumber-carrying vessels were driven ashore or wrecked on Long Point by the score. Others carried grain, salt, coal, block stone, dry goods, hides, machinery, hardware, canned goods, casked oil, furniture, kitchen ware, pottery, household items and ready-made clothing. The steamer *Evergreen City,* westbound from Buffalo, went ashore in 1871 with a miscellaneous cargo that included flour, butter, potatoes and onions, all welcome additions to depleted larders. The schooner *Merchant* went ashore with a full cargo of apples. Half the cargo was thrown over the side before she could be lightened and freed from the sands with a consequent surfeit of apples in Port Rowan and Port Dover that fall.

Would-be salvagers or patrolmen from the Point's life-saving station had to be hardened to strange and eerie sights when they walked the beaches. Early one December morning in 1880, after a bitterly cold and stormy night, patrolman William Porritt was startled to see a sixteen-year-old sailor sitting with his back to a pine tree, gazing out over the lake. It was a vigil of death, however, for he was frozen stiff. Behind him, in the shelter of a sand dune, were six more sailors also frozen to death. On another grim and cold December morning an ice-coated lifeboat was discovered aground on a sandbar off the beach. There were nine men in it, most of them sitting upright and still clutching their oars but also sheathed in ice and very dead.

Strangely, out of the lurid history of the Point and the re-counting of its violent and lawless era comes the heart-warming story of Abigail Becker, the great and noble lady who gave it its finest hour and Canada its own counterpart to Britain's Grace Darling.

Abigail Jackson was only seventeen when she married Jeremiah Becker, a widower with six children—one girl and five boys. Becker was a trapper by vocation and soon after the marriage took Abigail and the children to live in his sturdy cabin near the south shore of Long Point. There Abigail gave of herself wholeheartedly to the task of raising the children, a responsibilty made more difficult by the fact that Jeremiah was away on his trap lines much of the time. She and her stepchildren got along famously, and they soon became devoted to her, and she to them.

During the first severe fall gale and snowstorm of their

first year on the Point, when the wind hammered at their little cabin and sleet lashed its single window, there came a clump of feet and a frantic pounding at the door. Unafraid, Abigail flung it open to find four men, almost encased in ice and obviously close to death from exposure to the elements. They turned out to be sailors from a schooner that had gone ashore during the night. There had been six survivors, they told Abigail, but two of them had given up and collasped a mile or two from the cabin. Bidding the four men to warm themselves by the fire, Abigail gathered together some warm clothing and with two of the boys set out to find them. Somehow—the sailors thought it a miracle—she found them, too far gone to care much what happened. By sheer force of personality, cajolery, and promises of hot food nearby she finally got them to their feet, put coats around their shivering bodies and practically pushed them to the cabin. All lived to sail again and sing the praises of the courageous lady of Long Point.

During a late autumn gale a schooner laden with barley went ashore near the Becker cabin. All hands were saved except the woman cook, who unaccountably went missing during the excitement. The wet grain swelled and burst the hull, but some was saved by mainland salvagers. The shattered hull, full of lake water and bedded in the sand, became a convenient well or reservoir, solving one of the winter problems of life on Long Point. One had to walk out a long distance on the ice hummocks to get water clear of sand. So the Beckers simply dipped their buckets into the hold to obtain clear, sweet water.

One morning one of the Becker brood came running back with her little water bucket empty, crying, "Mother! Mother! There's a woman in the schooner waving her arms at me!"

Brave Abigail, who feared God but no man or woman living or dead, strode briskly to the wreck, half convinced that the girl was suffering from hallucinations. She peered down through the open hatch through which the winter sunlight beamed, and there in the clear, green water she did indeed see a woman. It was the schooner's cook, floating upright, her arms waving gently as the level changed with the heave of the seas through the broken hull.

In the blackness of the night on November 24, 1854, the three-masted schooner *Conductor*, Henry Hackett master, was laboring in mountainous seas off the Point's dreaded south shore. The *Conductor* had loaded 10,000 bushels of grain at Amherstburg and was bound for Toronto by way of the Welland Canal. Caught in a prolonged westerly gale that had piled up seas of terrifying stature, Captain Hackett tried desperately to wear his vessel to starboard and round the Point, when it became apparent that the seas would not permit a safe approach to the Old Cut channel. But the schooner's aged sails blew out and she lay helpless in the trough of the merciless rollers a-building the length of Lake Erie. When at last the *Conductor* imbedded herself on a sandbar a hundred yards offshore, Captain Hackett and his crew of seven followed the only course open to them. They climbed into the rigging, lashing themselves to masts and spars, there to spend a hellish night as spray froze to their clothing and the relentless breakers stripped the schooner of her hatch covers and looted her of the grain cargo.

That was the situation the next morning when Abigail made another early morning trip to the beach for water. Jeremiah, after an unusually productive early fall season on his trap lines, was off on the mainland disposing of his pelts and purchasing supplies. But he had left plenty of food and a big supply of firewood. Abigail's attention was attracted by an unusual but persistent snapping and popping sound—sharp reports made by the *Conductor*'s shredded sails fluttering and cracking in the wind. The vessel was grounded about a mile from the Becker cabin, but even from that distance Abigail could see the crew clustered in the rigging, obviously suffering from the cold. Returning quickly to the cabin, she dressed the children, explaining, "There is a vessel ashore about a mile down the beach. We must hurry there to see if we can be of any help."

At the scene she quickly kindled a fire, sent the children to harvest more driftwood and went about the task of making hot tea. The combination of a warm fire and hot drink, she calculated, might tempt the freezing sailors to abandon their perches and swim for their lives. When the fire had reached cheering proportions, Abigail waded into the surf and made beckoning, encouraging motions, indicating that she was prepared to help them. Captain Hackett was the first to try.

"If we stay here, we will be lost," he told the crew. "I'll go first, and if I get to shore safely, the rest can follow."

Pulling off his coat and shoes, he plunged in. But the roaring surf was more than the captain had counted on. Exhausted, bowled over with each cresting sea, he was helpless and being swept down the beach until Abigail, up to her shoulders in the raging waters, caught him by an arm and dragged him ashore to the fire. The mate then made the same journey and was buffeted unmercifully and nearly drowned, when young Edward, fourteen years old and crippled, rushed into the water to save him. But the lad's crutches sank into the sand, and he, too, was being tossed about, when Abigail plunged into the combers and pulled them both ashore. The other sailors, viewing the near-drowning of their captain and mate, were reluctant to follow suit and only after two hours of Abigail's beckoning and holding up a hot bucket of tea as temptation did they jump from the rigging into the angry seas. Each one had to be dragged from the clutching surf by Abigail and carried to the fire. Daughter Margaret and the younger children had been sent back to the cabin to prepare hot food and more tea. The rescued men, with Abigail and Edward helping those who had dif-

ficulty walking, finally made their way to the Becker cabin.
Here, as they stood around drying their clothes and paper
money, all thoughts were of the one sailor who, unable to
swim, had steadfastly refused to leave his spray-drenched
niche in the rigging. He was the ship's cook and was doomed
to spend another night in the cold, sleet and snow. Miraculously, he was still alive the next morning when Captain
Hackett and his men fashioned a raft from driftwood and
rescued him, more dead than alive. He was bedfast in the
Becker cabin for some weeks.

Through the good offices of Captain Hackett and his grateful men the story of Abigail Becker received wide circulation. Shipowners, merchants and sailors in Buffalo took up
a purse of five hundred and fifty dollars, the New York Life
Saving Benevolent Association struck off a handsome gold
medal in her honor and the Royal Humane Society did likewise. Queen Victoria dispatched a warm letter of commendation, and Lord Aberdeen, Governor-General of Canada, sent
along his congratulations. Later, when on a duck hunting
expedition to Long Point, the Prince of Wales, afterwards
King Edward VII, made a point of seeking out Abigail and
presenting her with a gift. Immediately after the rescue,
when her name was the subject of household discussions on
both sides of the border and abroad, she was offered a substantial sum of money to tour America with a show company.
But Abigail, a quiet country lady, wanted no part of the
bright lights and would not leave her family, regardless of
the monetary considerations.

To the constant praise that was heaped upon her, she
would only reply: "I only did my duty as any other would
have done." Ironically, some time after the rescue of the
Conductor's crew, it was learned that Abigail herself could
not swim a stroke!

The modest heroine used the money given her by the

Buffalo group to buy a fifty-acre farm in North Walsingham Township. Here the Beckers started farming in a small way, with two cows and a yoke of oxen. But bad luck plagued the enterprise. One cow died from drinking sour sap; the other was killed by a falling tree. There was unfortunately no money for tools or other equipment. Jeremiah became very discouraged. After a few disheartening years at work he had little aptitude for, he went back to trapping on Long Point to augment the income from the farm. In January of 1864, as another terrific westerly gale pounded the south shore of the Point, he was forced to abandon his line shanty because of rising waters. Placing his trunk on the roof for safekeeping, he set out for his permanent cabin some three miles away. But the exhausting trek in the face of fierce and bitter winds and the driving snow must have been too much for Jeremiah Becker. A half mile from the safety of his cabin he sat down on a log to rest and there perished of the cold. He was still sitting there when searchers found him three months later.

Abigail, since she had presented five boys and three girls to her trapper husband in addition to the six stepchildren, was left to rear them on the farm, raising potatoes and corn, cutting wood and weaving cloth to make ends meet. Married to Henry Rohrer a few years after the death of Jeremiah Becker, Abigail bore him three daughters and took in her charge two adopted youngsters. Having loved and raised nineteen children under her roof, Abigail died on her farm in 1905 at the age of seventy-four. A public fund was established by the citizens of Norfolk County for the purpose of erecting a monument in her honor. Eventually, however, it was decided to use the money to furnish a ward in the Norfolk General Hospital and affix a suitable tablet bearing her name. Abigail, a modest, unassuming person, would have hated the monument but from her place in heaven her very nature guaranteed approval of the hospital ward.

The Point has had its good years and bad, the latter inevitably related to prolonged periods of foul weather. Ships that slid up on the shore or sandbars in foggy but calm weather were often released, sometimes unharmed. But those that "went on" in the furious fall storms usually left their bones, and sometimes those of their people, on the Point forever. Seven vessels were lost off, or on, the Point in 1851, five in 1852, six in 1855, five in 1864, six in 1870, four in 1874, six in 1877 and another six in 1883. But if the truth were known, probably many of the vessels sunk in collision off or near the Point were lost simply because it existed. Stretching across the lake to within eight or nine miles of the international boundary, it drastically narrows the shipping lanes. Today's big vessels, with radar and automatic directtion finders, round the Point and its hazards with ease. But earlier shipmasters, mindful of the clutching, shipwrecking sandbars, kept well off the Point if they could, thus making its offshore waters even more congested. Sometimes it was a case of successfully avoiding the perils of the Point only to meet a worse fate in the rumbling finality of collision.

But while Long Point has its grim tales of disaster, starvation and heart-warming stories of rescues, it also has a classic tragi-comedy that still inspires chuckles around Port Rowan. And like so many humorous tales of the good old days, it happened when "dry" Ontario was in a state of perpetual and enforced thirst by virtue of the Ontario Temperance Act. It was not unlawful for distilleries to manufacture whisky, or to sell it if the purchaser intended to ship it to distant points where a more tolerant viewpoint prevailed. Bootlegging thrived, and most Ontario residents regarded the legislation with the same disdain that Americans exhibited toward their own tragedy, the Volstead Act of 1918.

Canadian vessels, from fishing tugs to cargo steamers, could legally take on cargoes of hard liquor, providing they filled out official clearance papers with customs officials, their destinations listed as somewhere other than Ontario or a port in the United States. Thus armed with the implement of deceit, skippers regularly and cheerfully cleared with cargoes supposedly consigned to Cuba, Mexico or Puerto Rico. The fact that they returned with holds empty after surprisingly brief voyages, sometimes only a few hours, was of no concern to the authorities. They had cleared port properly, and that was that. Obviously, the cargoes were landed in secluded Ontario ports or across the lake in the United States.

Such a vessel was the *City of Dresden*, an impressive name for the aged and infirm steamer owned and operated by sixty-five-year-old Captain John Sylvester McQueen, of Amherstburg, Ontario. Old when he bought it in 1914 and the object of considerable tinkering, he had abandoned the original power plant, replacing it with the boiler of one tug, the engine of another. But it worked, provided employment for him and a crew and was every bit as good as a number of other Canadian bottoms he could name offhand.

The saga of the *City of Dresden* begins on Friday, November 17, 1922, as a modest gale from the north was giving Lake Erie a nasty chop. Captain McQueen had cleared his vessel from Belleville, on Lake Ontario, with a heavy cargo of whisky in kegs and cases, all of it Corby's Special Selected or Old Crow, consigned, so the clearance papers said, for Mexico. Much of the whisky was stowed below decks, but a considerable number of cases were carried as deck cargo, possibly so the captain could keep an eye on the liquid treasure. After leaving the Welland Canal, the *City of Dresden* took quite a dusting from the seas and was beginning to show her age and lack of adequate power. These considerations being uppermost in his mind, Captain McQueen wisely dropped his anchors in Gravelly Bay, on the north shore of Long Point, two and one-half miles from the lighthouse. The vessel was still exposed to the north winds except for the little shelter she got from Bluff Point, but with her anchors down and her bow swung into the wind, she rode easier and labored less. Before noon the next day, however, the wind began to blow with even more authority, and the ship began to pitch and roll, showing every indication of dragging her anchors should the prevailing conditions continue or worsen. Early in the afternoon Captain McQueen decided to move around the Point and anchor off the south side, there to wait in protected waters until the strong north winds abated. But the underpowered *City of Dresden* showed her displeasure at leaving her anchorage, wallowed heavily in the seas, seemingly intent on going ashore then and there. In desperation —and only desperation and the proximity of known sandbars could account for such a decision—Captain McQueen ordered his crew to lighten ship by throwing overboard all the whisky stowed on deck! Regretfully, probably with tears in their eyes, the crew obeyed. This did the trick and the creaking *City of Dresden* finally began to make progress around the Point.

The lifesavers of Long Point were accustomed to finding strange and unusual things on their beach patrols, from deceased bootleggers to baby buggies, but never such a bonanza as came bobbing in on the breakers that stormy but delightful Saturday. The lonely lifesaver who spotted the first case while walking his route gave a joyful whoop and sprang to the rescue. Incredibly, others followed, case upon case, forty-two in all, and rather evenly spaced. With the intuitive judgment of a man who sees his drinking problems solved for a long time, and working with the frenzied industry of a woodchuck, he buried them, one by one, a single case stashed near each of forty-two of the spindly poles that supported the primitive telephone line to the lighthouse. It was like money in the bank—forty-two banks.

Unfortunately, Captain McQueen's troubles were really just beginning. He had brought the *City of Dresden* safely around the Point into the comparative calm on the other side, when the wind shifted swiftly and ominously to the southwest. With practically the length of the lake in which to build up momentum and seas, it took only a short time for the elements to belabor the vessel again into a dangerous position. Working heavily as she rose and fell in the trough of the seas, seams began to spout water, only a few at first, but soon many. Engineer Ray Sawyer did his best until the fireman climbed from the stokehold and refused to return.

When Peregrine McQueen, the captain's twenty-one-year-old son, came to investigate the falling steam pressure, Sawyer explained and said: "Better tell the old man to beach her!"

Captain McQueen, considering his precious cargo, was obviously reluctant to do so, keeping the *City of Dresden* headed down the south shore toward Port Rowan as long as he could, blowing the distress signal with what steam he had left. Finally the choice was made by the sea and wind even as the captain turned his vessel to shore. The *City of Dresden* hit a sandbar, broached to, and almost immediately began to break up.

The wailing of the whistle, however, had alerted those on shore, particularly in the home of cattle buyer Delbert Rockefeller. Delbert had chosen that Saturday to take the family car to Simcoe on business, but his wife, Pearl, and a niece, Viola Blackenbury, and Mrs. Rockefeller's mother recognized incipient disaster. Quickly the two younger women hitched up a horse and buggy and raced full speed around an area of swampland and down to the beach.

The first lifeboat lowered from the *City of Dresden* capsized almost immediately. A second boat was lowered and into it climbed the crew—Captain McQueen, his son, engineer Sawyer, fireman Joe Antio, J. D. Hunt and the cook, Jackie McBridge. But it, too, soon rolled over, spilling the men into the water in a wild tangle of arms, legs, the tossing boat and debris from the ship. Young Peregrine McQueen was having a hard struggle to stay afloat, and Sawyer started to swim to him. But Peregrine vanished in the crest of the next breaker and was seen no more. The others, although cold and exhausted, finally managed to right the boat and climb in. But without oars they were helpless to beach their craft. A strong undertow kept it some yards off the beach but subjected it to a merciless pounding, cresting one moment on a breaking sea and dropping the next instant into the valley beyond it. Sometimes the conflicting undertow and incoming combers would spin the boat around. The occupants could do little but hang on and pray.

Pearl Rockefeller and Viola Blackenbury, their horse sweating and steaming from its mad gallop, arrived on the beach opposite the wreck just as the second lifeboat capsized. They saw the survivors climb in and drift helplessly downwind, so near yet so far from safety.

Pearl waded out chest-deep into the seas, signaling for one of the sailors to throw her a line. One of them finally did. Pearl, now joined by her niece, both buried frequently by the breaking seas, slowly dragged the reluctant lifeboat to shore. Engineer Ray Sawyer must have been having his own very special thoughts the moment his feet touched land. It had been exactly sixty-eight years earlier, less six days, when his grandfather had been rescued off the dreadful south shore of Long Point, also by a woman—Abigail Becker!

Captain McQueen, badly chilled and shaking, was hustled into the buggy and taken to the Rockefeller home, where, out of his head with fever, he was put to bed. He had about a thousand dollars in his trouser pocket, which Pearl carefully dried out for him.

The ladies of the Rockefeller household were not the only ones aware of the stranded and broken *City of Dresden*. The whistle had also triggered considerable action in Port Rowan where, as in every small town, Saturday night was very special. The clarion call of "shipwreck," coming at dusk, emptied the barbershops, the pool halls, stores and homes as well as dispersing the street-corner gabfests. To the scene they rushed, some running, others on bicycles, by horse and buggy and by automobile as far as the sandy track above the beach would permit. And by that very mysterious and special ingredient that symbolizes but does not solve the enigma of the jungle telegraph, word of the stranding spread like wildfire all along the Norfolk County shore, from the fishing docks to the tobacco farms. They came by the score, some laughing and yelling most of the way, others running or walking in silence, conserving their breath. Many had arrived while Pearl Rockefeller and Viola Blackenbury were still desperately hauling in the lifeboat, constantly being swept by the breaking seas in the last light of day. Strangely, the ladies' efforts and obvious distress brought no offers of assistance, for the nature of *City of Dresden*'s cargo was already being revealed in the wild surf. Inflamed by the discovery, the men and boys plunged into the seas with little regard for the perils thereof, dragging their loot to the swamps and sand dunes for quick burial, then returning for further salvage. One would stop to help another, waist-deep in water and knee-deep in sand, and in second they would be fighting over the prize. Hijackers noted the burial spots and stole from the original salvagers, only to have others note their sly markings and carry away the loot. Some quickly organized a more systematic way of getting as much as possible by sending friends home for wagons on the promise of splitting the haul. Kegs and cases were loaded into wagons, wheelbarrows, even baby buggies and trundled off into the dark of night. Hundreds of quart bottles were stashed in the sand or swamp while a couple of sturdy specimens of manhood marched off toward Port Rowan with a case on each shoulder. Some of the late arrivals, missing the cases, kegs and barrels by their tardiness, but finding individual bottles tossing in the surf, repaired to the comfort of the sand dunes to sample the spoils in darkness but in good company. They concluded, after a thoroughly scientific series of tests, that Corby's Special Selected was a mellow drink, but that Old Crow was a much sterner blend, a corn whisky that efficiently separated the men from the boys.

Possession of ardent spirits was punishable by a stiff fine by the provincial authorities, and ingenious were the methods used to hide the loot when the happy salvagers got it home. Farmers concealed cases in haystacks, digging in from the top to evade the probing of pitchforks in the hands of inspectors. Bottles were arranged in long lines in freshly plowed furrows and neatly covered. Other bottles dangled from ropes suspended in cisterns and wells. Cases were lowered into pits dug in the sawdust of icehouses. Householders stacked bottle after bottle in recesses created by loosening the floor boards of their homes or in hastily built false ceilings. Excavations beside barns were quickly filled with cases and covered with manure. It was a mad, hilarious, once-in-a-lifetime adventure.

Another of Captain John Sylvester McQueen's sons, Captain J. E. McQueen, who had hurried to the scene from Amherstburg, said that the *City of Dresden*'s cargo consisted of one thousand cases of whisky valued at $40,000 and five hundred kegs worth another $25,000.

Not all of the loot found its way to Port Rowan hiding places. Bootleggers from adjacent communities were on hand, paying hard cash on the spot and hauling the liquor away.

Much more was lost in the swamps and sand dunes because darkness prevented establishing proper landmarks to locate the caches later. For weeks some of the early salvagers prowled the Point with long sticks—probing, probing, probing.

By Sunday morning not a single bottle of spirits remained to be rescued from the sea or shore. Visitors at first light found only the shattered timbers of the *City of Dresden*, hundreds of whisky labels, what appeared to be the remains of splintered wooden cases, and the body of young Peregrine McQueen.

Through some strange, inexplicable delays, the authorities in Simcoe, the county seat, were not notified of the wreck until Sunday evening. Properly outraged by the tardiness of the news and suspicious of the circumstances and motives, Police Inspector Edmonds, Provincial Constable Lawrence and County Constable Alway marshaled forces and set out for the scene of the debauchery. Port Rowan, strangely for a Sunday night, was curiously bustling with activity, its citizens either nursing the agonies of momumental hangovers or in high good spirits. It was two o'clock Monday morning when the gendarmes, carrying lanterns, arrived at the wreck scene. Despite a long, cold tramp along the beach in both directions, they found naught but hundreds of paper wrappers, splintered whisky cases, telltale marks of kegs being rolled along in the sand and the tracks of many feet and wagon wheels.

Pursuing their investigations with customary diligence, the constables and Inspector Edmonds spent a week in the Port Rowan area, probing the sands of the Point, poking under buildings, examining haystacks, peering along basement rafters, asking embarrassing questions and making uncomplimentary remarks as to the honor and pride of Port Rowan's menfolk. The men of the community had plenty of honor, but swallowed their pride along with some of Canada's finest whisky. Inspector Edmonds, a thorough, methodical man, was particularly suspicious of one innocent-looking farmer whose breath consistently reminded him of spirits. For the better part of a week he persisted in sporadic, unannounced visits to the farm, searching the buildings, even going so far as to shift all the hay in the barn. He found nothing.

"Thank God it didn't rain that week," the farmer later confided to a friend. "I had the eaves troughs of that big barn lined with bottles all the way around."

Furtive transactions went on for months with the asking price for a case of whisky finally stabilizing at a modest sixty dollars. The established bootleggers in the area whined plaintively about the undercutting of prices but could do little but complain to each other. The patrolman from the lifesaving station had little to fear about his forty-two caches being discovered, for neither the amateur salvagers nor the minions of the law were aware that part of the cargo had been jettisoned on the north side of the Point hours before the *City of Dresden* came to grief on the south side. It was rumored that the lifesaver disposed of his "plantings" for a handsome price to a single bootlegger and paid off the mortgage on his home.

Later, after Ontario had abandoned its ill-conceived Temperance Act, but while the United States still persisted in the Volstead Act disaster, rumrunning to the south shore of Lake Erie from ports east and west of Long Point continued at a brisk and sometimes perilous pace. Dominion authorities still had no restrictions on exports other than to the United States, and numerous sympathetic Canadian citizens, anxious to aleviate the parching thirst south of the boundary line, regularly cleared their little liquor-laden launches and fishing tugs for such exotic ports as Havana and Port-au-Prince. Only when the craft were intercepted by United

States authorities or an exchange of shots inspired an official international gnashing of teeth did the law seek explanations for the unseemly short voyages or disposition of the cargoes.

So flourishing was the trade and so frequent became instances of musketry at sea that many Port Dover and Port Rowan boatmen had George Gamble install a modest shield of armor plating above the water line of their craft. Mechanical wizard, blacksmith, boat builder and one of today's liveliest raconteurs, Gamble, now ninety-four, came to Port Dover in 1922, when the hulks of thirty-five wrecks were still visible on the Point. Looking back on almost a century, he still fondly recalls the rumrunning era as the good old days, when the friendly lighthouse on the Point winked a sly "good luck" to the departing adventurers with its 100,000 candlepower beam and a warm "welcome home" when they returned.

Now, gone are the old lifesaving station, the frame homes that housed the crews and the wagon road once kept open by supply wagons and the mysterious journeys of man. No longer do the thrifty farmers of Ontario's south shore come to the Point to harvest ship timbers or lumber cargoes for their barns and houses or edible cargoes for their larders. Long Point is still unique in its loneliness and only the intermittent flashing of its light every eight seconds, casting fleeting beams over the graves of its victims, gives evidence that the Point is still a potential death trap for the unwary mariner. When the dreadful gales blow from the southwest, its sheltering arm still protects the long vessels that flee to safety in the lee of the Point and anchorage in Long Point Bay. At night their myriad lights appear to be those of a small city to shipwatchers in Port Dover and Port Rowan. And the booming, haunting blasts of the fog signal seem to be sounding an eternal requiem for those now asleep in the shifting sands.

⚓

4

Ghouls, Gold and the Prevarications
of Henry Priday

David R. Stebbins was a careful and thoroughly practical
man—attributes which seemingly go hand in hand with successful bankers and marine engineers. Mr. Stebbins was of
the latter persuasion, given to great care, considerable fussi-
ness and close rapport with engines in his charge. Perhaps
it was just these commendable characteristics that inspired the
owners of the steamer *G. P. Griffith* to offer him the post of
chief engineer, sweetening the deal by making it possible for
him to purchase a one-eighth interest in the vessel, thus sharing proportionately in her profits, if any. The *Griffith,* in
early 1847, was still a-building at Maumee, Ohio, ten miles
from Lake Erie on the historic Maumee River. As part
owner of the *Griffith,* named for a prominent Maumee busi-
nessman, Stebbins had more than a little to say about her
construction, the placement of her machinery and the center-
ing of the big thirty-one-foot side-wheels. It was a responsible
role and one to which he responded with his usual diligence.

Appointed to "bring out" the *Griffith* was Captain Charles
C. Roby, a popular skipper from Perrysburg, Ohio, just
across the river from Maumee. Like engineer Stebbins, Captain Roby was tendered a small interest in the vessel and

quickly accepted. The pair had been acquainted for some years and got along well. The major investors in the *Griffith* were sure that the dual financial interest of the captain and engineer would augur well for the anticipated earnings, since both would have every incentive for safe, economical and efficient management of the ship and her business. The communities of Perrysburg and Maumee, facing each other across the wide Maumee, were, as they are today, fierce rivals in civic affairs, but the representatives of each, in command of their respective domains aboard ship, could be counted upon to function smoothly as a team with the interests of the ship and her owners always in mind.

Beyond the exacting meticulous, sometimes incomprehensible habits peculiar to his trade, Mr. Stebbins was, by nature, a chronic worrier, especially about fire. It amounted almost to an obsession. To say that it was understandable, in view of his occupation, would be an understatement. Mr. Stebbins was well aware of the dreadful frequency of fire and the deplorable annual toll of lives on the Great Lakes due to wooden steamboats catching fire. He was mindful, too, that the survivors almost always reported that the conflagrations originated at or near the smoke stacks, funnels or "pipes," as they were sometimes called. Horrendous tales were still current about the steamer *Washington*, Buffalo to Cleveland, lost by fire off Silver Creek, New York, in 1838, and of the almost predictable disaster of the *Erie,* loaded with two hundred immigrants, most of whom perished when the ship caught fire, again off Silver Creek. Six painters in the employ of a William G. Miller had boarded at Buffalo and with almost unbelievable carelessness had piled their containers of varnish and turpentine on the deck directly over the boilers. Only twenty-nine persons survived, including one of the guilty painters.

The conscientious Mr. Stebbins was determined that a

similar fate would not strike the *Griffith* or the people who entrusted their lives to her management. On his orders and under his careful supervision the two big smokestacks were surrounded by a wide water jacket where they passed through the wooden decks. Furthermore, he left a substantial gap between the water jackets and the deck planking as an added safety factor.

While capable of carrying a considerable freight tonnage, the *Griffith* was designed primarily for the immigrant trade. She had accommodations for nearly fifty first-class passengers and plenty of deck space for the strangers to our shores, most of whom were content to bed down on the deck, surrounded by piles of their treasured personal belongings. Some were city folk with trades, but many were farmers, laden with sacks of seed and implements that were lowered into the hold. Bewildered by the strange sights and new surroundings, they arrived at Buffalo by the hundreds every week, some by the primitive railroad from Albany but most of them by the canal packets which were infinitely cheaper. Germans, Irish, English, Scandinavian and Dutch, they had burned their bridges behind them, taking hope for the future in the challenges and rewards the new world offered. Some would be going to the homestead lands of upper Michigan, Wisconsin or Minnesota. Others would join established friends in cities or buy farms in communities suggested by previous arrivals. In any event, at Buffalo they had to make a choice among three alternatives for reaching their eventual destinations. They could walk, take the lumbering and uncomfortable stages or book passage on a lake steamer. Not only were the steamers the lesser of three evils, but they afforded space for the trunks, bags, boxes and crates loaded with treasured and necessary personal belongings. For those bound for the wilderness of the homestead lands, far beyond primitive roads, there was really no choice.

The immigrant and passenger business was belatedly coming under the critical and disapproving eyes of the public press, alarmed at the frequency of disaster, usually in the form of fire or the exploding of high-pressure steam boilers. Safety regulations or mandatory inspections by qualified officials simply did not exist. Regrettably, too, when tragedy struck, captain and crew usually departed the craft with whatever means were at their disposal, leaving the paying guests from faraway lands to shift for themselves.

Charles Dickens, the eminent British novelist, touring America in 1842, had a caustic comment for the Great Lakes steamboat situation after taking passage from Sandusky to Cleveland on the steamer *Constitution:*

> She was a large vessel of 500 tons, and handsomely fitted out, though with high pressure engines, which always conveyed that kind of feeling to me, which I should be likely to experience, I think, if I had lodgings on the first floor of a powder-mill.

Into this booming, free-wheeling, often confusing trade, the *Griffith* found her place soon after launching, trial runs, Mr. Stebbins' expert appraisal and his verdict that she was "ready." For the most part her route was consistent, Buffalo to Toledo with stops wherever freight consignments dictated, or where immigrants were scheduled to depart. Occasionally, if the human cargo revenue justified the expense, she went as far as Chicago. Moreover, when she arrived in Toledo the *Griffith* was only a scant few miles from home for both Mr. Stebbins and Captain Roby, affording them an opportunity to see their families with some regularity. But whatever the time or whatever the port, there was Mr. Stebbins, puttering around his water jackets, filling them to the brim and noting, with great satisfaction, that the deck area around them was comfortable to the touch.

The Buffalo to Toledo routine provided a familiar course

for Captain Roby although he had a great respect for the known and unknown hazards inherent with command, a respect sharpened, no doubt, by memories of 1845 when, while skipper of the steamer *Indiana*, he had unhappily and to his great surprise sunk her after striking a snag in Maumee Bay.

The *Griffith's* first season, 1847, or what was left of it when she entered the trade, was brisk and profitable. But the imigrant hauling business as a whole was under sharp scrutiny again due to the November 21 holocaust aboard the steamer *Phoenix* in Lake Michigan, when two hundred Dutch immigrants perished. Again, the fire had started near the "pipes," and could not be controlled. Again, too, the ship's two lifeboats made their way to shore safely bearing Captain Sweet, the first mate, other crewmen and a few first-class passengers. The immigrants, as usual, were left to their fate.

The season of 1848 brought a respite from the usual calamitous happenings with the only significant loss by fire or explosion being that of the propeller *Goliah*, far out on Lake Huron. She was witnessed to be ablaze, with her mast and smokestack overboard, about eight miles from shore. Whether her condition was the result of fire or a boiler explosion is not known. It was a moot question, however, as a short time later she was blown to atoms by a tremendous explosion when the two hundred kegs of blasting powder in her cargo were touched off by the blaze.

Likewise, the 1849 season proved to be one relatively free of tragedy beyond the usual collisions, groundings and strandings. A tally near the season's end showed 140 steam-powered craft in the passenger, immigrant and freight business, ninety-five of them were side-wheelers, forty-five propeller-driven. As to sailing vessels in general commerce there were 784—548 of them schooners.

The winter of 1849-1850 was an auspicious one for Captain Roby. He had, as newspapers of the time would put it, "good connections," one of them being his brother-in-law, Mr. William V. Studdiford, of Monroe, Michigan. Mr. Studdiford was disposed to make an investment in another steamboat. What more likely, then, than the one skippered by his wife's brother, the esteemed and highly respected Captain Roby? Between them they bought out the original major investors with the provision that chief engineer Stebbins would retain his one-eighth interest. Mr. Stebbins, who spent most of the winter tinkering with his beloved engine, was highly pleased with the arrangement.

Almost as if the elements themselves smiled on the transaction, the shipping season of 1850, thanks to a mild winter, opened much earlier than usual. Buffalo, often plagued with ice until early May, saw the first boat depart on March 25. The early start had ominous overtones, however, for two days earlier, off Bird Island, in the Niagara River, the steamer *Troy* burst her boilers, killing twenty-nine of her passengers and crew.

Undaunted by the inauspicious beginning of what promised to be a long and profitable season, the fleet of immigrant, passenger and freight vessels, the *Griffith* among them, began their annual shuttle from Buffalo to points west and north. They were joined by scores of other steamers not in the immigrant trade but which regularly plied from port to port, always managing to book a few passengers and garner their share of the freight offered.

Among them was the creaking old *Anthony Wayne*, whose engine room was presided over by Edward E. "Eureka" Elmore, a gentleman of choleric disposition who had complained long, loud and frequently to Captain Gore about the sad state of the boilers. Captain Gore, however, had been unable to persuade Charles Howard of Detroit, who owned

three-quarters of the boat, that the matter was critical. She
was an old vessel, built in 1837, and doubtless Mr. Howard
considered a major expenditure in new boilers a waste of
money in view of her age.

The *Anthony Wayne* left Toledo on the morning of April
27 with twenty-five passengers, arriving in Sandusky that
afternoon. During the afternoon and evening she took on a
cargo of 300 barrels of high wines and whisky from Sandusky's famed distilleries, and added forty to her passenger
list. Departing late that evening, she was off Vermilion and
eight miles from shore when the starboard boiler exploded.
Captain Gore was blown rudely from his bed, relatively un-
injured, but Eureka Elmore, who chanced to be on duty in
the engine room, was catapulted into eternity, thus depriv-
ing him forever of the opportunity of telling his employers,
"I told you so." Sixty-five perished as the ship went down
within minutes, but Captain Gore, the ship's clerk and a
couple of passengers launched a lifeboat and drifted safely
ashore.

The variables of lake shipping being what they were—fog,
wind, overcrowded docks and myriad problems with cargoes
—the *Griffith*, on Saturday afternoon, June 15, 1850, found
herself at her Buffalo dock after a routine voyage from Toledo. Things had gone well on the previous trip and the
Griffith, as scheduled by her agents, would sail at ten o'clock
on Sunday morning. In a way it was a special occasion for
Captain Roby; it was his first opportunity since assuming
ownership of the vessel to have his family accompany him.
His wife, a thirteen-year-old daughter, an infant son and his
mother were quartered in the most commodious and comfortable of the first-class cabins. The weather had been favorable,
and for Mrs. Roby the run from Toledo had been a pleasant,
relaxing respite from the cares of life ashore.

A noisy, cosmopolitan, almost carnival-like atmosphere prevailed on the Buffalo docks that Saturday afternoon and evening as the *Griffith*, her engine wheezing, but at rest, disgorged her modest cargo and prepared to accept a substantial assortment of boxes and barrels for the return trip. A break in the bank of the Erie Canal had resulted in an eleven-day delay for the canal packets and a consequent avalanche of packets and immigrants when the break had been mended. Mr. Stebbins, the inveterate experimenter and tinkerer, after routinely checking his precious water jackets and surveying the clamorous scene, was pleased to note that the new and supposedly superior type of lubricating oil he had ordered from New York was among the waiting ship's stores, in six superbly coopered kegs.

But it was the human element, strange clothing and the confusion and babble of foreign tongues that created the air of a romantic, far-off port. Among a monumental collection of valises, handbags, bundles, boxes, crates and trunks that towered mountain high over several docks, lounged, dozed or roamed hundreds of immigrants. There were two hundred and fifty-six, half of them children, ticketed for the *Griffith*. They were predominantly German and Irish, but the roster included an odd Frenchman or two and a group of about forty English from Yorkshire, Devon and Gloucester, most of them bound for Medina County, Ohio, where friends, immigrants themselves only a few years earlier, were making ready to welcome them. Tiffany & Lockwood, the *Griffith*'s Buffalo agents, had done their job well. Henry Wilkinson, the ship's clerk, went among them explaining to the Germans as best he could, mostly by pointing to his watch, that the *Griffith* would leave at ten o'clock Sunday morning, as advertised.

The more affluent of the outbound passengers were permitted to go to their first-class cabins almost at once, and as soon as the freight had been discharged, the immigrants began carrying their belongings aboard. Most of them ticketed steerage; they bedded down on either the lower or hurricane decks, among their treasured belongings, in family groups and preferably in company of others speaking the same language. Their heavy baggage, trunks, crates and boxes went into the cargo hold with the general freight. Mothers were kept busy quieting exhausted and querulous youngsters, while the men gathered in knots, exchanging views of the steamer and impressions of this imposing new country that held their hopes and futures. All in all it promised to be a long and restless night despite the apparent mental relief at departing on the last stage of what had been a vexing and enervating journey from their homelands. But the common bond of a promising new life made the discomforts and inconvenience of the moment of small importance.

Robert Hall, fresh from the fields of Cambridgeshire, headed a family group that included his mother, his wife Sophia, two sons, two daughters, two brothers and two sisters. They found a spot forward of the lower deck cabins, well ahead of the noisy side-wheels. At the aft end forty-four-year-old Henry Priday, of Quedgely, England, somewhat more prosperous than most, found cabin room for some of his flock that numbered his wife Elizabeth, eighteen-year-old daughter Kate and eight relatives. They were headed for Deerfield, Ohio, where friends had previously settled. Priday kept in his possession at all times a strongbox containing the family's modest collection of heirloom jewelry and his total cash resources of $2250. It had been a rather pleasant trip from Liverpool until the break in the canal which had delayed them eleven days. To make things worse, one of the party, Ann Hooper, had taken ill and was removed to Rochester, there to await repairs to the canal and resumption of the journey. Henry Priday had utilized the time to visit his son William, who had emigrated to America earlier and was living not far from Rochester. But for fate in the form of the canal mishap the Priday clan would have been safely at their destination on that Saturday night instead of waiting impatiently for the *Griffith* to depart.

A peculiarity of the German men, noted by Mr. Wilkinson and others, was that a majority of the older family men seemed to be somewhat encumbered by girth, not all of which could be accounted for by the good dark beer of the Fatherland. It soon became obvious and generally known that the similarity was inspired by common accouterments— money belts. The thrifty and wise Germans, unfamiliar with the currency and monetary exchanges they might encounter on their voyage, stuck with the one form of tender they knew would be good anywhere—gold! Nearly all were heavily laden with the capital they anticipated needing to start life anew in America, all of it in gold coins. Little wonder, then, beyond the matter of language difficulties, that they stayed among their own and slept but fitfully.

Franz Hugel, of Baden, Germany, was alone and bedded down among his few pieces of baggage near the bow on the top or hurricane deck. Bound for Cleveland where he had promise of a job in a brewery, he had passed the early part of the evening in animated conversation with new friends, the Bohling family, nine in all, destined for Sandusky and a reunion with relatives who had preceded them from Germany. Pierce Hill, from Ireland, had little in the way of possessions but found room for his wife and daughter along the port bow rail on the lower deck. Nearby was Joseph Wildes, a lone Englishman who carried only a simple canvas sack which he used as a pillow. It was after midnight when things settled down, when snores replaced muted conversation and the silence was broken only by the occasional whimpering of a restless child.

The first hours of the voyage which began when the *Grif-*

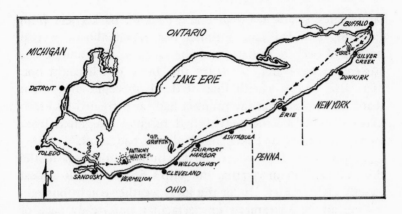

fith departed her Buffalo dock shortly after ten o'clock on Sunday morning were all that the most optimistic tour director could have asked for. A gentle breeze from the southwest added to the enjoyment of a bright, sunny day. Inbound steamers blew friendly salutes to the *Griffith* and received a booming answer. Miles of the south shore of Lake Erie slipped by, providing a most enjoyable panorama of modest bluffs, and in the distance a storybook vista of hills and farmland, rolling away into the blue of infinity brought forth heartening and reassuring comments among the immigrants. Many of them found space along the the port rails, some chattering and exchanging impressions with those of the same tongue. Others were lost in their own dreams, almost a minor state of shock brought about by the nearness of their objectives after months of travel and literally living with their few belongings. Mr. Stebbins, following his several-times-a-day ritual, passed among them as he inspected his water jackets and felt the decks.

At noon, in the open space forward of the pilothouse on the hurricane deck, first porter Lawrence Dana supervised the setting up of a table of food, a sea-going smorgasbord, so to speak. Fresh fried lake perch was the main course with sandwiches, salads, tea, coffee and cookies. Barkeepers John Paulding and William Tillman had taken aboard several barrels of beer at Buffalo, and the German men among the passengers were anxious to try this brew which could not, of course, compare with that of the Fatherland. But when word got around that the product had been created by brewmasters who, like themselves, had recently emigrated from Germany, the verdict was "not bad; not bad at all."

The distance from the *Griffith*'s Buffalo moorings to the dock at Erie, Pennsylvania, the ship's first stop, was almost exactly eighty miles. Under the ideal weather conditions prevailing and the steamer's unspectacular but steady pace of ten miles per hour, she made the Erie dock only moments after six o'clock. The stop was brief, only long enough to trundle off twelve barrels of cargo and pick up a half dozen passengers, among whom Dr. William Maronchy was the only one of note. Dr. Maronchy, of Washita, Louisiana, had been spending a few days in Cleveland but had brief but compelling business to attend to in Erie. He had arrived on another steamer, but Mrs. Maronchy, considering herself a poor sailor, had remained at the Weddell House in Cleveland, awaiting his return. The doctor obtained first-class accommodations, sharing a cabin forward with another gentleman of substance.

The next scheduled stop was Fairport, Ohio (now Fairport Harbor), where more freight would be discharged and whatever was offered in the way of freight or passengers would be accepted. As it developed, no freight was on hand and only two passengers awaited the *Griffith*'s arrival. One of them was Stephen Woodin, of Hambden, Ohio, some fifteen miles south of Fairport; the other was Hiram Knapp, of Munson, Ohio. Both were en route to Toledo and much preferred to go by steamer than to suffer the rigors of stage travel. Woodin noted a distinct smell of wood smoke as he made his way to a cabin, but there was activity in the ship's galley and since the stove burned wood, thought nothing of it. He did, however, mention the fact to first mate William Evans, who responded with curses and the suggestion that Mr. Woodin mind his own business. Mate Evans gave every indication of intoxication.

Engineer Stebbins who had been up and about utilized the time at Fairport to check his water jackets again and oil his beloved engine, using the supposedly superior new oil he had taken delivery on at Buffalo. At 2:30 A.M., as soon as the *Griffith* had turned and steamed from her dock, Mr. Stebbins went to bed, leaving the engine room in charge of second engineer Maxim Juno and the boilers in care of fireman Hugh McLain. Captain Roby and his family had retired much earlier. The obstreperous first mate turned in as soon as the vessel was out of the harbor and headed for Cleveland. Second mate Samuel McCoit and wheelsman Richard Mann checked the steering course. A short time later the second mate and deck hand Theodore Gilman went forward on the lower deck to re-coil the lines in preparation for making the dock in Cleveland. They worked quietly to avoid disturbing the tired immigrants, but many of the men among the German steerage passengers, excited at nearing their goal, were sleepless and helped with the lines as best they could. The job was simple and required no communication beyond Mr. McCoit's gestures and nodding. The night, like the day, was warm although at midnight the breeze had freshened somewhat, providing welcome relief.

The *Griffith* was approximately two miles from shore and directly on the Cleveland course when mate McCoit was interrupted by a call from wheelsman Mann:

"Mr. McCoit, can you come here a moment, sir?"

The voice was calm but something in it told McCoit that

all was not well—a tremor of excitement that the deliberately subdued summons could not hide.

Mann, nodding over his shoulder when the mate arrived, said: "Look, there's sparks coming up around the stacks!"

McCoit looked, and sure enough a steady cascade of sparks was flying upward from between the water jackets and the deck, from the very void that engineer Stebbins had provided to lessen the danger of fire. They streamed up steadily in the draft the gap created, bright red but fading into an iridescent glow as they swept back over the skylight and the walking-beam of the engine. McCoit dashed a couple of buckets of water down through the openings but with little or no effect. Indeed, steady tongues of flame were succeeding them!

A capable and determined officer, McCoit recognized at once the dread potential of delay and instantly ordered wheelsman Mann to steer for shore. The mate then began to arouse the crew, beginning with Captain Roby and engineer Stebbins. The fire could not have originated in the engine room or it would have been detected earlier. More likely it had started aft of the boilers, in the cargo hold or around the wooden bulkhead between the boilers and hold. It was where a fire could be expected to gain some headway before being detected, and where the draft supplied by the openings around the smoke pipes might carry the smoke and sparks upward and out without being seen promptly by the busy firemen.

Whatever its cause or point of origin, the fire spread with astounding speed. And it was no secret. The running and shouting during the crew's efforts to extinguish it had long since aroused the sleeping and bewildered passengers. With the fire raging midships and spreading aft rapidly, the immigrants quartered there were endangered first. The ship's two big lifeboats hung just aft of the side-wheels and were among the first casualties, dropping into the sea in flames as

soon as their ropes were burned through. Terrified children
were being calmed by parents near a point of hysteria themselves. Those quartered forward of the fire made their way
to the bow, milling about in the dark in such confusion that
families were quickly separated. Some tried to carry their
personal belongings with them, others threw theirs overboard. Down below, before he and second engineer Maxim
Juno abandoned the engine room, Mr. Stebbins had made
sure the throttle was fixed in the full ahead position. His
engine, he knew, would operate at maximum efficiency until the steam pressure dropped substantially. Hopefully, by
then the *Griffith* would be ashore and in water shallow
enough for her people to save themselves.

Henry Priday and his family, asleep in their cabin aft on
the lower deck, were aroused by the cry of "fire." Both Priday
and his wife hurried out on deck, carrying with them daughter Kate and a young companion, Lydia Humpidge. They
were quickly joined by Thomas and Ann Hooper, other
members of the Priday contingent. Seeing that the bow was
still clear of fire and smoke, they climbed to the hurricane
deck and fought their way forward, the flames singeing their
hair, and the hot deck blistering their feet. They were not
alone. Blinded and choked by smoke, scores of others battled
their way madly toward the bow amid the booming of the
fire, the thrashing of the side-wheels and the hellish din
created by the shouts and screams of nearly three hundred
fear-crazed passengers.

Dr. Maronchy, asleep in the upper berth of his forward
cabin, had been aroused by the sound of running feet and
distant shouts. So was his cabin mate in the lower berth.

"Something's wrong," he said to the doctor, panic in his
voice.

"No," countered the doctor. "We're nearing Cleveland
and the crew is just getting the lines ready."

His own fears still paramount, the man in the lower bunk ran out on deck in his underwear but returned almost instantly shouting, "The boat's on fire!"

Dr. Maronchy donned his trousers hurriedly and went out to see for himself. The forward cabins were still relatively free of smoke, but midships aft the ship was a crackling sheet of fire. The flames, fanned backward by the motion of the ship, were swiftly devouring every temporary haven of refuge. When they could no longer endure the searing heat, those quartered aft, cabin or steerage class, jumped overboard, sometimes singly, often entire families hand in hand. Captain Roby was observed to be making some hopeless attempt to direct the crew's fire brigade, but was much handicapped by his own family, which clung to him in terror.

The bow, on both decks, was now jammed with milling, clawing and shouting passengers. Some jumped overboard but were drawn alongside by the ship's motion and crushed in the big side-wheels. Some on the lower deck stood on the outside, feet on the wooden fender, clinging tenaciously to the rail. The bullish surge of immigrants forward had separated husband from wife, both from their children. Those who lost their footing were trampled underfoot. Hysterical with fear, many still continued to throw their trunks and luggage overboard, down upon those below, then jumped blindly into the swirling waters dotted by discarded luggage and the laboring forms of their fellow passengers—a maelstrom of thrashing, shouting and cursing humanity.

Wheelsman Richard Mann, almost blinded by smoke and suffering terribly from the heat, vainly sought lights ashore to give assurance that the *Griffith* would soon be in shallow water. There were no lights and he could not be sure that the dark mass he did see was land. Mate McCoit was standing on the bow fender, almost at the stem, calmly throwing the sounding lead and shouting out the depths. It was a useless gesture, for his voice was lost in the tumult. A large, bull-voiced German man, separated from his family and crazed with despair, kept pulling his hair and shouting "Mein Gott, Mein Gott!"

The *Griffith*'s steam pressure was about gone, as indicated by the slower pace of the side-wheels. Finally they stopped completely and for a moment or two the ship continued on her course through sheer momentum. Practically at that moment she ran up on a sandbar and stopped dead. Now, the flames once fanned aft by the ship's forward motion swept toward the bow. Wheelsman Mann, still at his post in the pilothouse and already badly burned, now jumped overboard. Hope now gone, the rest of the passengers began jumping by the score, leaping down upon others or throwing themselves at floating objects, trunks, boards, chairs and other bits of flotsam. Captain Roby was seen to leap off the starboard side with his family. The sea, now brilliantly illuminated by the blazing *Griffith*, was a dreadful panorama of chaos and despair, seething from the frantic thrashings of those who seemingly only moments before had been safely nearing the last stop on the long voyage to a new world. Some wasted their breath in hoarse shouts for help that could not come. Others husbanded their resources to fight their way free from the clutching, gurgling and flailing souls about them.

Henry Priday had been quickly separated from his family and went overboard against his will, caught up in the mad rush to the rails. He had scarcely hit the water when another person landed upon him, driving him down. Another clutched at his leg but was shaken loose. Priday struck out for shore, which he judged to be a half mile distant, but which was actually much nearer, slowing when he saw others sinking and reaching for him. Finally, numb from exhaustion, he crawled up on the beach and lay alone, too tired and weak to move.

Dr. Maronchy, cool and collected, worked his way forward until he reached the very stem. Hanging from the bowsprit, which also served as a steering pole, he waited until he saw a place clear of floundering immigrants and jumped. Not a good swimmer, he paddled cautiously, avoiding those who would grasp him for support. Progress was painfully slow and he had about given up when he finally felt his toes touch bottom. Too tired to swim further, he let the gentle seas carry him to the beach. He estimated the distance from the ship to shore as about two hundred yards. One by one Dr. Maronchy and Henry Priday were joined by others, speechless with exhaustion, numbed by the horror they had experienced and content to lie prone as reality slowly replaced the dreamlike agonies of the past hour. Others came crawling in from the surf. There were not many—probably between thirty and forty—among them heartbroken engineer Stebbins, first mate William Evans, second mate Samuel McCoit, wheelsman Robert Davis and ship's clerk Henry Wilkinson. Mr. Stebbins was morose, shaking his head from side to side as if in utter disbelief of what had happened. The ship's yawl, hung over her stern, had burned loose and fallen into the lake. John Chichester, the steamer's headwaiter, had swum to it, splashed out the fire and in his oarless craft had saved himself and seven others, among them the wife of the ship's barber, thrown overboard by Captain Roby after the vessel grounded.

The *Griffith* had "found" the sandbar a couple of miles west of the Chagrin River, off Willoughby Township, in a sparsely settled farming area. Even so, the flames had attracted considerable attention in the village of Willoughby, and the first dawn arrivals at the scene, coming by horse and buggy, found the pitiful survivors still sprawled on the beach, dazed and limp from their ordeal. Offshore, naught remained of the *Griffith* above water but her heat-warped smokestacks and the metal framework of her side-wheels. The wreck had swung around broadside to the beach and over it still hung a pall of smoke. Along the shore the victims lay rolling gently in the surf—scores of them. Offshore more could be seen, floating in or being carried eastward with the wind and sea. Reinforced by new arrivals and an armada of small boats rounded up from shoreside residents, the farmers and villagers from Willoughby began the unpleasant job of recovery. Recognizing the enormity of their task, the group appointed a committee of prominent Willoughby men to supervise the grim program of identifying the victims through personal effects, physical characteristics and clothing worn. It was an almost hopeless task from the beginning. Few had any personal belongings except rings or lockets with initials. Although the beach was strewn with a monumental collection of spectacles, combs, shawls, sweaters, slippers, skirts, vests, dresses and coats, none could be specifically related to any of those in the long and growing lines of victims laid out on the sand. The exception was a nightgown marked: "William Hooper, 1850." Hooper, identified by Henry Priday, was one of the first to be found and identified.

Small boats shuttled to and from the wreck as others cruised in the area between the sandbar and the shore. Many victims were sighted on the bottom, often in clusters of six or eight, the result of the mad clutching and grabbing in the fight to stay afloat. A single probe by a pike pole brought up six, still locked together in death as they had been when they went down.

The counting, tagging and noting of physical descriptions and clothing went on—one German woman, age about thirty; English woman, age about twenty-seven; Irish boy, age fifteen; a Frenchman, age thirty; child, one and one-half years old, shirt marked J.H.; an Englishman, twenty-five years old, shoes, corduroy pants, plaid worsted vest, cotton shirt, hair auburn; American lady with dark brown hair, black silk dress, gold earrings; German, thirty years old, gray socks, moleskin vest and gray coat; an English girl, corset marked M.S., with green calico dress; English woman, age thirty, with large English watch; German man, very large with blue calico jacket, German papers and a large snuffbox; an English girl, about eight years old, hair brown, black dress and spotted purple apron; American lady, twenty-five to thirty years old, green dress and size four slippers; German girl, eighteen years old, chemise marked W.; two flaxen-haired girls, six and eight, supposed to be sisters. On and on it went as morning turned into afternoon and a hot sun beat down upon the dreadful scene.

There were two instances when identification posed no problem. John Ham Northy, who left his Devon home in March, carried a letter from his mother—a letter full of forebodings and a slip directing where his friends could be written to in case of an accident. He had sailed from Plymouth on March 27, according to a passage receipt found in one of his pockets. Louisa Taylor, a comely girl from Cambridgeshire, carried with her a letter to be left with William Burnswick, Bloomfield, Medina County, Ohio.

The citizens' committee of twenty-four, which had volunteered to render whatever assistance possible, was now faced with an unenviable decision. The day was growing progressively hotter and identification, in most cases, was turning out to be an impossible task. Something had to be done quickly about interring the unfortunate people stretched out on the hot sands of a land still foreign to them. Chairman of the committee Samuel Wilson, along with George Skiff and A. T. Sharp, sought the guidance of Dr. Orson St. John. After numerous consultations with other committee members and much soul-searching and on the advice of a clergyman, it was decided to dig a couple of long trenches well back from the beach and bury them then and there. It was a painful decision, but one that obviously could not wait. Two sizable trenches were dug, thirty feet long, six feet wide and eight feet deep and into them were lowered the bodies of twenty-four women, forty-seven men and twenty-five children. Others, who had been identified, were taken to Cleveland on lake craft which had come to the scene. The steamer *Diamond* and the scow *Sylph* carried twenty-nine of the dead, including Captain Roby and his family, wheelsman Richard Mann, deck hand Theodore Gilman and fireman Hugh McLain. Taken to Buffalo on another steamer were Clarissa Heth and her two children, Francis and Helen. Only Franklin Heth, husband and father, survived. With the still forms of the Heths were those of barkeeper William Tillman, second engineer Maxim Juno, first porter Lawrence Dana and cabin maid Christine Hood. The steamer *Delaware* brought seven surviving cabin passengers to Cleveland—all that were left of the forty-five booked first-class. Among them was the cool and collected Dr. Maronchy, who was obliged to relate the grim tales of the disaster to his wife and a gathering of journalists at the Weddell House.

Every disaster has its miracles, and the *Griffith* was no exception. First to reach the burning steamer was William Melton, a commercial fisherman. Melton and his helpers were about to depart their little dock in the pre-dawn darkness to lift their big seine net when they saw the blazing steamer headed for shore. The distance was considerable, but they rowed to the scene as quickly as possible. The steamer, now an inferno from stem to stern, could obviously support no life, so the fishermen began dragging bodies into their boat for transfer to the shore. The first load included a five-year-old boy, apparently dead. On the beach they were met by

Captain Kennedy, who lived nearby. The captain saw the boy's lips move slightly, quickly grabbed him by the heels, held him up and shook him vigorously, emptying the lad's lungs and stomach of much water. Rushed to the Kennedy home, the boy recovered in a remarkably short time. In the afternoon he was well enough to inquire about his mother. He gave his name as Johnny Rhodes and answered all questions put to him by the strangers quickly and intelligently. When the long rows of bodies were about to be interred, Captain Kennedy took the boy in his arms and went around among the dead to see if the little fellow could identify any of his friends. Shortly he pointed to a corpse in the group of women. "There," said Johnny Rhodes, "is my mother and she has five hundred dollars sewed in her petticoat." Seconds later he pointed out the bodies of his brother, sister, and, finally, his father. Little Johnny Rhodes was the only member of the family to survive, and that by a miracle.

The Hall family group, eleven in all, was decimated. Only Robert Hall, the Cambridgeshire farmer who had hoped to find a better life in Ohio, was left. His close friend William Waters also survived, but he, too, lost his entire family. Of the group of thirty-one immigrants from Cambridgeshire, only three remained to complete their journey.

Joseph Money, a lad of twelve, was saved, but his father, mother and two sisters were lost. The William Walker and William Taylor families were wiped out. Every member of the Bohling family of nine, the Germans bound for Sandusky, either perished in the hull or were drowned. Franz Hugel, the new friend, died with them.

At dusk on that grim Monday chairman Wilson and secretary Sharp of the citizens' committee reported that one hundred and forty-one victims had been recovered, but noted that many more were missing and would be reported as they were found. Some of them, as though reluctant to admit the end of their dreams, were slow in making their rendezvous with land. Nor did they stay in the vicity of the ship that had been their undoing. Many eventually wandered ashore miles down the beach, others drifted out into the lake to spend eternity looking for their loved ones. By Tuesday night the count had grown to two hundred and twenty-one.

Now alone and penniless, with only his shirt, pants and a watch to his name, Henry Priday, wild with grief, walked the beach in search of his wife Elizabeth, daughter Kate and the eight relatives in the party. Kate was found quickly, but Mrs. Priday was not recovered until Friday. Near her were Lydia and Albert Humpidge, others in the group. It was an appropriate time for sympathetic new friends to put in an appearance, and one materialized in the person of John Mosier, of Willoughby. Mosier offered to permit burial of the wife and daughter in his family burial plot. It was an exceedingly kind gesture and a grateful Henry Priday accepted.

Summoned from his home in Perry Township, Johnathan Coolidge, wreckmaster for Lake County, noted in his little brown book each and every item recovered, mostly things the surf had distributed on the beach:

          1 fiddle bow
         16 odd shoes
         10 bonnets, all worthless
          4 clothes brushes
          1 pocket flask
         27 cotton handkerchiefs
          1 snuff box
         19 hats
         35 caps

Altogether the list filled five pages without recording any item of intrinsic value. Strangely, however, Mr. Coolidge did not compile his inventory of the beach harvest until

Friday, June 21, a full four days after the disaster. Others had preceded him when the picking was easier and infinitely more rewarding.

During the first hours of work by coroner Samuel Brown and the citizens' committee, seeking clues to identification, hundreds of dollars in paper money were turned over to the coroner, hats were filled with gold and silver watches and from the pockets of the poor came a small collection of guilders, franc pieces, ha'pennies and shillings. One man had nine $100 bills and other money amounting to $1100 in his pockets.

In the utter panic in progress as the *Griffith* struck the bar and burned with renewed fury, a young man threw overboard a sack containing $1800 before jumping himself. The sack was recovered later by first mate Evans and a bitter dispute followed as to the true owner. The authorities eventually returned the bag to the young passenger, who proffered the mate a $100 reward which he quickly accepted.

The ship's books had, of course, been lost in the inferno. Clerk Henry Wilkinson, however, stated positively that there had been three hundred and twenty-six persons aboard when the vessel departed Fairport. With two hundred and forty-one accounted for a day after the disaster, and an odd one or two turning up day by day, a substantial percentage of the total were still among the missing. It was presumed that some had been entirely consumed in the burning hulk, but obviously not as many as were still unaccounted for.

The tragedy of the *Griffith*, coming swiftly on the heels of the explosion aboard the aged *Anthony Wayne*, fanned anew the flames of public protest. Citizens' groups in several cities, but particularly in Cleveland, called for public meetings. At Empire Hall, Mayor William Case was appointed chairman of a committee to draft resolutions to Congress—a committee that included many prominent and influential civic, business and political leaders. Some were responsible for drafting the resolutions, others for the printing of the documents and distribution of copies to every member of Congress. The resolutions called for safer construction of steam vessels then afloat or hereafter built; a law requiring every steam vessel on leaving port to have latches on her cargo hold secured to prevent fire from the deck; a provision for appointment by the President of the United States of three competent engineers for the examination of furnaces, boilers, etc., of every steam vessel; the lakes to be divided into three districts, with one inspector to each; establishment of a board for the examination of engineers and to permit no person to act in that capacity without the board's certificate of ability; to authorize each inspector to prosecute all infractions of the law in his district; and further requiring each inspector to appoint a competent ship carpenter for the examination of hulls, the government paying him an adequate compensation.

So prompt and decisive had been the public outrage in Cleveland that other lake cities quickly cast the voices of their citizens in the role of protesters to the daily examples of criminal carelessness and negligence cloaked in the guise of steamboats. Impetus was added to the campaign, and perhaps at a critical time, by the exploding of the boilers of the steamer *America*, off Barcelona, New York, only forty-four days after the *Griffith* holocaust, killing eleven. Captain Phillips, her owner, had been informed that the *America* was carrying 115 pounds of steam pressure, far more than the condition of her boilers warranted, but he had postponed repairs. Again the immediate outcry of the citizenry, given maximum exposure in the public prints, sent pressure waves in the direction of Washington. And although it took nine years for Congress to establish legislation, substantially as suggested by the Cleveland resolutions, the era of irresponsible operations of steamboats was coming to an end.

One of the most energetic forces in drafting the Cleveland resolutions was Edward L. Hessenmueller, justice of the peace and leader of the German residents of the city, many of whom had been waiting to welcome friends and relatives aboard the ill-fated *Griffith*. The Germans had been appalled by what they concluded was precipitous haste in burying their beloved relatives in the sand along Lake Erie and there was much talk of recovering the bodies, purchasing a large vault, coffins and a suitable plot of land.

In a week the lonely shore on which the *Griffith* had made her last landfall was much the same as it had been on that horror-filled early Monday morning of June 17. Only the blackened timbers and iron jutting up from offshore and the two long mounds of sand marked the end of so many immigrant families' dreams a scant fifteen miles short of their goal.

Survivors were warm in their praise for the sympathy and help rendered at the scene by individuals and groups, particularly the St. George's Society and several church missions. The Fisher family had been extremely kind, taking several of the injured and destitute into their home. Helping at the beach, too, were neighboring farmers, Robert Bales and Zophar Warner. Warner's farm was about on a line from the sandbar on which the *Griffith* grounded, but both men were shortly to share in a grim bounty.

A depressing story was related by the curious who visited the beach five days after the disaster. They told of finding the mass graves desecrated and victims exposed, supposedly by ghouls who heard the story of the $500 sewed in Mrs. Rhodes' petticoat and presumed that the other women bore similar riches.

Ten days after the disaster, when the beach was deserted by all but the gulls, the *Griffith*'s missing began to appear on the beach, wandering in singly, in pairs or sometimes in groups, like expected guests who have gone astray only to arrive apologetic and penitent after the welcoming festivities are over. All were men, most were German and all wore the encumbering money belts, the "prosperity anchors" that had spelled their doom and accounted for their tardiness. It had taken ten days for the chemical changes in the bodies to overcome the weight of the gold.

Alone with the horrible harvest on the beach and without the army of helpful and sympathetic citizens who had first been drawn to the scene by the flare of fire and pall of smoke, the two farmers set about burying the long overdue victims. But instead of interring the bodies in the sand, they loaded them on "stone boats" and hauled them up the embankment to the flat farm fields. The victims being unrecognizable and impossible to identify, it was a desperate, loathsome task, made endurable only by the growing pile of money belts and the treasures within, a reward Bales and Warner obviously felt was justly theirs in payment for the hideous labor that had befallen them. The gold yield must have been considerable, for in the division of it, according to tales handed down, there came a bitter quarrel that left the two, although related, bitter enemies for life. And as is so often regrettably the case, the ill feelings were handed down to future generations, persisting to this day, although the cause of the original breach has long since been forgotten, indeed if it was ever known to many of today's descendants.

Henry Priday, unwilling to put the news of the family disaster in cold ink, had journeyed the two hundred and fifty miles back to New York State to relate the details to his son William. Sympathetic Clevelanders contributed to a fund to make the trip possible. That done, Priday made his way to the family's original destination, Deerfield, Ohio, in Portage County. Two years later he remarried.

Time proved Priday to be an enigmatic soul. He apparently

believed all the wild, improbable tales related by other survivors, accepted them as the gospel and was not above embellishing questionable happenings as time went on, thus perpetuating doubts and suspicions that have lasted for years. Just thirty-six days after his crushing loss in the burning of the *Griffith*, he penned a long letter to his brother Samuel in England, apprising him of the details of the disaster and giving his own version of events. In it his only reference to possible laxity on the part of Captain Roby was a single sentence: "The captain seemed to be as much alarmed as any of the poor emigrants; he never had anything done to save life; he lost his own life."

But as time passed and his second wife bore him nine children, Henry Priday was unaccountably blessed with improving memory, freely recalling details which were not only in direct conflict with his earlier statments, but with known facts and the laws of probability and credibility. As later put down by his son Henry Charles Priday, born five years after the disaster, Henry Priday claimed that the boat was on fire before reaching Fairport, due to the fact that the captain was racing with another boat, and in order to keep up the increased speed the engine was fired to such an extent that the engine room became overheated, setting fire to several barrels of lubricating oil. Furthermore, he related at subsequent family gatherings of entranced listeners, "The captain was urged to put in at Fairport, whereby all on board could have been saved." But again, according to Priday's more recent recollections, the captain replied: "I will run her into Cleveland ahead of the other boat or run her to hell." He stated, too, although he made no mention of it in his letter to brother Samuel or his earlier references to Captain Roby: "He (Roby) was a drinking man and under the influence of liquor at the time."

The fact is that the boat did put in at Fairport as regularly scheduled and was not on fire, as attested by Stephen Woodin and Hiram Knapp, who boarded her there, and by other officers, surviving passengers and witnesses at the dock. Neither did any of them mention a race with another vessel. Captain Roby, as his friends and associates in Maumee would gladly testify, was a sober, industrious man. Nor does it make sense that a man with his personal fortune invested in a steamer and with his family aboard would participate in a senseless race with another steamer with his own vessel afire. Indeed, had there been another steamer about, she would quickly have come to the rescue of the *Griffith* and her passengers. The matter of the lubricating oil was debatable. Authorities had tested some of Mr. Stebbins' new oil and found that it truly did have an exceedingly low "flash point" and burned furiously when ignited. But had the fire originated in the engine room or boiler room, those working there would have been the first driven topside instead of being able to remain at their posts for some time to keep precious steam pressure up.

Substantiating Mr. Stebbins' claim that his new oil was not at fault was the statement of Mr. Woodin. Woodin told several officials that when fire was evident, auger holes were drilled in the bulkhead between the fire hole and the cargo hold, and that through the opening the fire could be seen raging in the cargo, much of which consisted of the belongings of the immigrant passengers. And while this statement exonerated the grieving engineer, it was certain that the lubricating oil added to the ferocity of the blaze once the ship had run aground and the flames were no longer driven aft by the vessel's forward motion.

Mr. Priday's judgment of his swimming ability had taken on new stature with the passing years, too, for in his letter to brother Samuel he had related how he had barely made shore, and then in such a state of exhaustion and shock that he could not stand for some time. But in the reminiscences chronicled by son Henry Charles, he related that he had swum underwater and out into the lake, making a wide detour so as to escape being drawn down by the struggling mass of drowning passengers, the last part of the perilous journey being made side by side with the first mate, who, being too weak to make the beach, perished before his very eyes. This would have been somewhat of a shock to first mate William Evans, who not only lived to give testimony at the coroner's inquest, but was the man accused of salvaging the bag with $1800 in cash, the one thrown overboard by the impetuous young passenger.

The observant Dr. Maronchy had been quite accurate in his estimate of two hundred yards as the distance from the sandbar to the beach, as compared to Mr. Priday's guess of one-half mile. Fisherman Melton knew exactly, for it was between the very sandbar that was the *Griffith*'s doom and the shore that he had stretched his seine net to trap sturgeon. "It was just the distance of my seine line, forty rods or 660 feet," he explained. A rod being sixteen and one-half feet, Dr. Maronchy had been in error by only sixty feet.

Time is a great healer and its passing a compelling reason for the daily meeting of new challenges, new problems, a relentless process during which the importance of today's happenings quickly become obscure and of little significance. The *Griffith*'s victims, never having had an opportunity to make their marks in the new life they so avidly sought, were all too soon forgotten. The area along the lake shore east of Cleveland experienced rapid growth and in due time an amusement park, Willoughbeach Park, occupied the flatlands overlooking the beach burial site. Roller coasters and fun rides were built over the land where Robert Bales and Zophar Warner dug graves for the ship's tardy arrivals and reaped the harvest of their money belts. It was a gay and convenient location, serviced frequently by interurban streetcars and where every summer generations gathered for sheer enjoyment and family picnics.

The plans of the German community in Cleveland to retrieve and honor in a more fitting manner their lost countrymen apparently never came to pass, however sincere the original concept of a vault, coffins and a suitable plot. Or, if the fine sentiments of June of 1850 were ever translated into action, those responsible were selective in their work. Sixty-three years later, in the summer of 1913, ten-year-old Homer Hunter, son of the manager of Willoughbeach Park, and a park concessionaire, Clifford Smith, uncovered the skull and bones of one victim while digging idly in the sand. They dug no further.

Time, too, put an end to Willoughbeach Park. The mushrooming eastern suburbs of Cleveland made it impractical to maintain an aging amusement park in the light of rising land values and taxes. The park, quickly demolished by the wrecker's hammers, was succeeded by acres of new homes and streets, now all part of the city of Willowick. It is doubtful if any of its thousands of residents ever heard of Captain Roby, the steamer *G. P. Griffith* or her meticulous engineer, David R. Stebbins, to say nothing of Henry Priday, whose memory grew more acute, if more undependable, as the years flowed on. Nor, probably, would they care that their modest homesteads are shared with the bones of almost three hundred immigrants who almost made it to Cleveland.

〽〽〽〽〽〽〽〽〽〽〽〽〽〽〽〽〽〽〽〽〽

⚓

5

A Scot Comes Home for the Harvest

It's a long way from North East, Pennsylvania, to Donegal County, Ireland, but that in itself is a revealing insight into the character of eighteen-year-old ordinary seaman Donald Sutherland McDonald who, on the afternoon of January 27, 1878, found himself clinging to the broken mainmast of the Norwegian brig *Hilding* as the North Atlantic seas picked her to pieces and drowned her men in the shallows off Donegal Head. It is significant to note, too, that the determined Scot was still there the next morning, after a night of freezing wind and spray, when Captain James McCandless and a volunteer crew in a large fishing boat came out to rescue him and a single remaining young Norwegian sailor.

The story really begins in the summer of 1877, back on Lake Erie, when young Donald took a pleasure trip on the little steamer *Georgian*, owned and operated by his uncle, Captain John Burgess, of Port Ryerse, Ontario. Donald liked the life of a sailor so well that he stayed on for the season as a crew member. When the *Georgian* was laid up for the winter, the desire to sail still burned with such a fury that he decided to "go salt water" and made his way to New York.

On November 11 he shipped out as a boy on the steamer *State of Pennsylvania*, bound for Glasgow. From there, on January 14, 1878, he shipped as ordinary seaman on the *Hilding*, bound for the West Indies. But January was a bad month to be on the North Atlantic in a sailing vessel. Not only was progress slow and erratic, but on the tenth day a great storm carried away the lifeboats, top masts, sails, yards and the topside casks of fresh water. In such a distressed condition the captain decided to square away with what little canvas was left to run for the north coast of Ireland, thinking he could work his vessel into anchorage at the entrance to the Londonderry River.

The highlands near the entrance to the river were sighted, but the gale still raged and the seas ran high. When the captain tried to work the *Hilding* into the estuary, the remaining sails were carried away, leaving crew and ship at the mercy of the sea, driving them in toward the beach. The anchors were dropped in seven fathoms of water. The bottom was quicksand and they refused to "bite." The ship's ensign was then hoisted, union down, the universal signal of distress. This done, the crew's duty to their ship was over. It was now time to save themselves if they could. The *Hilding* struck on rocks offshore, the shock sending the foremast and all the headgear overboard, leaving only the lower mainmast standing. Two of the crew were lost when a monstrous sea swept the forward cabin away, at which time the remaining nine made for the mainmast and its rigging. Young McDonald, learning the horrors of shipwreck quickly, climbed to the grating around the trestle trees. The captain, mates and the other seamen stayed in the netting underneath. By now the seas had carried away the other cabin, bulwarks and hatches. At midnight the hull began to break up, the mainmast heeling over at a rakish angle. The captain and the other men jumped into the sea only to be drowned or killed by the floating spars. McDonald and his youthful shipmate stuck to their perch although lashed by rain and hail throughout the night. Ashore many people stood watch with bright fires burning on the beach.

Donald Sutherland McDonald first touched the soil of Ireland in an extremely impoverished condition—an empty stomach, weak from exposure, without shoes, coat or hat and his shirt and trousers torn in many places and heavy with sand and salt water. Taken to a nearby farmhouse, he found that there were two other survivors, both in bed and very ill.

The rescue had scarcely been completed and the two young seamen taken to warm shelter when a fine carriage drove up to the door of the farmhouse. In it was Lady Bruce, mistress of nearby Downhill Castle and estate, inquiring as to the health of the survivors. Spying young Donald, obviously a fellow Scot, she had him taken to the carriage and whisked him away to Downhill Castle where he ate ravenously, slept around the clock and was provided with new clothing. The shipwreck and exposure had taken its toll, and, at the insistence of Sir Harvey and Lady Bruce, it was several weeks before he set off for nearby Londonderry to seek another shipboard berth. It was typical of McDonald, too, that in expressing his gratitude to his kind hosts of Downhill Castle he made a promise that if fate ever blessed him with an heir, his name would be Bruce.

During the next four years the indefatigable young seaman circumnavigated the globe twice, visiting India, China, Australia and many exotic ports. Meanwhile he studied navigation and received his official papers as an able-bodied seaman and navigator. On April 2, 1881, he sailed on the *St. Patrick* from Glasgow, arriving back home in Montreal early in May.

Returning to the family home in North East, Pennsylvania,

he began his career on the lakes almost immediately, serving on schooners and steamers in a variety of capacities before receiving his license as a first-class pilot. After working three years as second mate and three more as first mate on several steamers, he took command of the *Nyanza* of the McBrier fleet, out of Erie, Pennsylvania, in 1894, and two years later was appointed master of the *Emily P. Weed* when the Mc-Brier interests purchased her. The next year the vessel's name was changed to the *Sevona* and thereafter in Great Lakes history the names *Sevona* and McDonald were synonymous.

It was characteristic of Captain McDonald that he always kept his promises. In December of 1888 he had married Jessie M. Town and in due course of time a son was born and promptly christened Bruce, in honor of Sir Harvey Bruce of Downhill Castle. Later another son, Jay, was born.

A man of vast energy, Captain McDonald found other outlets for action when the Great Lakes vessels were ice-bound and laid up for the winter. Big, hearty and outgoing, he liked nothing better after a good snow than to test the speed of his horse and sleigh in friendly jousts with other North East citizens on the town's Main Street. The sport was so popular that the town council passed an ordinance reserving Main Street for racing from one-thirty to three-thirty every afternoon when conditions permitted. Active in civic and church affairs and a brilliant host at many social gatherings during the winter, his comings and goings were frequently recounted in the columns of the local papers, the North East *Sun* and the North East *Breeze*.

He was too shrewd to put all his eggs in one basket, as the saying goes, and perhaps cognizant of some of the uncertainties of the lake shipping industry, he sought other outlets for his time and talents during the winter months. Like others, he was aware of the boom in vineyard properties along the lush lake shore between Erie and Buffalo, and in 1891 bought eleven acres himself, just east of town on the Buffalo Road. Later he founded his own real estate firm, specializing in vineyard properties, and during the winter of 1901-1902 sold twenty-eight farms. His own eleven acres were, of necessity, entrusted to the care of a neighboring grower who, in exchange for his work, received one-third of the crop revenue. The fact that his steamboating career kept him away from home during the busy late September harvest season was a cross he bore philosophically, if not always in silence. "Never home for the harvest," he often grumbled.

Even in 1904, when vessel captains and mates staged a long work stoppage to enforce their demands for higher pay, the dispute was settled and Captain McDonald was back aboard the *Sevona* when the grapes were ripe and fragrant. He missed another harvest season.

Early in 1905 he moved his family out to the farm and in true, proud sailor tradition named the property "Snug Harbor." There all through the long gloomy winter he looked out upon his eleven acres, dreamed of the gaunt, dark vines blossoming out and perhaps had happy visions of seasons to come when he would be home for the harvest.

Very early in 1905 the *Sevona* went into the Buffalo drydock to be lengthened seventy-two feet. At the time there was considerable discussion in marine circles about the principle of lengthening boats to keep them competitive with the newer and longer vessels then being launched. The *Sevona* was only one of several "stretched out" or scheduled for the procedure. Most experts agreed that the program was thoroughly practical from a standpoint of increased carrying capacity, but pointed out that the *Sevona* had a beam of only forty-three feet, whereas greater capacity could best be gained by lengthening boats with beams of fifty feet or more. At the same time she was in drydock for major surgery other improvements were made, including new boilers and an electric lighting system powered by a single generator. The tonnage capacity was increased to 4800 as compared to her former maximum of 3300 tons.

Normally the shipyard workers would have completed their work by the time the ice was out of Buffalo harbor, but a disastrous fire destroyed many of the yard's facilities, seriously delaying work on the *Sevona*. This would have greatly disturbed any shipmaster but Captain McDonald, who looked upon the affair as a heaven-sent reprieve—a special dispensation from above permitting him to stay at home in good conscience, happily puttering with his grapevines.

It wasn't until June 29 that the *Sevona,* "practically a new boat," according to the Erie *Evening Herald,* loaded her first cargo of the season, hard coal taken on at the Lackawanna dock in Buffalo. If there was any dissatisfaction with the work done on the "patching up," as skeptical old sailors persisted in calling the lengthening operation, it was not in evidence as the *Sevona* resumed her place in the lake trade, hauling iron ore from Lake Superior ports to Buffalo, Erie or Cleveland, returning with coal. And it was a rare trip when she went up without "guests"—relatives or friends of either the owners or of Captain McDonald. The hundreds of snapshots they took always showed the genial skipper wearing his badge of office aboard ship—a derby hat.

Such a trip began in Cleveland on August 24 where, before the *Sevona* took on her last car of coal at the dumper, Mr. James McBrier ushered aboard two young ladies. They were Kate Spencer and Lillian Jones, both from Erie and family friends of the McBriers. Owner McBrier stayed aboard as far as Marine City, Michigan, along the St. Clair River, there leaving his young guests in care of the affable Captain McDonald.

The voyage to Duluth proved to be all the girls had expected and they soon became firm friends of the other two women aboard, Mrs. William Phillipie, wife of the chief engineer, making her first trip of the season, and Louise Cluckey, second cook and wife of the steward, C. H. Cluckey. The weather was delightful all the way up the lakes and the *Sevona* arrived at Duluth on Monday, August 28, Captain McDonald's forty-fifth birthday.

Delays, usually associated with cargo problems, had plagued the *Sevona* ever since she had reentered the trade, and it was no different this time. Some time elapsed before the vessel was able to moor at the unloading dock and the clamshell buckets seemed to take longer than usual in dredging out her coal cargo. But when the last of the coal had been removed and the hold swept clean, Captain McDonald hauled his boat over to Allouez Bay and the long, towering iron ore loading docks. But again, quick dispatch was not to be the lot of the *Sevona*. There had been an unusual rush of ore cargoes and a shortage of cars to move the ore from the mines to the dock. The *Sevona* was scheduled for a specific grade of ore consigned to Cleveland, and had to wait three days before it arrived. The time was spent sightseeing in Duluth or Superior and just lounging around the deck in the warm sun.

The *Sevona* finally departed the ore dock late Friday afternoon, at 6:03 P.M., as recorded in chief engineer Phillipie's log. By this time the young ladies had enjoyed dinner in the ornately paneled dining room and had repaired to the deck, the evening breeze being slightly cool but the seas calm. Captain McDonald brought out a .22 caliber target rifle he had purchased in Duluth for his son Bruce, and proceeded to challenge Miss Jones and Miss Spencer to a bit of marksmanship. The girls were spectacularly poor shots, but the captain hit the little tin can target with great regularity.

All the while he spoke glowingly of his son and the pleasure he would have learning how to shoot.

At dusk the girls joined Captain McDonald in his cabin, where they took turns reading aloud from *The Clansman,* by Thomas Dixon, Jr. The wind by now had taken on a distinctly bitter edge and a modest bit of sea was running from the northeast. The *Sevona,* with the Apostle Islands off to starboard and Devil's Island Light winking from afar, was beginning to roll, but not enough to cause any discomfort. At nine o'clock, as was his nightly custom, Captain McDonald excused himself and went aft to check his boat and consult with chief engineer Phillipie. The girls went to their cabins fully prepared to be rocked to sleep by the motion of the boat.

Unbeknownst to Captain McDonald, and apparently to other mariners on Lake Superior, the night of September 1, 1905, was to spawn and hide a diabolical gale, gathering in secrecy in the upper altitudes before descending like an avenging angel on the vessels plodding the steamer tracks. It was the worst weather many masters could recall and, strangely, no inkling of what was to come was indicated in weather reports issued by the United States Weather Bureau at either end of the lake. The wind reached gale intensity before midnight and built up dark seas that creamed up over the *Sevona*'s bow and marched down her deck to spend themselves in a swirling lather among the hatch coamings. She was rolling briskly and beginning to pound. The air was laced with flying scud as the wind whipped the tops from the seas and sent them on ahead, like advance agents for calamity. At two o'clock on Saturday morning Captain McDonald apparently considered it foolish to continue on and decided to turn and seek shelter behind one of the Apostle Islands. The *Sevona,* having already passed Devil's Island, sixty-eight miles out from the Allouez Bay dock, was then beyond Outer Island, easternmost of the Apostle group. Shortly after he decided to seek shelter, Captain McDonald knocked on the door of the girls' cabin with a warning: "I'm going to turn the boat around in a few minutes to try to find shelter behind one of the islands. You had better put away any small articles which might be thrown about and broken."

The turn was completed successfully and the *Sevona* retraced her course, hunted down now by billowing black seas that welled up over her fantail and kept chief engineer Phillipie busy throttling down his engine as the valleys between the seas rolled under the stern.

Such was the confidence that Captain McDonald inspired that both Kate Spencer and Lillian Jones promptly dropped off to sleep again. But at 3:30 A.M. came his heavy knock on the door again and the calm words: "Girls, I want you to get up and dress, as I am going to send you aft."

A half hour later he was back with four seamen. Meanwhile he had arranged for a life line to be rigged between the fore and aft winches. With a sailor on each side, one of them holding the life line, the young ladies were taken aft although cold seas sometimes swept waist-high over the deck. At 4:15 A.M., with the smell of fresh coffee and graham muffins prevailing, they were safe in the dining room. The boat's porter, with the dinner bell in his hand, was ready for the breakfast call but kept mumbling that he couldn't get around the deck to ring it. The *Sevona* now began to pitch heavily, and the girls quickly rallied forces to help Louise Cluckey gather up dishes to keep them from sliding off the table. At 5:45 A.M. steward Cluckey, a complete realist, sidled into the dining room from the galley and said portentously, "You would all better get on life preservers. I think this is the end!"

Captain McDonald, meanwhile, must have had a terrible time in the pilothouse. The flying spume, along with a lashing rain, had blotted out the navigational aids that would have guided him in good weather. Raspberry Island Light was seventy-two feet above the water and the captain and the watchmen strained their eyes looking for it. Somehow, in the blur of rain, scud and spume, they missed it! The Apostle Islands group provided good passages but also dangerous, unmarked shoals. It is not an area where a shipmaster willingly takes his vessel, particularly in bad weather and with little or no visibility. It was a course that involved a calculated risk, but it was a risk that had to be taken. The vessel could no longer stand the punishment of wind and seas rolling unchecked the length of Lake Superior!

Unable to see, his boat assaulted by hurricane winds and

vengeful seas, Captain McDonald desperately sought the lee of one of the islands. At this point he was not particular which island offered salvation—any one would do. He had little idea of exactly where he was, how far the elements had carried him off course, or how many miles he had retraced his tracks. It would have been a splendid bit of seamanship to find shelter under the existing conditions even with today's aids—automatic direction finders and radar. But the *Sevona*'s pilothouse, like others of her era, had only the bare essentials—a steering wheel, telegraph, clock, compass and a cuspidor. Even so, he almost made it. Some say another one hundred yards to port would have been sufficient to escape Sand Island Shoal, a murderous ridge of granite. In good weather there was sixteen feet of water over the shoal, but with the *Sevona* pitching into the yawning valleys between the seas there was much less—much less.

Captain McDonald must have had an instinctive premonition that extreme caution was now in order, for at 5:45 A.M., as steward Cluckey was making his gloomy prediction of impending doom, he signaled the engine room for half speed, an order chief engineer Phillipie immediately acknowledged. Fifteen minutes later the *Sevona* struck the shoal, three distinct shocks being felt by Phillipie before the boat came to a halt and promptly broke in two near number four hatch, about the point where one end of the new hull section had been attached. Deck hand Charles Scouller had been aft and below when the first shock came. With others quartered below, he rushed through the engine room, up a ladder to the deck, and from there climbed on top of the boiler house. Every sea was rolling over the deck, now broken and with the two halves of the ship badly out of alignment. It was just growing daylight.

Even though isolated on the forward end of the boat, Captain McDonald was in full command, bellowing through his megaphone: "Lower the boats, put the ladies in and hang on as long as possible!"

Under chief engineer Phillipie, calm and resourceful, the starboard boat was lowered and the four women helped into it, the operation carried off without mishap, thanks to Captain McDonald's insistence on frequent boat drills. Charlie Scouller had kicked off his heavy boots but, like the others, was poorly attired in just a shirt and overalls. The cold, driving rain persisted and the wind still blew a gale. Although in the water, the starboard boat was still tethered to the vessel while Scouller and another man used their oars to keep it from being smashed against the freighter. Others of the crew, meanwhile, were trying to drag the smaller portside boat over to the starboard davits, since the seas on the weather side would have smashed it instantly. To accomplish this they had to remove a fresh water tank and cut away some stays on the smokestack. But the port boat was also launched successfully and moored to the afterrail of the *Sevona*. Unfortunately, the men on the aft end were not sailors, but engineers, oilers, firemen and the cook. The real sailors and boat handlers were up forward, cut off without a lifeboat or raft and, with the prevailing wind and running sea, inaccessible to those aft.

The complete absence of lifesaving gear up forward was really an ironic aftermath of official measures to save lives. After the tragic burning of the *General Slocum* in New York harbor the previous year, when over one thousand lives were lost, hasty corrective measures were instituted. The fearful loss of life was blamed on the fact that steamer's lifeboats had been stored on deck and were quickly consumed by the fire that swept the ship. Thereafter inspectors had condemned the practice of carrying lifeboats on the decks of vessels. Before her lengthening and rebuilding at the Buffalo dry dock, the *Sevona* had carried a lifeboat on the forward deck, immediately aft of the forward house. The new rules required davits for all boats. Because on lake boats the davits interfered with the loading and unloading machinery, they were located aft and out of the way. But they were also inaccessible to those quartered forward in the event of a disaster such as had just befallen the *Sevona,* her hull broken, the halves separated. The seven men on the forward end of the boat, Captain McDonald, first mate Louis Darwin, second mate George Hamilton, wheelsmen Otto Willett and Nels Salverson, and the two watchmen, Gus Drews and Orville Valette, were marooned and left to their own devices. They were observed by those aft to be salvaging some of the big wooden hatch covers and removing cabin doors, obviously in an attempt to fashion some sort of raft.

Chief engineer Phillipie apparently reconsidered his earlier decision to abandon ship, at least for the time being. The after end of the *Sevona* seemed to be firmly planted on the shoal and for the moment her cabins offered protection from the rain and cold. He ordered the ladies and the crew out of the boats and into the dining room, with two men detailed to keep the lifeboats from being smashed against the steamer's hull. He had ordered the whistle blown with the distress signal from the moment the boat "went on," with the hope that the lightkeeper on Sand Island would note the *Sevona*'s plight and phone to Bayfield for a rescue tug. The whistle sounded only briefly, as rising water in the boiler room put out the fires.

Keeper Emanuel Luick of the Sand Island Light was indeed aware of the wreck but was scarcely equipped to do anything about it. He had only one small boat, actually a skiff, which would have been but a pawn in the seas that were running, assuming that he could have launched it by himself. Nor was the light equipped with a telephone to notify authorities at Bayfield or the distant lifesavers. It was now seven o'clock on Saturday morning and still no sign of rescue craft. The storm, rather than abating, seemed to increase in intensity and power, as though determined not to rest until the poor *Sevona* was no more.

In the dining room the men relieved from tending the lifeboats came in periodically, dripping wet and practically frozen. The ladies did their best to warm them by wrapping their bodies in curtains and tablecloths. Deck hand Charlie Scouller, still without shoes, was supplied with a pair by one of the young guests who found some belonging to the steward. But their plight worsened as the hours passed. By nine o'clock the seas had broken in the skylight, water was knee-high and debris from the galley and pantry began to wash through. The galley door was barricaded but it, too, soon broke in as the seas that poured aboard over the weather side ravished the rooms and companionways. Then, about eleven o'clock, section by section, the beautiful oak paneling began to burst in and the stern of the *Sevona* began to list to starboard. It was time to abandon ship for good!

This time the doors were so battered and twisted that the only way out of the collapsing dining room was through the starboard windows. Once more the four ladies were lowered into the large lifeboat with Mr. Phillipie directing the operation and first assistant engineer Adam Fiden taking the tiller. Into this boat, too, climbed Adam Fiden's son, deckhand Nick Fiden, steward Cluckey and firemen Otto Schmidt, Neil Nelson and Gretten Retner. The smaller boat was taken in charge by Charlie Scouller, the only occupant with any small boat experience. He was joined by William Long, Paul Stockel, Edgar Ryder, George Slade and the one-armed oiler, Harry Van Vlack. Altogether they made up a capable after end crew for a steamboat but were complete strangers to the skills of handling a small boat in the seas that were running that grim September Saturday.

Engineers Phillipie and Fiden had hoped to be able to maneuver the large lifeboat toward the bow to pick up Captain McDonald and the other six men, but found this to be an impossibility. The seas, rolling completely over the broken hull, offered no lee in which to work up to the bow and drove the lifeboats steadily away. Earlier the stranded forward crew had been seen trying to make rafts from hatch covers and doors, but when the two lifeboats cast off from the wreck, the men were nowhere in sight. It was Phillipie's conclusion that the seas romping over the deck had driven them into the cabins for shelter from the cold. He was also of the opinion that the forward end of the *Sevona* was firm and hard on the rock shoal and would likely stay that way until he returned with help. Earlier, too, the captain's men had been observed carrying the trunks of Miss Spencer and Miss Jones from their cabin to the forepeak, indicating that the captain expected the bow end to survive and a rescue tug to reach the scene eventually.

Miraculously, although few if any of the men had any experience in handling small craft, both boats reached safety. The larger boat, with Mrs. Cluckey taking a turn at the oars and the two young lady passengers bailing, reached the mainland of Wisconsin, fourteen miles from Bayfield. The smaller boat, with deck hand Charlie Scouller standing at the tiller and one-armed Harry Van Vlack bailing industriously with his cap, rammed ashore on one of few good landing spots on Sand Island, going in the last one hundred yards on the crest of a big sea.

Shortly after landing on the lonely shore, the eleven from the boat piloted by engineer Adam Fiden chanced to encounter a homesteader, out in the rain and wind hunting for a missing cow. He led them through muddy swales, heavy forest and cresting small streams to a lumber camp operated by Napoleon Rabideau. Here the hospitable lumbermen made them welcome around hot stoves while the cook quickly prepared food. Exhausted to the point of numbness, the grateful crew and passengers ate their fill and fell into a heavy sleep. They had arrived at the lumber camp at 7:30 P.M. on Saturday, thirteen and one-half hours after the *Sevona* had impaled herself on Sand Island Shoal. Outside the storm still raged and howled. Rain beat down on the tin roofs of the cabins and turned the countryside into a quagmire.

Out on Lake Superior the sudden and unexpected storm was really just beginning to show its true stature. Sweeping westward the full length of the lake, the wind built up formidable seas that bullied vessels into submission or placed them in grave peril. Off Keweenaw Point the steamer *Iosco* and her tow barge the *Olive Jeanette* both disappeared. Near the Apostles, off Outer Island, the schooner *Pretoria* parted her towline from the steamer *Venezuela* and foundered before the eyes of John Irvine, keeper of the Outer Island Light. A huge sea, overtaking the steamer *R. L. Ireland,* swept away second mate Frank Smith, and off Knife Island, seas pounding over the whaleback steamer *Samuel Mather* carried away seaman John Lindquist. The package freighter *North Wind,* trying to enter the Duluth ship canal, was smashed against a pier and sank. Ironically, because of the enormous loss in vessels, the storm that came in November of the same year has come down in history as the "great storm of 1905," but the one that began on the eastern end of Lake Superior about the time the *Sevona* departed Allouez Bay was far the most costly in lives, a total of forty-three seamen perishing!

Although he was most anxious to send help to his marooned shipmates, chief engineer Phillipie found it impossible to travel to Bayfield on Saturday night, but did arrange for a lumberman with a horse and wagon to start out early on Sunday. Even so, the trip took nearly all day. The rain still came in torrents and many times the pair had to stop to cut away trees that had fallen across the road. It was five o'clock Sunday afternoon when the fishing tug *Harrow* departed Bayfield with a worried and distraught Mr. Phillipie pacing the pilothouse. There was no reason to believe that the forward end of the *Sevona* would not still be there on Sand Island Shoal, probably with an even more worried Captain McDonald stewing in his own pilothouse. The stranded crew, the tug men agreed, would probably be very hungry.

The wind was still very strong and the seas high when the tug, utilizing the west channel and keeping in the protected waters between the mainland and Oak Island, rounded Point DeTour and headed for Sand Island, still getting some protection from the seas from little York Island. Yes, there was a familiar bulk of a boat there on Sand Island Shoal, but not as much as they had hoped to see. The after end which chief engineer Phillipie and his men had abandoned still loomed on the horizon, battered and flattened, but the forward end was gone. There was nothing left—no protruding spar to indicate that she had slipped off an uneasy perch into deep water; no familiar silhouette on the rocky shore of Sand Island. She was gone, and that's all there was to it! The storm, rising to its full fury during Saturday night, must have taken her off or, more likely, just pounded her to pieces.

If the hatch covers and doors Captain McDonald and his men were seen salvaging were instrumental in bringing them safely to shore on Sand Island, there was no evidence in the form of life on the beach or a signal from up on the rocks. But the seas were still running so high that anything approaching a thorough search or landing was impossible.

Charlie Scouller and the group in the small boat had quickly located an abandoned cabin, where they kindled a

fire to dry their clothes. Nearby, in another cabin, a Norwegian homesteader provided them with food and water. At
dusk he returned with the sad news that the forward end of
the *Sevona* and all her houses had disappeared.

On Monday morning Scouller and his men heard a whistle
hooting and ran down to the beach. It was the tug *R. W.
Currie*, out looking for them. The lake being calm now, they
boarded the tug and began to search the shores for any sign
of their missing shipmates. They had already found one of
them, wheelsman Nels Salverson, lifeless on the beach on
Sunday afternoon. Soon a fisherman signaled the tug and
pointed out another body up on the sand. It was Captain
McDonald and near him, half buried, was a single dollar
bill! Before the day was over, two more of the *Sevona*'s forward crew were found on the beach or wallowing in the
shallows—first mate Louis Darwin and wheelsman Otto Willett.

Strangely, although he was known to be carrying about
fifteen hundred dollars on his person, Captain McDonald,
with the exception of the one dollar bill found near him,
was penniless when found, about in the same financial straits
as when he left the stricken brig *Hilding* there on that wild
morning off Donegal Head. Captains were normally well
supplied with money, for it was an era in which most vessel
masters conducted their owners' business in cash. They paid
off crews, hired tugs, took on supplies and handled the man-
ifold vessel expenses on a cash basis. It was possible that the
captain had hidden his money aboard the *Sevona*, but it
would have been an act foreign to his nature and highly un-
likely.

Incidents of the next couple of weeks seemed to indicate
that others had found Captain McDonald before the fisherman had happened upon the body. In Bayfield several individuals, normally without funds, were noted to be sud-

denly prosperous, treating friends, feeling no pain and paying for their purchases and entertainment with bills that appeared to be watersoaked and somewhat mutilated. One of them, Ambrose Gordon, an Indian, was subsequently arrested and brought before municipal judge A. M. Warden by Bayfield County Sheriff H. J. Conlin. The case of the State of Wisconsin vs. Ambrose Gordon was set for trial on November 8. On the day in question sheriff Conlin produced the prisoner, but the prosecutor for the state failed to put in an appearance. After hearing the plea of defense attorney E. C. Alvord and the testimony of the accused, Judge Warden waited another hour before dismissing the case for lack of evidence. The defendant, too full of emotion to utter a word, was led from the courtroom by attorney Alvord, a free man.

The loss of the *Sevona* brought about the usual cries of protest and demands for changes that would prevent similar disasters. Vessel masters seized upon the incident to renew earlier requests that gas buoys be stationed at the Sand Island, York Island and Bear Island shoals, all of them unmarked at the time. Lightkeeper Emanuel Luick of Sand Island, who had witnessed the wreck and heard the distress signals, pointed out that had he been equipped with telephone communication to Bayfield he could have summoned a rescue tug in time to save everybody. He claimed further to have seen Captain McDonald and his men leave their shelter on the battered bow of the *Sevona* late on Saturday on some sort of improvised raft, only to have it break up in the surf while still some distance from the island. He was positive, too, that he could have saved them had the station been equipped with a larger boat and if he had another man to help launch it. And there were loud cries for regulations that would provide lifesaving equipment at both ends of the long lake steamers.

And while the sturdy wooden hatch covers did not bring the captain and his men safely to shore, they were put to good use by shoreside residents and homesteaders. There still stands, on Sand Island, a summer cottage whose sides are made from the hatch covers, marked from "A" to "J."

They brought Captain Donald Sutherland McDonald [1] home to North East, where the whole community turned out to pay their respects. Flags were at half mast and many businesses closed for the afternoon. The warm September breezes brought the tantalizing odor of the vineyards and ripe grapes. Out on the Buffalo Road where hundreds had gathered at "Snug Harbor" to say their good-bys, the first fragrant wagonloads of the harvest were clip-clopping into town.

Captain McDonald had at last come home for the harvest!

[1] At the urging of Captain McDonald, when he started to school, young Bruce began to use the original spelling of the family name, MacDonald. Two generations earlier his grandfather, James MacDonald, had changed the spelling after a bitter quarrel with a brother. Subsequently, some in the family have reverted to the original spelling. Others had never changed it. Robert J. MacDonald, of Erie, Pennsylvania, a grandson of the gallant captain and a capable Great Lakes historian in his own right, has faithfully chronicled the history of the MacDonald family, particularly the life and times of Captain Donald Sutherland McDonald.

6

Justice Evermore and the Gentle Man in Cell 24

Born to riches, destined for evil and cursed by the avenging ghosts of thousands, it is somehow eminently fitting that the ancient and grounded convict ship *Success,* the oldest vessel then in existence, perished violently on fresh water. There is an ironic sort of justice, too, in the fact that she went to her doom within cannon sound of Rattlesnake Island, off whose rock-bound Lake Erie shores a young nation wrested control of the Great Lakes from an empire that spawned and nurtuerd her as an infamous and diabolical link in the most contemptible penal system known to man.

Her story, and it is not a pretty one, begins in 1790 on the banks of the Salween River at Moulmein, Burma, a romantic setting if one forgets the heat, noise, labor and stench of the shipyard and recalls only the penned magic of the immortal Rudyard Kipling and his hauntingly beautiful "Mandalay":

By the old Moulmein Pagoda, looking lazy at the sea,
There's a Burma girl a-settin', and I know she thinks o' me;
For the wind is in the palm tree, and the temple bells they say:
"Come you back, you British soldier; come you back to Man-
*   dalay!"*

Her building was no more eventful or spectacular than any other merchantman constructed for British owners from plans approved on London's Fenchurch Street. Her main timbers, some of them two feet thick, were of Burmese teak —logs hauled from the jungle by elephants and squared at the yard. Less impressive in size but of the same material, her planking was steamed, bent and spiked to sturdy ribs by sweating shipwrights. Just over 135 feet in length and with a beam of thirty feet, she was duly registered at 1100 tons. Permanent ballast was Indian marble, tons of it. And because she would undoubtedly encounter occasional pirate craft, her bulwarks sprouted several brass cannons to discourage the brigands. While her fo'c'sle accommodations for the crew were typical of the day—stark, dark and decidedly uncomfortable—the aft quarters for her officers and passengers provided a considerable degree of comfort and luxury. Rich paneling, soft rugs, gilded scrollwork and exquisite carvings were the lot of the princes of the East who cast their fate with her for a voyage. Because the captain of a merchantman was himself literally a merchant, entrusted to bargain for the acquisition and disposal of cargo, always with his owner's interests in mind, wealthy traders, planters, potentates, nabobs and local trade magnates were royally entertained aboard.

For twelve years the barkentine *Success* enjoyed the prosperity her name implies, sailing thousands of miles, calling at the world's most exotic and romantic ports, returning periodically to London's West India Docks with rewarding cargoes of aromatic spices, ivory, priceless silks, jewels, rare woods, rum, wine and savory teas, the most profitable commodities carried on the seven seas. At sea, when suspicious craft hauled within hailing distance, the sun, reflecting off her brass cannons, kept brightly polished for just such occasions, gave them pause. The *Success* sailed safely on her course.

The stroke of fate that took the *Success* out of the merchant trade routes and their rich cargoes was due not to any short-comings of her own, but rather to the sordid affairs of man-kind ashore. These were years of crises in England, the predictable penalty of years of oppression and a monstrous penal system largely administered by dishonest political favorites for their own profit. Under a succession of rulers the laws had been so outrageously twisted that justice was a mockery. While London itself was beset with the vilest crim-inals and permitted unspeakable cruelty to children of the slums, a man could be sentenced to a lifetime in the dungeons or to hang for stealing a tupenny pie or a loaf of bread. There were one hundred and forty-five offenses, many of them petty, for which the decreed penalty was death. Little won-der, then, that by 1800 the nation's jails and prisons, from the modest county detention structures to the largest jails—infamous Wormwood Scrubs, festering Newgate Prison, the brawling and loathsome Fleet Prison and even dank and re-mote Dartmoor—were literally at the explosion point. In most there was no segregation by sex, age or crime. Debtors, thieves, murderers, perverts and idiots were jammed like sardines into squalid, unheated quarters abounding with vermin and totally devoid of sanitary facilities. Of Newgate a London *Chronicle* reporter once said, "Of all the seats of woe on this side of hell, few, I suppose, exceed or equal Newgate."

Although Captain Cook had landed and claimed the new continent of Australia for Britain in 1770, it was, according to all reports, "extremely unpromising." Nevertheless, when transportation of convicts to the American colonies ended of necessity, harassed British officials looked with new-found favor on the untamed wilderness Captain Cook had named

New South Wales. On Sunday, May 13, 1787, when George Washington was entering Philadelphia to preside at the Constitutional Convention, Captain Arthur Phillip was sailing out of Portsmouth, England, with the first shipload of unfortunate deportees. For the most part they were not desperate characters, but political prisoners, petty lawbreakers, debtors, vagabonds and scalawags. Once confinement barracks were built and penal compounds established, the more hardened criminals were herded aboard other vessels for the eight-month voyage. With them came hundreds of thieves, cutthroats, swindlers, footpads, prostitutes and the usual dreary legions of debtors. The deportation program, after a modest beginning, soon swelled to significant proportions.

To transport the growing numbers of undesirables, Britain established what was to become known the world over as the "felon fleet," an armada of ships converted into floating jails—hell ships into which hundreds of wretched souls were jammed in complete disregard of every humane consideration. Some in chains, some without, all herded like animals into the dark and airless lower decks, they spent weary months at sea, each day like an eternity. Deaths were frequent, disease ever-present and food unbelievably foul. Barbaric punishment was meted out to the malcontents and rebellious.

Into this evil trade, in 1802, came the *Success*. Chartered by the British government, she was altered extensively to accommodate a maximum of hard cases, the elite murderers who had somehow escaped with their heads, but whose deeds had made criminal history. Two decks of cells were constructed, tiny cubicles with but a small barred opening on the door to admit air and whatever light the guard's candle might admit. Inside the cells chains limited movement of the victims to a foot or two. Truly incorrigibles were put in "solitary," even smaller cells with no openings whatsoever.

Topside, and only madmen could have concocted them, were a variety of torture devices used all too frequently for real or imagined acts of insubordination or breaches of discipline. One heinous fixture was a cage in which a convict could be tightly chained. Known as the "tiger's jaw," it was so designed that a horizontal saw, fastened to the bars at either end, rested just beneath the prisoner's chin. With the motion of the ship with each sea, the "jaw" would rise to "bite" him. Here, too, was the dreaded iron maiden, the flogging rack where felons were tied and flogged with leaded cat-o'-nine tails, after which they were led to the "coffin bath" forward, their wounds bathed in salt water. Nearby was the ghastly "crouch iron," a restraining device in which the victim was looped into a question mark configuration, there to remain, sometimes for days at a time. After a session in the crouch iron many prisoners committed suicide by leaping overboard. Between malnutrition, disease and the tools of torture, little wonder that the arrival roster of the *Success* varied considerably with that of embarkation.

For forty-nine years the *Success* plied her hellish trade between England and Australia, each voyage a nightmare for her human cargo. How many people she carried is not recorded, but it must have been thousands.

But Australia, newest crown jewel of Britain's colonies, was having troubles of her own. In addition to the involuntary guests shipped to the penal colonies, free settlers had been migrating there by the thousands, their ranks swelled year by year by prisoners who had served out their sentences to begin life again as free men and women.

When immense gold deposits were discovered near Ballarat, in the Victoria territory in 1851, new troubles came to plague the country and its officials. Now it was invaded by a vast army of gold seekers from all over the world. Many were honest engineers, prospectors, laborers and adventurers, but others were brigands, murderers, thieves, con artists and plain opportunists. Their numbers included many far more dangerous and undesirable than the thousands shipped in on the felon fleet. With the astronomical population increase (300 percent in ten years) came a predictable boom in crime. Now, ironically plagued with their own problems of overcrowded jails, the Australian authorities ordered the *Success* to anchor in Sydney harbor to take aboard the prison overflow. Because she was so ideally equipped to handle them, she got, for the most part, only the vicious, case-hardened lifers and long-term prisoners. Anchored in various harbors, other vessels of the felon fleet were similarly employed as floating prisons.

Despite their effectiveness as temporary penal institutions, a swelling tide of public indignation was slowly bringing the days of the felon fleet to an end. A goodly percentage of the young nation's growing population was comprised of men and women who had come as involuntary guests of the British aboard the dreaded hell ships. Many had served out their sentences and were now solid citizens and had raised children who were making substantial contributions to the national development. The very presence of the hell ships was a constant reminder of evil days and the barbarous British penal system. As new confinement institutions were completed ashore, the hulks were gradually emptied of their notorious guests. From 1860 to 1869 the *Success* was utilized as a prison for women and later as a reformatory vessel. Still, the Australians continued to denounce the very existence of these living symbols of a past they would like very much to forget. Mounting pressure finally brought an order from England that all prison hulks were to be sold or broken up. But the very complexity of ship registry procedures permitted a clerical error that did not specify the *Success* by name, and she remained afloat in Sydney Harbor, still a nagging reminder. Eerie tales abounded along the waterfront —tales of ghostly figures that clambered about in her rigging during the night, of moans that originated in her lower cells and cries of pain from the iron maiden and flogging rack. Several times her night watchman, who saw no ghostly figures nor heard any moans or cries, was forced to drive off boarding parties of angry citizens intent on burning the ship.

The registry oversight was not corrected until 1885. Then under a cloudless blue sky, while thousands cheered from ashore and hundreds of small craft rendezvoused at the scene, the *Success* was scuttled in seventy-two feet of water. It was, the witnesses thought, the end of an era, or at least the last painful reminder of an era of which humanity could not be proud.

Strangely, five years after she slipped placidly below the surface of the sea, by virtue of a long and expensive salvage operation the *Success* was brought up from her watery grave. It was the work of visionary promoters who saw her as a money-making curiosity, a floating exhibit of horrors—horrors once inflicted by mortal man upon his fellow creatures. They knew, too, that another generation with no personal recollections or memories of the felon fleet, would flock to see one of the real and authentic hellships that brought their antecedents to Australia.

Refitted, rerigged, painted and exactly one hundred years old, the *Success* was still a solid and staunch vessel. Her new owners, entrepreneurs of the morbid, pursued every aspect of her shameful past in re-creating the agony and futility of life aboard a ship of the felon fleet. The bolted cells were occupied by realistic wax dummies of former occupants, all of them with expressions of utter hopelessness and despair. Some had made criminal history by the very nature of their crimes, the ghastly details made available on small plaques on the cell doors.

Others had been jailed for trivial offenses, but became so embittered by the injustices and barbaric treatment that they, too, became savage, dangerous men.

In Cell 26 was Daniel Morgan, called the arch-fiend of Australia. Placing absolutely no value on human life, he was personally responsible for ninety-two murders, many of them involving barbaric tortures. In Cell 25 was "Captain Starlight," a mysterious fellow said to be of noble birth. He had led a pack of bushrangers who specialized in stealing cattle and race horses. A bold and audacious fellow, his exploits read like an improbable romance. In Cell 23 was George Lovelace, one of the "Six Men of Dorset," whose only crime was the effort to secure a better way of life for his kind. A farm laborer who, by virtue of the pittance lavished upon him by a landowner, was forced to exist on barley meal and turnips, Lovelace sought to organize fellow laborers in a demand for more money. A proclamation was issued threatening seven years in the penal colonies for any man daring to join a trade society. Lovelace and his group, which included his brother James, Thomas Stanfield, James Hammett, James Brine and a man named Clarke, gathered to consider their position. This was judged a "conspiracy" and all six were arrested and sentenced to the chain gangs in Australia, the first martyrs in the trade union movement.

Cell 47 held William Brown who, at sixteen years of age, was sentenced to ten years for what would now be considered a trivial wrongdoing. Frank Gardiner lived in No. 52. A bushranger, he had received a thirty-two-year sentence for a highway robbery and complicity in the great Lachlan gold escort caper of 1862 in which 2400 ounces of gold were pirated and two guards done in. He was pardoned in 1874 on condition that he leave Australia. This he did, taking up residence in San Francisco. Richard "Lawyer" Bryant was incarcerated in Cell No. 46. He was "transported" for seven years as the result of some minor misdeed that would draw a two-dollar fine today. No. 49 held John Chesley, who began his sentence ashore but had been wounded in an escape attempt. For this he was given an extra term on the *Success*, in thirty-five-pound irons. Henry Garrett, in Cell No. 55, served out his original sentence on the *Success*, but then became a notorious bank robber and burglar. He got another twenty-two-year term. He died at the age of seventy-one, boasting on his death-bed that he had spent fifty-two Christmas days in jail. In Cell No. 45 was Francis Brannigan, a perfect example of how a cruel administration of the law could turn a harmless country lad into a hardened convict. Transported for a minor agrarian offense for which he incurred fourteen years, he escaped and joined forces with outlaws, the group becoming known as Brannigan's Gang. All were caught and sentenced to fifteen years on the *Success*.

Richard Jones had arrived in Australia a free man. A successful gold digger, he was mild-mannered and well-behaved. But one night, while celebrating an unusually rewarding day in the gold pits, he was arrested on a charge of being drunk, disorderly and resisting arrest. For this he was given seven years. Kept in Cell No. 60, he was so embittered that he frequently attacked the warders, resulting in banishment to the "black hole" for months at a time. He was found dead in his cell on July 21, 1856.

Most unusual of the lot was the gentle man who lived in Cell No. 24. Harry Power was born at Waterford, Ireland, and was but still a lad when he was arrested for poaching and injuring the squire's gamekeeper in the struggle that followed when he was nabbed. Sentenced to the penal colonies for a considerable period, he escaped from the chain gang one day and thereafter devoted his time to bushranging and highway robbery. Caught again, he was given fourteen years on the *Success*, seven of them in solitary confinement. During his escapades as a road agent he had developed quite a reputation for his quiet, kindly manners and courtesy to the ladies who chanced to be among his robbery victims. Strangely, Harry Power came out of his solitary confinement cell the same quiet and mannerly man he was when the cell door slammed shut on him seven years earlier. Thereafter, while in Cell No. 24 he remained unchanged despite the living hell that was still his lot. Though the men quartered near him turned into vile, animal-like creatures from bestial treatment and maggoty food, Harry Power remained his old imperturbable self—soft-spoken, mannerly and obedient to orders. His hair was white when his day of deliverance finally came.

Topside, the promoters had resurrected the dreaded tiger's jaw, the iron maiden, the flogging rack, the crouch iron and the coffin bath. It was a dreadful display and only the physical evidence of the torture devices gave proof that such things did, until recent years, actually exist. In gauging public reaction to their horror ship, the shrewd salvagers had judged well. Hundreds of thousands flocked aboard as the *Success* toured all the major Australian port cities—Sydney, Melbourne, Brisbane, Adelaide and Freemantle. When possible, she tied up to public docks, but when the available water could not accommodate her considerable draft, she anchored out in the harbor where fleets of launches were hired to ferry the visitors to and from the boarding ramp.

Despite the morbid drama of the grim deck fixtures and the still, pathetic figures in the cells, perhaps the ship's most valuable asset, for a time at least, was gentle old Harry Power. Quite aged now, but with his shock of snow-white hair adrift in the breeze, the impoverished Irishman came aboard one day shortly after the *Success* had been refitted and when she was moored in Melbourne harbor, drawn by some strange, incomprehensible force, perhaps to see if the wax figure in Cell No. 24 really looked like him. Stranger yet, when he was offered a job as guide, and few could be more knowledgeable, he accepted. For months he led wide-eyed visitors through the dank lower deck companionways flanked by rows of cells and their life-like occupants. Significantly, although the owners of the ship had quickly publicized his past and unique personal knowledge of the ship and her tools of torture, Harry, while amiable and talkative enough on deck, became somewhat subdued, even morose on the tours of the confinement galleries, hurrying his awed guests past Cell No. 24 with never more than a furtive glance.

The flood of memories evoked by daily exposure to the appalling cell decks and the grisly artifacts topside must have been too much for Harry Power. One day he finally ended them by jumping overboard.

But even in death Harry Power could not be separated from the dreadful ship that had been his home for fourteen years. Owners of the *Success,* seizing his parting as a promotional gimmick, quickly pointed out in their subsequent literature that so diabolical had been the ship that a man, long free, had been driven insane merely by the sight of her ghastly relics. The sad story of Harry Power was henceforth one of the morbid but thoroughly believable legends of the *Success.*

Australia was just the beginning of a new life for the *Success* as a vessel for exhibition. After three years, her owners, deciding that her drawing power was diminishing, hired a group of skilled officers and capable seamen and cleared her for London. Under a good press of canvas she stood out of Bass Strait on a voyage that took 165 days. It had been over a century since the *Success,* as a merchant ship, had thrust her figurehead through the fog on the Thames to bring rich cargoes to her counting-house owners. Now all she carried was the damning evidence of the warped justice once practiced by past generations of Britons. And it was just this malevolent system that her present owners counted upon to bring thousands of the morbidly curious aboard—people who would pay good money to see to what lengths their antecedents had gone to suppress crime, dispose of political enemies and punish thousands whose only wrongdoing was that they were in debt.

The *Success* proved to be an amazing drawing card. In London, over a period of several years, hundreds of thousands found their way to her dock, tramped her deck and toured the cell tiers. Included, in special visitations, were several members of the royal family, including King Edward, the Prince of Wales and the Princess and Prince Henry of Battenberg. Doubtless they left her with a new dimension of outrage in assessing the deeds of their predecessors.

Twice, when attendance lagged, the *Success* made extended trips around the British Isles—Southampton, Plymouth, Liverpool, Glasgow, Belfast and Dublin. In each port she found new and enthusiastic crowds. They queued up to gaze wide-eyed at the torture implements, muttered sympathetically at the story of Harry Power, and took in every detail of the hellship responsible for much of the colonization of Australia, now the brightest jewel in the Empire's tiara of commonwealth nations.

But all profitable things come to an end, and after her second tour of the islands the *Success* was moored at an out-of-the-way Liverpool dock, her boarding ramp down, but rarely used. A single watchman lived aboard to keep away unwelcome visitors and to check her bilges daily.

Her earning potential now extremely limited, the old hellship might have stayed in Liverpool indefinitely but for the vision of an American, Captain D. H. Smith. Convinced that the *Success,* properly exploited, would be as interesting to Americans as it had been to Britishers and Australians, he purchased her "as is and where is." But his project involved sailing her across the Atlantic, no mean feat when one considers that she was the oldest ship then afloat, had spent five years on the bottom and had received only superficial attention for the past seventy-five years. Certain involved and expensive tasks loomed before Captain Smith could hope to get a crew. The vessel required rerigging, all new cordage and considerable caulking before she could hope to weather the Atlantic's big graybeards. Finding room for a crew was still another matter. Her once comfortable officers' quarters had been largely gutted to make room for her grisly displays. Any arrangments for the crew would necessarily be temporary in nature. It was also the age of steam and there were not many qualified men of sail looking for berths. Those that were physically capable of making such a voyage also had superstitions that precluded sailing on a ship of such age and with such an infamous reputation. Some marine men stated flatly that an Atlantic voyage in a vessel as old as the *Success* was little more than folly. Somehow, though, Captain Smith rounded up a somewhat reluctant and grumbling crew, took on provisions and cleared his ship with the proper authorities.

She left Liverpool's Glasson dock on the morning tide of April 10, 1912, without even the friendly hoot of a tug to bid her Godspeed. Ironically, to the south of England, at Southampton, accompanied by the greatest fanfare ever accorded a vessel on her maiden voyage, the super-queen of the Atlantic, the *Titanic,* was making her departure on what many assumed was to be a record run. Aboard the *Success* were some good men and also some of the scum of Liverpool's waterfront. But the *Titanic* boasted a picked crew and a blue-ribbon passenger list that included some of the greatest names in finance, politics, literature, music and high society on both sides of the ocean. They were sailing on the most luxurious passenger vessel ever created by men, a vessel so constructed that her owners declared her "unsinkable."

Though he failed to note that the oldest ship in the world, and also the newest, made simultaneous departures from England, a ship news reporter for a London paper, compiling the passages from the major ports, was struck by the disparity in ages, noting in print: ". . . just like a wedding today—something old, something new."

Four days later, in one of the great disasters of all time, the *Titanic,* pride of the White Star Line, was on the bottom, ripped open by an iceberg. Lost with her were 1517 souls.

The *Success,* meanwhile, plugged along as best she could, meeting truly ghastly weather but making the best of it. Unfavorable winds drove her far from the projected course and mountainous seas boarded her rudely and with great frequency. The days—cold, gray and boisterous—dragged on. Food supplies ran low and fresh water was rationed. The seamen recruited at Liverpool were an old and superstitious lot. Some claimed the ship was haunted and refused to sleep belowdecks. They told of weird noises and groans at night down in the cell galleries and of strange apparitions in the form of arms protruding from the barred openings in the cell doors, as of mortals sore beset with despair, beseeching release from their eternity of loneliness. The men who had been patrolling the lower deck corridors for signs of leaks now refused to continue this loathsome duty.

The mate, believing that the seamen had spent too much time reading the advertising literature left over from the exhibition tours, particularly the story of Harry Power, proved the point to himself.

"And," he questioned the watchmen, "just where do the noises and waving arms seem to be coming from?"

"Ah, sir," quaked one, "from Cell No. 24, sir, from Cell 24, to be sure."

Ninety-six days after departing Liverpool, the bedraggled *Success,* her canvas torn and her hull salt-streaked, sailed slowly, almost apologetically, into Boston harbor. It had truly been an epic voyage.

The Boston *Globe,* duly impressed, paid tribute to her in the issue of July 19, 1912:

The *Success* has created a record in Atlantic voyaging. No other ship of anything approaching her great age could even have attempted the task. It certainly speaks for the builders of wooden walls of olden days. It is undoubtedly the most noteworthy feat of seamanship since Christopher Columbus sailed his gallant little fleet to fame in 1492.

Like his Australian counterparts, the new owner of the *Success* had judged public interest shrewdly. The horrors of the felon fleet had been a part of history now for over a century, but to free Americans the hardships, barbaric cruelty and oppressive punishment practices were so remote and unbelievable as to become myths. The *Success,* with her exhibits of torture devices, wax dummies and dungeonlike cells, dispelled those myths. She was, to make wry use of her own name, an instant success. Bostonians thronged aboard in great numbers, and in the following two years she proved equally popular in New York, Philadelphia and other eastern seaboard ports.

After what must have been another incredible journey, the old ship turned up in San Francisco in 1915 as one of the star attractions of the Panama-Pacific International Exposition. Over nineteen million people were logged through the exposition's gates, and it is a fair asumption that many trod the aged teak decks, peered with horror into her dark cells and left with a new perspective of mankind.

It was here, too, that Frank Gardiner, formerly of Cell No. 52 and drummed out of Australia, was earning his living as a hotel host. His back to the bar and arms waving, he regaled visitors with the legends of the past, reliving every holdup, battle and peccadillo for their edification. While Gardiner himself, an old man now, shunned the *Success* as he would the embrace of a boa constrictor, many of his friends peered in at the wax figure in Cell No. 52 and reported back that "It's the spittin' image of you, Frank."

After the exposition closed, the *Success* retraced her watery tracks on a protracted series of stops that included the Gulf of Mexico ports and a leisurely fresh-water tour to cities along the Mississippi, Missouri and Ohio Rivers. Here, too, incredulous visitors trooped aboard in numbers pleasing to her owners.

Long stays in many ports having again diminished her earning potential somewhat, the old brigantine languished again in Boston until 1923, when her owners, envisioning a couple of profitable years on the Great Lakes, contracted for a long overdue overhaul. Here, for the first time in one hundred years, the *Success*, seven years older than the U.S.S. *Constitution*, had her hull scraped and painted. Thus, like a maiden aunt, much refreshed and rejuvenated after a lengthy session in a beauty salon, she appeared in the Gulf of St. Lawrence in 1924, bound for the Lachine Canal, then the gateway to the fresh water of the Great Lakes.

The *Success*, as an exhibition, had proven to be a lucky vessel moneywise—far luckier than she had been for the poor wretches she carried in the convict trade or those she housed in the years she served as a floating penitentiary. And her luck held on the Great Lakes. Unable to move on her own power now, since she carried no crew knowledgeable in sail, she was towed from port to port, in each of which she attracted paying crowds. Highlight of her long stay on the inland seas was at Cleveland. There, after considerable periods of inactivity, she was once again a feature attraction at an exposition, the Great Lakes Exposition of 1936. Moored at the East Ninth Street Pier with her rigging festooned with lights, she belied her age when viewed from afar. But close-up it was a different story. Time was running out, for she was barely earning her keep. More miles, more ports and finally in 1939 she came back to Cleveland. Once again the big bright signs "See the Convict Ship" drew modest patronage, but the end was in sight.

Taken to Sandusky, Ohio, in 1942 when her Cleveland dock was needed for other vessels, the tired old *Success* lay idle while her neglected hull, badly in need of caulking, slowly, almost imperceptibly, began to fill. Finally there came a day when she just gave up and went down. She couldn't go far, for she had only a foot or two of water beneath her keel, but she listed to port, snapping her mooring lines. Altogether she presented a hopeless picture.

Salvation, temporarily at least, came in 1943 in the form of an imaginative salvager and marine contractor from nearby Port Clinton, Ohio. Walter Kolbe had visions of a complete refitting and a permanent mooring for her at Port Clinton, in the center of the famed Lake Erie Islands area, one of the most popular tourist meccas in the midwest. After acquiring title to the *Success*, he pumped her out, made temporary repairs and began the tow to her final port of call, Port Clinton.

The *Success* dutifully followed her tug through the South Passage and swung to port after rounding Mouse Island Reef. Doubtless none aboard the brigantine or tug gave it thought, but the voyage was over hallowed waters. It was here, slightly to the north, that the British fleet of Commodore Barclay fell victim to the savage fire from the hastily built, modest armada of Commodore Oliver Hazard Perry, thus ending forever the British Empire's control of the Great Lakes. From here, too, Perry dispatched by schooner to his superiors ashore the memorable, but laconic message: "We have met the enemy and they are ours; two ships, two brigs, one schooner and one sloop." The year was 1813 and the *Success* had already been in her infamous trade for eleven years.

Walter Kolbe either misjudged the deep draft of the ship or the modest depth of the Port Clinton channel and harbor. A half mile from what was to be her final home and rest, the *Success* "took the ground" on a sandbar, heeling to port and settling herself comfortably. Dismayed but not discouraged, Kolbe figured that a season on the sandbar would do her no harm. Meanwhile he would set about digging a channel into what he hoped would be her mooring forevermore.

But Lake Erie ruled otherwise. The savage seas of several autumn gales did what the hurricanes of the tropical seas and the romping gray monsters of the Atlantic had failed to accomplish. They finished her. As if they were determined to wash away the stench and stigma of nearly a century and a half, the relentless combers that pounded in from the northwest smashed in her starboard ribs and planking, laying the entire hull open to the seas. Down below the heavy cell doors swung to and fro with each surge of fresh water, the ironwork groaning and complaining with the strain. The onslaught of winter brought roving fields of ice to hammer her anew. And later on, when ice was solid across the bay, vandals crossed over it and pillaged the ship of many relics, stole her steering wheel and cut the top from her impressive figurehead. Spring found the *Success* shorn of her valuables, a useless hulk. Kolbe, however, still hoped to recover some of his investment by selling the teak timbers, said to be as good as the day they felt the shipbuilder's adz, and by disposing of the heavy cell doors for conversion into coffee tables or decorator's pieces. Down below, too, were tons of Indian marble, the ship's original ballast. Meanwhile, Lake Erie continued the methodical process of demolition, each storm tearing rents in the hull and twisting her cruelly.

The final blow came on July 4, 1946. Considering the date, perhaps it was a prophetic and appropriate one. World War II was over, and the island area was experiencing its first postwar tourist season. All the cottages, motels and hotels were filled, the summer-only business booming and traffic along the highways was bumper to bumper. Lake Erie and Port Clinton's harbor were bustling with small craft. At about ten o'clock that night flames were sighted a half mile offshore. Many thought a small craft had exploded, but the conflagration grew to such proportions that there could only be one answer. Once again vandals had visited the *Success,* and this time she was finished. Her upperworks, thoroughly dried by the summer's sun, burned furiously while along the beaches and highways thousands gathered to watch the spectacle. The ship's foremast, the only one remaining and now a pillar of flame, crashed down over the port bulwarks, sending a towering geyser of sparks and embers high in the air. Big timbers, steam-bent to the hull shape, twisted as the iron stays and bolts grew white-hot. Her poop deck and fo'c'sle collapsed and what was left of her figurehead flared brightly, like a torch seeking to light the way to freedom from this damnable fate.

Dozens of small craft clustered around the flaming hull, like insects drawn to light. Over the cries and shouts of their occupants could be heard the many hellish noises of a ship going to her final reward. Heated bolts and ironwork parted in an agony of sound while the crackle and roar of the inferno finally overpowered the puny mortal shouts from the pleasure boats witnessing the funeral pyre. Doubtless those phantom figures dancing a macabre saltarello on the fringes between the red halo and the gloom of night, the shrieking ghosts of a thousand convicts, went unseen and unheard. One wonders if white-haired Harry Power, the man in Cell No. 24, was among them!

But what of the tortured soul of the old *Success,* writhing in the agony of flames? Every ship has a soul, as every sailor knows, although it is often abused by thoughtless or evil owners. Would she, too, in the horror of falling embers and billowing flames, while the ghosts danced about her, turn her thoughts back there, somewhere east of Suez . . . ?

For the temple-bells are callin', and it's there that I would be—
By the old Moulmein Pagoda, looking lazy at the sea; . . .

7

A Question of Lights, Birthdays— and a Farm

Probably because the dockside din would have thwarted his great desire for rest and made sleep improbable if not impossible, the Hon. Herbert Ingram, member of Parliament and proprietor of the *Illustrated London News,* leaned resignedly on the hurricane deck rail of the steamer *Lady Elgin* and surveyed the pandemonium that reigned below. It was ten o'clock on the night of Friday, September 7, 1860, and the *Lady Elgin* was scheduled to depart her Chicago River dock at eleven o'clock for her regular passenger, mail and freight run to Mackinac, the Soo and Lake Superior ports. All afternoon noisy drays had rendezvoused at the steamer's side, raucous teamsters voicing their commands, the horses whinnying their discontent. Now, with evening waning, stevedores were still trundling crates and barrels through the gangways, accompanied by the thumping, shouting, cursing and commotion that inevitably attends such strenuous rituals. Adding to the confusion was the bawling of some sixty head of cows being prodded, one at a time, through still another gangway. Destined for a lifetime of browsing in some newly cleared upper Wisconsin pastures, they had been quiet enough in their temporary stalls during the day but now, doubtless annoyed at being rudely aroused at such an unseemly hour to be marched over cobblestones to even more questionable quarters aboard the ship, they became exceedingly vocal in their displeasure, mooing querulously and frequently. Beyond this discordant blending of barnyard and steamboat, overpowering the dockside hubbub as the evening wore on and their number grew, was a veritable flood tide of humanity—everybody laughing, shouting and singing as departure time neared. Impromptu paraders tramped the cabin deck voicing strange slogans. Bands on the dock and on the ship materialized as if from thin air, each playing on the premise that volume alone denoted musical superiority. Torchlights flared along the quay, songs of the day were seemingly taken up by hundreds of willing voices. Altogether the clamor was rather unnerving. It was a macabre scene such as might inspire a sensitive English gentleman to conjure up images of witches, vampires and demons. It was as though the whole teeming mob of revelers had been mesmerized and held in a permanent state of hilarity by the inhalation of vapors from some sorceress's magic brew. Ingram, who noted that many wore uniforms he could not identify, wished most fervently that he, too, could be endowed with the blissful sleep of youth now being enjoyed by his sixteen-year-old son Herbert, Jr., in their cabin berth, unmindful of the tumult without. His fears that the entire trip would be endured under pain of such deplorable bedlam were alleviated by the remark of a sailor who volunteered the information that the roisterers would debark at Milwaukee in a few hours and that peace would once again reign. This news had delighted the Hon. Herbert Ingram, member of Parliament.

Still another publisher witnessed the strident celebrating from the boat rail but without registering the bewilderment

of Mr. Ingram. He was Col. Francis A. Lumsden, co-owner
of the New Orleans *Picayune* (now the *Times-Picayune*),
bound on a leisurely vacation journey to Mackinac with his
wife, son and daughter. Similar dockside festivities were
rather common place in New Orleans. Colonel Lumsden had
not only witnessed many, but had probably participated in
a few. After watching for a brief time, he joined his wife
and children in their roomy family cabin. The Lumsdens,
the Ingrams and about fifty others were regular cabin passengers, with quarters assigned them. The noisy revelers took
over the remaining cabins, parlors, saloons and deck areas
for dancing, band playing and singing. It was a frightful
hullabaloo that made a mockery of the steamship line's advertised assurances of peace and repose while enjoying the
soothing breezes of the great inland seas.

A late addition to the cabin passenger roster was twenty-
three-year-old Cyrus H. Walrath, a bookkeeper for the Marine
Bank of Milwaukee, returning from a very pleasant vacation
at his home town of Evans Mills, New York. He had originally been booked for passage in the propeller *Sun,* but some
difficulty had arisen and he had transferred to the *Lady
Elgin*. He was due back at work on Monday morning. Despite
the fact that his uncle, Jacob Hoover, was president of the
institution and likely to deal leniently with errant and overdue bookkeepers, he meant to be on the job at the prescribed
hour. A fellow passenger noted that young Walrath was of
slight stature, had a delicate figure and wore a natty gray
suit. Considering the distance from Evans Mills and the
vagaries of travel, Mr. Walrath, despite the commotion
aboard the *Lady Elgin*, considered himself most fortunate.

Perhaps the wealthiest person aboard the *Lady Elgin*, in
terms of ready cash, was Mr. Lacy, the ship's barkeeper. Since
the ship had picked up the high-spirited Milwaukee excursionists late Thursday night, business had been exceedingly

good, probably because a vast majority of them were Irish, uninhibited and determined to have a good time whatever the cost. As the *Lady Elgin* gave off a series of warning blasts and finally a protracted departure whistle, Mr. Lacy was known to have several thousand dollars in bills stuffed in assorted coat pockets and a money belt, heavy with gold, secreted somewhere in his trunk, chained and locked to his cabin berth. Still the merrymakers continued to rally forces at his place of business, as if each was determined to arrive home in Milwaukee stone-broke and feeling no pain.

Grand vizier, rajah and mikado of the *Lady Elgin* and her affairs was Captain Jack Wilson, an eminently respected sailor who had spent nearly a quarter of century on fresh water, and many years as master. He had delayed his departure somewhat for two sound and basic reasons. First, he did not like the looks of the weather. Squally weather could be expected, although it was pleasant enough at the time. Secondly, there were far too many people aboard his ship— many more than had boarded her at Milwaukee. He suspected that most of the surplus consisted of rollicking Chicagoans who had no intention of sailing with him, but who had followed their friends aboard and were loath to leave the festivities. When the *Lady Elgin* had departed Milwaukee on Thursday evening, there were between three and four hundred excursionists aboard. A rough estimate on the part of Captain Wilson put the number of added and unwanted starters for the homeward voyage, not counting the scheduled cabin passengers, at between thirty and fifty. Repeated warning whistles had proven ineffective. Even the shouts of crewmen, circulating in the crowd and calling out news of imminent departure, had gone unheard in the din. But there came a time when departure, if Captain Wilson was to maintain any semblance of a schedule and keep his non-excursionist passengers happy, had to become a reality no matter what the weather prognosis or how many dawdling Chicago celebrants remained aboard. Shortly after 11:30 P.M., then, the *Lady Elgin*'s stern hawsers were slipped and those forward slackened off somewhat. When her big side-wheels, churning slow astern, had worked her aft end into midstream, the bow hawsers were cast off and drawn aboard. With maneuvering room now, Captain Wilson grabbed the bell pull and rang "slow ahead." Once out of the river and a quarter mile into Lake Michigan, he rang up "full ahead" and ordered the vessel swung to port, heading her on the Milwaukee course.

The amazing scene of revelry witnessed by the distinguished British publisher had its genesis in what was really the most serious and corrosive issue ever to divide the American people, often pitting father against son, brother against brother. The issues were slavery and state's rights—matters in which many of the Milwaukee excursionists, despite their apparently carefree dispositions, were intimately and personally involved.

Governor of Wisconsin, Alexander Randall, was a radical Republican and fierce abolitionist. Whether they were inspired by Randall or others is not known, but by the spring of 1860 there were persistent rumors that unless the federal government abolished slavery, Wisconsin would secede from the Union. One state assemblyman from Waukesha County, an abolitionist bastion and a busy link in the underground railway, went so far as to introduce a resolution in the Wisconsin legislature, directing the governor to declare war against the United States and to appoint Brigadier General S. W. Smith commander of the state armies. Cooler heads, seeking to appraise the temper of the troops before taking such drastic action, dispatched agents to sound out the very considerable companies of the state militia as to their loyalty should the dread declaration become a reality. Milwaukee had several militia organizations, four of them of real importance numerically: the German Green Jagers, the German Black Jagers, the Milwaukee Light Guard, and Captain Garrett Barry's Irish Union Guards who drew much of their strength from an area reached by the shadow of St. John's Cathedral tower, in the center of the predominantly Irish third ward, sometimes called the "Bloody Third." Captain Barry was eminently qualified to lead his Union Guards. Upon graduation from West Point he had been appointed instructor of infantry tactics, an assignment that brought before him as students some whose names were later to become famous in the great conflict between the states—Generals Sherman, McDowell, Rosecrans, Thomas and Grant. When queried as to his allegiance, federal or state, Barry calmly declared that while he was as much against slavery as any man, he viewed the abolition problem as a national one, not sectional, and that his loyalty must be with the federal government, that any other course would be treason. Shortly thereafter the adjutant general of Wisconsin, J. S. Swain, ordered Captain Barry's commission revoked and the arms and equipment of the Union Guards surrendered to the Milwaukee Light Guard.

Shorn of all but their uniforms and intense pride, but determined to maintain their group as a meaningful unit for the common good, the Union Guards lost no time in formulating plans to finance new equipment. Thus a suggestion that a lake excursion, if heavily subscribed to, would benefit the treasury, met instant approval. The occasion would enable crusading excursionists to visit Chicago at a time when the city was to host a gigantic Democratic parade and rally. It was believed, too, that Stephen Douglas himself would be on hand to orate and to view the marchers. The Union Guards had already established themselves as one of the midwest's foremost military marching units and intended to per-

form in Chicago, with or without arms. The cause of the
Union Guards was sympathetically supported by the other
three large militia units. As a result the 500 tickets for the
gala excursion sold remarkably well. Many members of the
city's various volunteer fire companies seized the occasion
as an opportunity to visit their counterparts in Chicago.
There was a great spirit of camaraderie between men of similar selfless interests traditionally expressed by open-hearted
hospitality. Delegations from the police department also demanded to be included. Each group was accompanied by
family, relatives and friends, young and old. The city band
and the musicians in the military units were among the first
to sign up for the trip.

Rather than charter a ship for the specific occasion, a
course that would have been more expensive, and one that
would negate to a degree the original goal of clearing a handsome profit for the Union Guards, the committee had arranged to board the *Lady Elgin* on Thursday night as she
was downbound from her Lake Superior run, returning on
her upbound trip late Friday night. The *Lady Elgin* was a
commodious wooden side-wheeler built in 1851 at Buffalo
by Bidwell and Banta at a cost of $96,000. Named for the
wife of Lord Elgin, former Governor General of Canada, she
was 252 feet long, almost thirty-five feet of beam and boasted
1037 tons. Built originally for Lake Erie service, she was sold
in 1856 to A. T. Spencer & Company for service between
Chicago and Lake Superior ports. Early in 1860 she had been
purchased by Gordon Hubbard of Chicago but maintained
the same sailing route. Trim and well maintained, she was
referred to in her owner's advertising broadsides as the
"Queen of the Lakes," the result of a laudatory affliction
common to boat owners but often one not consistent with
performance. It is well to note at this point that the certificate
issued to the *Lady Elgin* by the United States inspectors

limited passengers to three hundred—two hundred in her cabins, saloons and public rooms, another one hundred on her decks.

The *Lady Elgin* was scheduled to depart Milwaukee at 7:00 P.M. on Thursday, September 6. She did not arrive at her dock, however, until well after 10:00 P.M. that night. The excursionists who had begun gathering at about 6:00 P.M. were by this time tired and discouraged. Indeed, many had concluded that the steamer had met with some mishap or bad weather and would probably not arrive until the next day. One who wearied of the long wait and finally returned home with her escort was Eliza Curtain, twenty-one, very popular with those of her age group. After waiting for over an hour, Eliza had her young man take her home, explaining to her mother that she felt uneasy about the trip anyway and would give up her excursion plans. Her mother, however, possibly because she was proud of her daughter's popularity, was adamant. Reluctantly, Eliza returned to the dock.

Milwaukee at that time had a population of just under 45,000, and many of the excursionists were known by sight through social, political or civic activities. Among those most frequently recognized and greeted were Captain Barry; school commissioner James Rice; teacher Cornelius O'Mahoney; Francis McCormick of the Milwaukee Common Council; Thomas H. Eviston, chief engineer of the fire department; Samuel Waegli, registrar of deeds; Martin Dooley, harbor-master; John O'Grady, clerk of the mayor's office; John Horan, deputy U.S. Marshal; and Timothy O'Brion, another member of the Common Council. Although all, or nearly all, of the tickets had been sold, the tardiness of the *Lady Elgin* and the discouraged departure of many who had intended to sail on her left the committee in doubt as to the exact, or even the approximate, number of people who finally boarded

the steamer. It was after midnight when the *Lady Elgin* left
Milwaukee, her prolonged departure whistle echoing through-
out the city, reminding nearly every home in the "Bloody
Third" that their loved ones were at last on their way to
Chicago.

Possibly because the dockside wait had been long and
parching, Mr. Lacy's bar did a rushing business all the way
to Chicago, where the excursionists disembarked without
incident on Friday morning. Although few had enjoyed
much sleep, most of them none, the day's program found
them lively and in full spirits. They cheered loudly and ap-
plauded heartily as the Union Guards marched by in the
parade. Speeches, the parade, sightseeing and an early evening banquet followed by dancing preceded the procession
back to the *Lady Elgin*. The arrival at the dock, the singing,
music and exuberant good fellowship created the incredibly
busy scene that had amazed the distinguished Britisher, observing quietly from his post on the hurricane deck. Quite
a number of the Milwaukeeans, exhausted by the rigorous
twenty-four hours, immediately collapsed on saloon sofas,
chairs, benches, quiet corners of the public rooms and on
deck. They were still there, unconscious of the tumult, when
the Hon. Herbert Ingram, thoughtfully picking his way
among the prostrate forms, wended his way to his cabin.

There were many ships, sail and steam, afloat and under
way on Lake Michigan that night of September 7, but only
two, the *Lady Elgin,* loud with revelry, and a lowly lumber
schooner named *Augusta,* going about her work-a-day task,
are pertinent to our tale. Just as relevant are the two men
who commanded them. Captain Jack Wilson of the *Lady
Elgin* was something special. Mature and vastly experienced,
his very bearing exuded confidence and faith. All through
his over twenty-four years of sailing he had possessed a certain charisma that resulted in loyal crews and charmed pas-

sengers. Starting at sixteen as a deck hand on the schooner *Boston* and later the schooners *Excelsior* and *Algonquin,* he had risen through the ranks on the steamers *Montezuma, Lady of the Lake, Monticello, Baltimore, Empire State, Southern Michigan, Illinois* and the *North America,* commanding some of them before succeeding Captain Tomkins as master of the *Lady Elgin.* Three times during his career he had exhibited great and noteworthy bravery—when the *Algonquin* was almost overcome by ice on Lake Superior, when the *North America* caught fire at Conneaut, and when the *Monticello* collided with the propeller *Manhattan,* again on Lake Superior. His deportment, record and reputation were such as to later inspire the Chicago *Daily Press Tribune* to comment editorially: "In all these years there has lived no man who could declare that he ever betrayed a trust, or deserted a friend, or proved faithless to duty. With a great generous heart, a clear head, a strong, warm hand, he was a thorough sailor and 'all in all' a man."

But for all of his achievements, his reputation and his dedication to command, Captain Wilson shared with sailors the world over a wistful, somehow incongruous desire to own a farm. To the sailor a farm seems to symbolize stability, security, a final home port—an end to the storms and endless wandering that have forever been his lot. But unlike most men of the sea, Jack Wilson had done something about his ambition. He had purchased a small farm near Coldwater, Michigan, at the extreme southern end of the state. It was in Branch County, an area favorable to fruit growing. Captain Wilson had fond visions of spending his declining years picking apples and peaches. Meanwhile, as the master of the homestead was absent at his shipboard duties much of the year, Mrs. Wilson and the children, two daughters and a son, kept the home fires burning. Despite his exalted station and the respect he was accorded, Captain Wilson was relatively a poor man. One of his daughters was an invalid, and medical expenses had been heavy. The $1500 mortgage on the farm was a matter that concerned him constantly.

Aboard the *Augusta*, with a full cargo hold and deckload of lumber, Port Huron to Chicago, Captain Darius Nelson Malott threw himself down on his bunk just as the ship's clock struck eight bells, midnight, thus signaling the start of another day, September 8. He did not bother to undress, and it is doubtful if he noted that the clock had just made him another year older. It was now Captain Malott's twenty-seventh birthday. But the captain was, as are most captains, concerned with matters of more moment. The *Augusta* was bowling along at a good rate with all sails set. But he expected a change of wind almost momentarily, for the fresh breeze was running from the northeast, while overhead the scudding clouds were running from the southwest. He got up at 1:00 A.M., took another look at the weather, then went below again.

Darius Nelson Malott, or "Nelse" as he was called back in Essex County, Ontario, had crowded much adventure into his modest years, beginning his sailing career, fresh from the family farm, as a deck hand on the schooner *Ellen Park*. It is perhaps interesting to note that he signed on with her skipper, "Red Dan" McKellar, on September 8, 1851, his eighteenth birthday. In the intervening short years he shipped on the schooner *Conductor* before going salt water on the *Gold Hunter*, Montreal to London, with timber. The *Gold Hunter* was dismasted and held on her beam ends by shifted cargo after encountering a severe gale soon after leaving the Bay of St. Lawrence. The captain and first mate were washed overboard. Their food supply soaked or under water in the lazarette, the men grew desperately hungry as the *Gold Hunter* lay on her side for an incredible forty-five days. Finally, nine members of the ravenous crew seized and bound

nineteen-year-old Malott and another young man named
George Dormer, with the announced intention of eating one
of them. The logic in the selection was based on the fact
that the others were married, while Malott and Dormer were
still single and without family responsibilities. In what must
have been a bizarre scene, the two were forced to draw straws
to determine who was to be devoured. Dormer lost and had
been partly eaten when the wreck was sighted by the mail
steamer *Tagus,* which took off the wretched sailors and released young Malott. In England he shipped out on the big
clipper-rigged *Edward Hyman,* London to the gold fields of
Van Dieman's Land. He continued on the *Edward Hyman*
when that voyage was completed, later touching at Hong
Kong before starting eastward across the Pacific. During this
voyage young Malott was promoted to second mate, just two
days before the ship caught fire. The ship's two small boats,
after provisioning, were lowered and cast off. The captain
took charge of the long boat, leaving Malott to command the
quarter boat and its crew of seven. The captain's boat was
never seen again, but thirty-two days later, Nelse Malott,
now twenty-one years old, brought the quarter boat safely
into the harbor at Callao, Peru. Here he signed on the *Star
of Empire,* which brought him to Liverpool. Shipping before the mast again, this time on the *Madeira Pet,* he arrived
in Canada once more, reaching the family farm home in late
November of 1857. Less than a month later he married Mary
A. Robson, the daughter of an Essex County schoolteacher.

Nelse Malott, probably because he was still so young, had
not yet succumbed to the sailor's vision of a farm as the
mecca of peace and tranquillity forevermore. He had been
born on one, had done chores for most of his early years,
and had no intention of resuming that routine, for the time
being, at least.

In the spring of 1858, casting about for a young and able

captain for their bark *Caroline,* the Detroit-based firm of Bissel & Davidson hired Malott. It turned out to be a wise move, for in 1859, by virtue of his deep-sea experience and obvious qualifications, he took the *Caroline,* with a cargo of copper ingots from Lake Superior, through the St. Lawrence canals and all the way to Liverpool, safely delivering his cargo and arranging for sale of the schooner to Londoners.

It was in late August of 1860 that his owners summoned Captain Malott to their offices. "We've just purchased the schooner *Augusta,*" he was told. "She is presently en route from Oswego, New York, under command of her first mate. Captain Jenkins had left her and you are to take charge when she gets here."

The *Augusta,* five years old, turned out to be a sturdy craft 128 feet long with a tonnage of 332. Bissel & Davidson had managed to keep the *Caroline* and another schooner, the *Sonora,* busy freighting general merchandise and supplies but were anxious to enter the lumber carrying trade, growing every day, thanks to the burgeoning cities along the Great Lakes. Chicago, already over 100,000 in population, was growing rapidly, and builders had an insatiable appetite for the fine white pine of Michigan. For that matter, so did builders in Buffalo, Cleveland, Erie, Toledo, Milwaukee and Detroit. Hauling it from the "sawdust" ports that sprang up along the Michigan shoreline was turning out to be highly profitable.

Along with the schooner, which the owners carefully inspected when it arrived in Detroit, Captain Malott had inherited her crew, including first mate John Vorce and second mate George Budge. After the owners took their leave, the schooner proceeded to a point three miles south of Port Huron to load lumber. The *Augusta* departed the lumber dock at 4:00 A.M. September 1.

Aboard the *Lady Elgin* an hour after departing Chicago,

the gaiety had subsided somewhat. The hardy still danced and the bands still played, but the roll of the ship had caused a minor epidemic of mal de mer—enough to dampen the enthusiasm for fun and games. Now almost every chair or bench held sick or tired excursionists. Many were stretched out on cabin floors. The lessening of activity was a welcome respite to Thomas Cummings, the ship's policeman. He was tired and after a circuit of the cabin deck found a chair in a small unoccupied cabin immediately forward of the port side-wheel. At the bar its proprietor, Mr. Lacy, was having "one on the house" with Charles Jotham, an old friend. Jotham had tended bar at Chicago's Rio Grande Hotel for several years but had not intended to go steamboating that night. However, like many another, he hadn't heard the warning and departure whistles. He had come aboard to see off and enjoy a bon voyage toast with Godfrey Hipelins, a young Milwaukee cigar maker. The three had mutual friends, and the conversation was good. Captain Wilson, pacing the deck outside the tiny pilothouse, paused frequently to ask the wheelsman what course he was steering. Patrick Maher and George Furlong, who earlier, while the *Lady Elgin* was loading her livestock, had made facetious remarks to one of the crew about turning an excursion ship into a cattle boat, had long since given up the battle with fatigue and were stretched out on benches on the aft cabin deck.

The squall struck just as Captain Malott was two hours into his twenty-seventh year. He had been awakened by feet clumping down the companionway and the knock on his door. "Looks squally, sir," called second mate Budge.

The captain threw on his jacket, but was only halfway up the companionway when the wind hit, heeling the *Augusta* over on her portside, practically on her beam ends. With the wind came jagged streaks of lightning and rain so violent that the captain thought at first it was hail. Most of the mainsail had already been dropped and other crewmen were forward, taking down the foresails. First mate John Vorce hit the deck seconds after the captain and heard someone call out that there was a light on the lee bow. Instinctively, mate Vorce looked for the schooner's own light, the only one required. It was a clear white light mounted on the five-foot Samson post forward of the windlass, on the bow. Captain Malott, almost automatically, although he did not hear the warning shout about the light, also noted that his vessel's light was burning as required by the existing regulations. The high deckload of timber, securely lashed down, limited visibility. Mate Vorce climbed to the top of the timbers in time to see the headlight of a big steamer crossing the schooner's bow. Captain Malott, running forward to assist in taking down the foresails, then saw the steamer's port and starboard colored lights.

"Hard up, hard up, for God's sake, man, hard up!" he screamed to wheelsman John Terrett.

Whether wheelsman Terrett obeyed instantly is not known. In any event it probably would not have mattered much. Both mates, although they had not confided in Captain Malott, knew that the *Augusta* was "pretty wild," meaning that she was inordinately slow in answering her helm when heavily loaded. And heavily loaded she was. Hanging on her beam ends when the two vessels approached, there was even less liklihood of her obeying the commands of her rudder.

Second mate Budge had been at work helping take down canvas, although he personally was convinced that they were about to capsize. There had been a foot of water over the lee rail when he started forward, but it was up to his waist by the time he reached midships.

Strangely, although both Captain Malott and first mate Vorce saw the steamer only when she was close enough for her red and green running lights to be seen, Budge had first spotted the *Lady Elgin*'s head or mast light much earlier, approximately ten minutes before he had aroused the captain, and twenty minutes before the steamer and schooner met on a collision course. Stranger still, he had not notified the captain, as was his duty, nor had he made any attempt to lessen the chances of collision by ordering a change of course. In his own testimony later he admitted that at the moment of impact the schooner's course was E by S, the same course she had been steering when he first sighted the white light on the steamer's foremast. By the same token there was probably little that could be done once the squall had struck. "The *Augusta* was unmanageable by then," he stated, "lying over on her portside with heavy water over the rail. I'm sure the helm was put 'hard over,' as the captain had directed, but it made no difference—she steered pretty wild."

Aboard the *Lady Elgin* the second mate, M. W. Beeman, on duty with Captain Wilson from the time of departure, saw the schooner's light off the port bow about fifteen minutes before the collision, but here again no immediate effort was taken to change course, it being assumed that the two craft would pass safely. Between brilliant flashes of lightning the torrential rain, driven with breathtaking force, blotted out everything on the weather side of the steamer.

Thomas Cummings, the *Lady Elgin*'s law-enforcement officer, taking his ease in the snug little retreat just forward of the ship's port side-wheel, was the first to be aware of the collision, and in a most startling fashion. Alternately dozing and puffing on a cigar, he was rudely awakened by the schooner's jib boom plunging through the side of his cabin, missing him by inches and penetrating through the inside bulkhead into the longitudinal passageway. With the next rising sea it charged in still farther, shredding the overhead beams, tearing out more of the bulkhead and wrecking the pantry on the far side of the pasageway. Paralyzed with fear,

Mr. Cummings sat there stunned until, seconds later, the massive jib boom twisted sideways and departed, taking with it almost all of the outside shell of the cabin.

Speared into the *Lady Elgin*'s portside and held there momentarily by the jib, the *Augusta* slewed around and was drawn abreast of the steamer. Side by side they stayed for a moment or two as the sailors aboard both vessels gathered their senses. The steamer continued on her course, dragging the schooner with her. Finally they separated, the schooner with her headgear collapsed and damaged, and, in the opinion of Captain Malott, badly crushed at the bow and in imminent danger of sinking.

Testimony of the crew of the *Augusta* later brought out the unanimous feeling that, moments after the collision, they were convinced that the schooner had received mortal wounds in the encounter, that the *Lady Elgin* had suffered only superficial damage above the water line. None believed that the schooner's bow had penetrated the steamer's hull below the water line. This impression was further confirmed when the steamer continued on her course, her walking-beam engine thumping away as if nothing had happened. At the brief moment when the ships were side by side, the *Augusta* the unwilling consort of the steamer, so to speak, a deck hand on the schooner, Dan Horigan, the watchman who first reported the steamer's light, heard another crewman, William Bonner, call over to men they saw in the steamer's aft gangway to throw him a line. There had been no answer from the *Lady Elgin* that any of the *Augusta*'s people could hear.

Wind, the unmanageable condition of the *Augusta* and the fact that the steamer continued on her way drew the two vessels rapidly apart. Certain that the schooner's bow was crushed and that she must necessarily sink, the *Augusta*'s crew prepared to launch the lifeboat but abandoned that project after the ship's cook, John Morris, inspected the fo'c'sle and reported some leaking but apparently no major damage. Thereafter all efforts were concentrated on making temporary repairs to the headgear and, under Captain Malott's direction, getting the fore-staysail up to get the schooner once more before the wind. The deckload of lumber had shifted somewhat from the collision, but there was nothing they could do about that for the moment.

After making his report of no severe damage, cook Morris glanced once more in the direction of the fast-disappearing steamer, when another crewman said the steamer was turning around to come back for them.

"I saw her partly winded around," said Morris, "headed more towards shore. I should think that was about five or six minutes after we hit; if the captain or the mates had been looking at the same time I was, they could have seen the boat heading for shore." There had been some grumbling on the *Augusta* about the high-handed manner in which the *Lady Elgin* had continued to steam ahead, unmindful of the fate of the schooner and her crew.

Stephen Caryl, the *Lady Elgin*'s clerk, noted that an instant after the collision all was quiet in the saloons and lounges. "Not a cry or scream but only the rush of steam and the surge of the heavy seas could be heard. Whether they were not fully aware of the danger, or whether their appalling situation made them speechless, I cannot tell."

The *Lady Elgin*, mortally holed, was indeed making for shore. The inrushing waters soon quenched her fires, thus allowing her engine to whisper to a stop.

First mate George Davis had been in his cabin asleep at the time of the collision but rushed to the pilothouse as soon as he could get dressed. Captain Wilson had already gone below to check the damage. The wheelsman was still steering the Milwaukee course, NNW, ½ N.

"Steer west, toward shore," ordered Davis.

Seconds later Captain Wilson ascended to the pilothouse, agreed that the course change was highly proper and confided to Davis that the ship was leaking badly and would probably sink. He ordered the whistle blown continuously and assigned a watchman to keep ringing the ship's bell. Mate Davis suggested that the cattle be driven overboard to lighten the ship. "Yes," agreed Captain Wilson, "the cattle and everything else you can get over."

Davis passed on the order to the second mate, but the attempted execution of the command resulted in a lower deck madhouse. The frightened cattle could not or would not be driven. Altogether the crew got twenty loose but only one overboard. Others broke out of their pens, bawling, sliding and piling up on the portside as the *Lady Elgin* took on a significant list. It was chaos.

With evidence of desperation now in his voice, Captain Wilson sought out Davis. "For God's sake, Davis, get a boat overboard and outside to try to stop the leak."

This was pretty much standard procedure under the circumstances. Often ships have been saved by stuffing canvas or mattresses in collision-incurred holes, the material held in the opening by the pressure of water against the hull. Mr. Davis did his best. He, the second mate and a watchman threw over a small boat from the stern and jumped in. Davis grabbed a rope, and volunteers among the passengers held the other end to pull the boat along the side of the ship to the area of damage.

But rarely was a boat for such a purpose so poorly equipped. By the time the three men jumped into it, the boat was nearly filled with water from the rough seas. Mr. Davis was obliged to drop his end of the rope to start bailing frantically. There was only one bucket, and that one was being energetically employed by the second mate. Mr. Davis and the watchman used their uniform caps.

"It was about five minutes before we could lighten her up and head her into it again," reported Mr. Davis to the authorities. "We pulled for five or six minutes toward her before she went down. It was the last I saw of her. She settled by degrees, rows of lights going out as the decks slipped under. We could hear the screams but were never able to get within 150 yards of her."

Mr. Davis, although he must have been aware that the schooner had suffered topside damage and a shifted cargo and thus could not be maneuvered as a steamboat might be, was petulantly critical of the schooner and her captain for not coming to the assistance of the steamer.

"Had the schooner lain to and put out a bright light, we could have run our steamer towards her and boated our passengers to her in about twenty minutes. We had our whistle going and the bell ringing." Aboard the schooner neither could be heard.

Captain Wilson had one more attempt made to reach the leak after the first mate's boat had been swept away. Thomas Cummings, the man who had so nearly been felled by the schooner's jib boom when it burst into his cabin, was one of those instructed to launch another boat, this time with men who knew how to handle it. It was the same story. The boat was launched without oars. Some were thrown to her, but they went astray in the gale. There were eleven men in the boat including ship's clerk Caryl, a coal passer and the ship's barber. The rest were passengers, who, in the belief that the crew was abandoning ship, jumped in. Thomas Murphy, deck hand, and Mr. Rice, the *Lady Elgin*'s steward, must have had the same impression. They jumped from the hurricane deck and were pulled aboard. Without oars the boat was helpless, and like Mr. Davis', drifted away in the spume.

Only two boats remained for the estimated three hundred souls still aboard. One had a capacity of twenty person, the other twelve.

The sinking of the *Lady Elgin* in the dark of night and in weather the first mate later testified had changed from squalls to a gale, inspired some of the most tragic and heart-rending scenes in the history of Great Lakes transportation—horrendous scenes glimpsed in the intermittent flashes of lightning and lashing rain, seascapes no artist could imagine or reproduce.

At the instant of the collision the dancing had stopped. As yet all the excursionists remained calm, reassured by Mr. Cummings and other crewmen that there was no danger. But the list that developed so rapidly changed calm to fear and, in some cases, utter panic. John Jervis, a passenger who had earlier spotted the schooner's light, minutes before the collision, had brought his wife and sister-in-law, Agnes Keogh, on the trip. After the collision he had gone below to survey the damage, saw the black gang futilely trying to stuff mattresses into the hole from the inside and heard the engineers tell Captain Wilson that there was no more steam, nor could there be any. The water was rising rapidly when Mr. Jervis climbed back to the cabin deck to get his wife and her sister. They refused to leave their cabin, so he carried both up to the hurricane deck. By now Captain Wilson was urging all the passengers to go above. The women, numbed by fear, had to be pushed or carried up bodily. Mr. Jervis estimated that he had helped up about twenty-five or thirty.

Brave Captain Wilson was everywhere, reassuring, calming, and recruiting men to help pass out life preservers. Mate Davis had said that there were about four hundred wooden life preservers piled on the hurricane deck.

Jervis recalled hearing one lady ask the captain if he was

going to leave them. "No," replied Captain Wilson. "No, I will die with you."

Two of the ladies assisted by Mr. Jervis were the wife and daughter of councilman Timothy O'Brion. O'Brion himself was helping to launch the larger of the remaining two boats. He tried to return for his wife and daughter but the pressure of panic-stricken passengers pushing toward the boat was too great. He never saw them again.

When she went down, the *Lady Elgin* did so swiftly, the rush of air and water upwards successfully dismembering the cabin deck and breaking away the hurricane deck, which remained intact for a short time. Insanely, the watchman Captain Wilson had instructed to ring the ship's bell continued to clang it with a fury. It was as though he was calling the Almighty's attention to his faithfulness to duty, perhaps thus justifying some merciful dispensation from what appeared to be the end. In the convulsion of debris spewed up like a volcano from below were the thrashing cattle, sections of paneling, chairs, cabin doors, lounge furniture, the ship's piano, trunks, picnic baskets, desks, railings, crates, cattle pens, boxes, barrels, mail bags, framing timbers, clothing, cans, benches, the steward's meat block, kegs and hundreds of bottles from Mr. Lacy's bar. Before the battering ram seas, rolling shoreward in the face of the gale, the hurricane deck rapidly distintegrated, plunging over three hundred terrified passengers and crew members into the heaving, grinding flotsam.

Captain Wilson had been everywhere, advising his people to hang onto whatever wreckage they could find and, above all, to be calm. The shore was not far away, he explained, and if they remained calm, they would undoubtedly be saved. "Hang on tight when you hit the breakers near shore," he cautioned. "Hang on tight."

Captain Barry of the Union Guards was also prowling the

hurricane deck before it broke up, doing his best to help the
ladies to ease the fears of an estimated forty children who
had somehow congregated near the bow.

At the time of the collision first mate Davis had estimated
that they were about ten miles from the Illinois shore, off
Winnetka. The ship had made some progress after the course
was changed and before steam power was lost. But even with
the seas driving her shoreward, she had gone down still nine
miles short of where she could have been beached with a
minimum of danger to her people.

Mr. Jervis got his wife and sister-in-law on top of the pilothouse seconds before the boat went down. "It seemed as if
the upper works all spread out when the boat sank," Jervis
later told rescuers. "Cabin doors and boxes all came up together, and then soon after cattle and passengers; the pilothouse capsized almost at once after the boat went down. I,
my wife and Agnes sank at once. My wife had her arms
around me. Her sister was hanging onto her. My wife and I
came up together, but somehow Agnes was lost. We got on
the pilothouse again. The water was covered with cattle,
women, children and men, screaming and sinking. It was
thundering and lightning. I stood on the pilothouse perhaps
fifteen minutes. We then got on another raft, a section of
the hurricane deck, on which were twenty-odd people."

Captain Wilson found himself on a section of the hurricane deck that held about forty people. But as the hours
wore on, the wracking seas broke up even this tenuous mes-
senger of safety. When it reached breakers, only eight remained. One of them, a woman, lost her hold and fell into
the surf. Captain Wilson dove for her, but both were
drowned in the boiling, confused seas created by the strong
undertow. Many who would otherwise have survived were
fatally injured by the thrashing and plunging field of wreckage that had accompanied the victims ashore. It is estimated

that more than half of the people floating on or hanging to wreckage lost their lives in the surf a scant hundred feet from shore.

"Five, including my wife, were alive when we were the width of the Courthouse from shore," sobbed Mr. Jervis. "They were all swept off and drowned by the upsetting of the raft."

Franz Christine was the only one saved from a raft that contained twenty people, and Charles May was the only survivor from a section of hurricane deck that came into the breakers with a dozen hopeful souls clinging to it.

There were, of course, the usual tragicomic incidents that attend nearly every disaster. James Rodee, floundering in the welter of wreckage, came across a snare drum of a band member and used it successfully as a life preserver all the way to shore. Patrick Maher and George Furlong, the young men who had made disparaging remarks as the cattle were being loaded, found their raft to safety was one of the cattle pens, with four of the drowned beasts still inside. John B. Quail, who had been seeing a friend off and was inadvertently carried with her when the *Lady Elgin* sailed, found himself astride the ship's piano. During the night he was sighted by the friend, George Locke. They had exchanged words of encouragement, but the piano came ashore without Quail.

The boat bearing first mate George Davis reached shore north of Winnetka just after daybreak. Those aboard quickly fanned out to nearby homes to spread the alarm. Their own experience had proven that help—much help—would be needed as the survivors were borne relentlessly into the surf. Word spread from house to house that ropes, manpower and warm clothing would be in great demand for the next few hours. The shore here has a rather high bluff and a modest beach that at the time was being combed constantly by the unusually high seas.

Ex-Alderman Artemas Carter of Winnetka was one of the first to respond, running to the bluff with a coil of rope and whatever clothing he could find in a hurry.

"Very soon," said Carter, "we could see small objects to the northeast floating, or rather pitching and tossing on the mad waves. As they came nearer, we saw that they were fragments of the steamer, and freighted with human beings —some with one person, some with two, three or a dozen persons. People began to rally on the shore with ropes."

The news had reached the nearby railroad station and from there quickly spread to neighboring Evanston, where parties of students from Northwestern University and the Garrett Biblical Institute rallied forces to help. While hundreds watched from the bluff, brave men plunged into the boiling surf to save those too far gone to help themselves. Hero of the day was a Northwestern student, Edward W. Spencer, who, tethered by a long rope held by fellow University classmates, plunged into the surf sixteen times, saving a total of seventeen exhausted people who had only eight hours earlier been among the *Lady Elgin's* tired but happy passengers.

By seven o'clock that morning of September 8 the dread news of the calamity and indications of its magnitude had spread through Milwaukee like a prairie fire. The morning train from the city to Chicago was jammed with hundreds of parents, brothers and sisters, most of them tearful, each dreading what they would find there on the windy bluff at Winnetka. They moved slowly between the still rows, sobbing and crying aloud when the form of a loved one came in view. When positive identification was established, men of a special Milwaukee committee, all good men and true, fastened a tag on the right wrist of the victims—Thomas Fitzpatrick, Christian Nickol, school commissioner James Rice, Amelia Ledden, councilman Francis McCormick, Sarah McManus, schoolteacher Cornelius O'Mahoney, Elias Diehl, marshal John Horan, Henry Schneider, harbormaster Martin Dooley, Joanna Kennedy, Samuel Waegli, Maria Dunnavan, the Hon. Herbert Ingram, Peter Riley, Mary Crehan, Michael Rich, Homer Goff, Col. Francis A. Lumsden, Honora McLaughlin, John Newton, bookkeeper Cyrus H. Walrath. On and on it went, the lines of silent forms growing longer as volunteers toiled up the bluff with their terrible harvest from the breakers. Among the first to be recognized was vivacious and popular Eliza Curtain, who hadn't wanted to go in the first place.

But if bravery and the finer instincts of humanity were exemplified along the Lake Michigan shore that day, so were the other extremes. The Chicago *Daily Press Tribune* noted in a frowning editorial comment the next day:

> Among the rubbish of the wreck came ashore numerous kegs of spirits, wines and beer from the barkeeper's stores. We regret to note among the incidents of the day its use to the extent of creating a drunken fight among some of the shore party.

Many of the pocketbooks recovered from the debris had one thing in common—they had been opened and the cash contents removed. Several persons were arrested on suspicion of having robbed the bodies; two of them were nabbed as they stood over the corpse of barkeeper Lacy, his pockets turned inside out. The several thousand dollars he was known to have had on his person when the *Lady Elgin* left Chicago was missing. Nearby was his trunk, also in the possession of the two suspects but broken open and the money belt stripped of gold. Another trunk, the property of Colonel Lumsden or members of his party, all of whom were lost, was spirited away from the beach by two men and taken to Evanston. Informers passed the word to Justice of the Peace Huntoon of that community. The trunk was recovered, but not without bitter argument. It contained much valuable jewelry.

Again in editorial wrath, the Chicago *Daily Press Tribune* said:

> The quest for bodies and baggage washed ashore will be main-
> tained for some time most vigilantly. As to the latter, it is a
> disgrace to our common humanity that the harpies in shape
> of men are so numerous and have recently given such repul-
> sive tokens of the same. We can only remark that during the
> great emergency they were on the *wrong* side of the breakers.

Also piqued at incautious remarks made by Chief of Police Beck of Milwaukee and quoted in the Milwaukee *Free Democrat* relative to the finding of a body upon which was found considerable gold and jewelry, the publication lashed back:

> This is the body upon which was found some $200 in gold,
> about which the Milwaukee *Free Democrat* and Chief of Po-
> lice Beck of that city have raised such an unseemly disturb-
> ance, and in such a spirit as almost induces the conviction
> that it is more than fortunate that these valuables did not go
> to Milwaukee, but were retained by the Coroner here.

Because the authorities were never able to determine exactly how many passengers had been aboard the *Lady Elgin*, the specific death toll has always been in doubt, ranging from 279 to 350. Neither was it possible, because some of the survivors recovered quickly and departed the scene, to establish the exact number saved. Here again the figures vary, from 100 to 155.

Unaware of the hellish hours as the *Lady Elgin* went to her doom and most of her passengers and crew to theirs, Captain Malott brought the battered and leaking *Augusta* into Chicago when the drama on the beach was about over. To a member of the tug crew that took a line to tow the schooner to her river dock, he passed the remark that they had been in collision during the night with a large steamer. Only then did the men of the *Augusta* hear that the ship they had struck was the *Lady Elgin*, and that there was every reason to expect a heavy death toll. Captain Malott later vociferously denied that he had referred to the vessel they hit as "an old scow that knocked some of our gingerbread off."

Following correct procedure with regard to his owner's interests and possible later litigation, Captain Malott promptly made a protest to the marine inspectors, taking his crew with him to verify the facts. With regard to his navigation immediately preceding the collision, the captain explained that the schooner was out of control, lying on her beam ends and in the trough of the seas. Confirming the ferocity of the squall was Captain Green of the brig *Saxon*, who stated that the squall had developed its full-blown fury in a space of ten minutes. Also bearing mute testimony of the destructive winds on Lake Michigan that night was the disappearance of the schooner *St. Mary*, with all hands.

It was apparent that there was no love lost between Captain Malott and his officers. First mate Vorce and second mate Budge both testified before the jury of Cook County Coroner William James that they were aware that the *Augusta* steered pretty wild when loaded, but admitted that they had not communicated this knowledge to Captain Malott, who was making his first voyage as her commander. Perhaps they resented his assignment as master when both considered themselves qualified for advancement, Vorce to captain, Budge to first mate.

Coroner James and others of the jury, along with marine inspectors, were aware of an ugly rumor that had been sweeping Milwaukee and already responsible for veiled threats against Captain Malott's life. The rumor was to the effect that the *Augusta* had been showing no light and that this omission was entirely responsible for the disaster that had brought bereavement to nearly every home in the city's Bloody Third ward. Aware, too, that persistent repetition breeds firm conviction, they sought quickly to establish the truth of the matter, beginning that very morning of the tragedy. Although under the circumstances their stories would be suspect, particularly in Milwaukee, the entire crew of the *Augusta* testified that their white light had been working and was in good order, and was mounted on the Samson post forward of the windlass about five feet above the deck.

"I expect it could be seen for about three-quarters of a mile," said Captain Malott. "I held to the law and rule that when a sailing vessel meets a steamer, it is required to hold its course. I assumed, too, when the steamer did not alter her course, that her lookout was sheltering himself from the rain, which was really quite furious. I also thought when I first came on deck that my second mate had not been doing his duty in not calling me sooner. But it depends on what the weather was. I can only judge from what they say."

Supporting the words of the *Augusta*'s men, however, was sworn testimony from those who had been aboard the *Lady Elgin* that nightmarish early morning of September 8. Second mate Beeman admitted that both he and Captain Wilson had seen the schooner's light, that the course had been altered somewhat and both thought the schooner would pass them safely. "But she just kept coming," repeated Beeman. "She just kept coming."

Even passenger John Jervis had seen the sailing vessel's light and saw it while looking out one of the lower deck gangways, without the advantage of height such as had been the captain's and the second mate's. Jervis had even remarked to a fellow passenger that, in his opinion, a collision was very probable.

While the hastily formed jury delved into the matter and

continued to interview survivors and witnesses, a small group of Milwaukee businessmen, although sympathizing heartily with the bereaved, breathed a collective sigh of relief once the list of the lost had been tabulated and the victims identified. They were the officers of the struggling, three-year-old Northwestern Mutual Life Insurance Company. It was known that a number of its policyholders had planned to make the trip with the *Lady Elgin*. They knew, too, that the deaths of just a few could spell financial disaster and ruin in view of the company's still limited resources. A final review showed that only one Northwestern policyholder, Milton Townsend, had been lost. His widow's claim was paid immediately.

So admired was Captain Wilson by all who had known him, that scarcely had his passing been verified and his brave conduct recounted, than Chicago businessmen and citizens began organizing a fund to pay off his farm mortgage and to assure care for his family. In less than half a day the fund was over one thousand dollars. Eventually, swelled by contributions from all along the lakes, it reached an eminently satisfactory total.

The seething rage of those left in the decimated Bloody Third, however, demanded revenge and action, not explanations, testimony or expressions of sorrow and regret. Several times chief Beck got wind of plans to burn the schooner and had issued stern warnings. There were rumors, too, that small groups of Irish had pledged to follow the future wanderings of the schooner and destroy her at any cost.

Cognizant of the potential danger, owners Bissel and Davidson quickly sold the *Augusta* to another firm, also aware of the mood in Milwaukee. They painted her black and changed her name to *Colonel Cook*.

The verdict of the coroner's jury, released on the afternoon of September 9, the day after the tragedy, was about what could be expected, considering the times, the circumstances and the sworn testimony. They found both vessels at fault to a degree, censuring the *Lady Elgin*'s officers and owners for overloading the steamer, confirming that she had her lights properly placed, but lamenting the fact that her hull was one big open cavern without the protection of compartments or bulkheads. As to the *Augusta*, the jury, while agreeing that the schooner had the proper number of officers and crewmen, censured second mate Budge for not informing the captain of the *Lady Elgin*'s light which he, Budge, had observed for some time before the collision, and further for not continuing to observe the progress of the light. Budge, they concluded, was not competent to handle the vessel. Captain Malott was censured for not immediately coming to anchor to assist the steamer. What good this would have done in light of the fact that the steamer had continued on her course for some time somehow escaped the reasoning of the official body. The primary cause for the collision, the jury ruled, was not directly attributable to any human failure but to the existing navigation laws—defective laws, they concluded, in the case of sailing vessels, which permitted such a vessel, when carrying a bright light, to vary her course as much as eight points without being obliged to alter the color or the arrangement of her lights. The variation in the course of such a vessel at one of those points, was liable, at any time, to prove fatal to lake craft.

The report that resulted from the inquest, conducted by twelve good and lawful men on behalf of the People of the State of Illinois, in the City of Chicago and in said County of Cook, merely confirmed pretty much what everybody already knew—that it was a most regrettable affair.

Collisions, strandings and other mishaps being considered part and parcel of lake shipping in those days, Captain Malott continued to serve the same owners, coming out in 1861 as master of the bark *Ravenna*, freighting between Buffalo, Cleveland and Detroit for the entire season. In the spring of

1862, again in the *Ravenna,* he took on a cargo of copper ore at Eagle Harbor, on Lake Superior, delivering it to London, England, returning to Detroit with china, crockery and miscellaneous ironware goods. In 1863 he made two cross-Atlantic voyages in the *Ravenna*—one with copper, the other with barrel staves.

Meanwhile, the *Colonel Cook,* nee *Augusta,* although repaired after her brush with the *Lady Elgin,* fell upon evil days. She had difficulty getting crews for one thing, many sailors avowing that she was haunted by the ghosts of the *Lady Elgin's* people. Although she sailed for thirty-four years after the tragic collision, she fell victim to an almost unbelievable number of mishaps and changes in ownership. Finally, in 1894, she stranded and went to pieces on Lake Erie.

Early in 1864, Bissel & Davidson took delivery on a spanking new bark, the *Mojave.* Nine feet longer than the old *Augusta,* requiring a crew of ten and so arranged as to carry cargo more efficiently, she was put in charge of Captain Walter Perry temporarily, Captain Malott being en route home from a voyage to England.

Captain Malott took over the *Mojave,* designated as the flagship of Bissel & Davidson's modest fleet, when he brought the *Ravenna* home. Captain Perry transferred to the *Ravenna.*

On September 8 of that year, in mid–Lake Michigan and with ideal weather conditions prevailing, the *Mojave* was bespoken by the schooner *J. S. Miner.* Apparently all was well aboard the *Mojave* at the time, but the fact remains that sometime later that day she and her crew and captain vanished forever, the victims of some catastrophic occurrence. Whatever happened, one wonders if Nelse Malott had time to note that it was again September 8, the fourth anniversary of the *Lady Elgin* tragedy and time again for another birthday, his thirty-first!

⚓

8

The "Big Blow"—an Introduction

Early in November of 1913, a monstrous low-pressure area, spawned in the Aleutians and moving steadily over the great grain-growing provinces of Canada, came in violent collision over Lake Superior with another low-pressure system born in the Rocky Mountains and beating a northward path from lower Minnesota. This hurricane-breeding wedding of the elements brought savage and sustained winds and seas, often from conflicting quadrants—a hell's brew of weather that produced protracted snow flurries of unprecedented fury. But as deadly and destructive as this blending of fronts was, it reached a degree of violence hitherto unknown when it was later joined by still a third low-pressure front originating in the Gulf of Mexico and sweeping northward from Georgia in an abnormal pattern. This diabolical third element brought record-breaking snowfalls and high winds to West Virginia, western Pennsylvania, Ohio and along the Lake Erie shore of New York. Towns and cities were isolated, each of necessity becoming a self-sufficient oasis as all railroad and interurban lines were overwhelmed by drifts and winds. Telegraph networks were decimated as miles of poles, overbur-

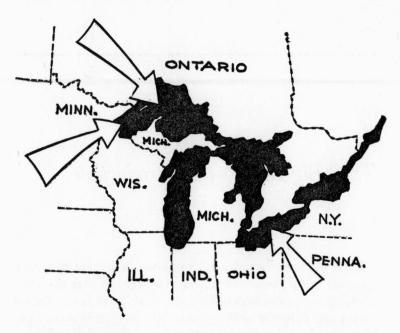

dened with ice and snow, lay prostrate like regiments of soldiers fallen in battle. In Cleveland a two-foot snowfall, whipped by driving winds into six-foot drifts, brought all traffic to a halt for the better part of three days. Householders were marooned, supplies of coal, food and milk ran low, electric lights failed and the remaining stocks of candles and kerosene were soon depleted. About one hundred people died of natural causes during the period of the storm and remained unburied, but by the same token approximately the same number of new citizens were ushered into the blizzardy world without the attention of physicians. Across Lake Erie, at Chatham, Ontario, the city was completely storm-bound and isolated for over thirty-six hours.

The northerly gales brought their own crushing winds and driven snow pounding down the length of Lake Michigan. In Chicago, which narrowly escaped the snow, the seas wiped out dozens of shoreside luxury homes, plucked away retaining walls and ravished breakwaters. Two Chicagoans, literally carried away by the winds, were cast into the Chicago River and lost.

Over lower Lake Huron, where the witch's broth of the blended northerly gales met the advancing low front from the south, the cataclysm defied the laws of probability and survival. Seas of unbelievable stature roared ashore, the whole lower lake churned into such a state of convulsion that its heaving and rearing surface was a frothy white. Again, the cyclonic nature of the maelstrom resulted in shipmasters bravely confronting the monstrous lathering seas from one direction while being asaulted by hurricane-force winds from another. And all the while there was the hellish shrieking of the wind and the terrible, driving snow, rattling like buckshot against the pilothouses as every inch of exposed wood and metal accumulated a swelling meringue of ice. Stentorian steam whistles blew frantically and continuously, but such was the tumult of the hail and the density of the snow that they went unheard, even by the men who sounded them.

Unprecedented in both intensity and duration, the storm has gone down in Great Lakes history as the "Big Blow," a four-day weather convulsion whose dates vary, in local legend, with wherever one chanced to be at the time. On Lake Superior the days of November 7th through the 9th are remembered as the violent ones. Southeast from the Soo, in Georgian Bay and Lake Huron, the ninth and tenth were the bad ones. In lower Lake Huron and Lake Erie, the time span between dawn of the ninth to noon on November eleventh were regarded as the disastrous days.

The dates matter little, really, for in its course the storm wrought such havoc, ashore and afloat, that the normal routine and processes of living were brought to an abrupt halt. When it was over, although it took nearly a week to assess the tragedy on the lakes, twelve vessels and their crews had vanished forever. Another twenty-five had been driven ashore, six of them listed as total constructive losses!

Due to the rather casual manner of keeping crew lists current in that era, nobody will ever know exactly how many sailors perished, or who some of them were, but the estimates vary from two hundred and fifty to nearly three hundred. It was typical of the times, too, that many men below the licensed grades were known even to their own shipmates by whatever name they chose to give when they signed on. Often it was only a nickname—Spike, Red or Blackie. Sometimes only by an abbreviation of his given name—Tom, Joe or Bill. Some of them still lie in the cemeteries of little communities along the eastern shoreline of Lake Huron, known but to God.

They are remembered today by the words on a historical marker near Port Sanilac where, in summer, tourists often stop to observe the peaceful panorama of Lake Huron and wonder that its tranquil waters could rise to such wrath:

THE GREAT STORM OF 1913 [1]

Sudden tragedy struck the Great Lakes on November 9, 1913, when a storm whose equal veteran sailors could not recall left in its wake death and destruction. The grim toll was 235 seamen drowned, ten ships sunk, and more than twenty others driven ashore. Here on Lake Huron all 178 crewmen of the eight ships claimed by its waters were lost. For sixteen hours gales of cyclonic fury made man and his machines helpless.

This, then, in the following five chapters, is the story of the "Big Blow," of some who survived and lived to spend

[1] The historical marker is in error in the number of vessels lost. Ten were indeed lost on Lake Huron and Lake Superior But somebody forgot to count the barge *Plymouth*, lost with all hands on Lake Michigan, and *Lightship No. 82*, overwhelmed and lost with her crew on Lake Erie.

their declining years telling their grandchildren about it, but also of ships and men who never came back up from those yawning, frothing valleys between the seas. For many the decisions that made the difference between life and death were made by others—men who worked in the high place called the pilothouse, wore uniforms and were called "Captain." But captains had a hard row to hoe, too, and were under constant pressure from men who worked in high places ashore and who kept reminding them of schedules, lost time and seasonal tonnage commitments. The often beleaguered shipmasters could not possibly have foreseen the monumental forces of nature that were to join in a four-day orgy of devastation. And because they were mere mortals, there were some who wouldn't have changed their decisions in any event.

9

"He Went Away and Never Said Goodbye"

Saturday, November 8 of 1913, following a pretty ordinary Friday, started out to be a rather ordinary day itself, considering the season. It found a number of pretty ordinary vessels on Lake Michigan going about their routine tasks. That their voyages ceased to be ordinary before the day was over can be credited to the whims of nature, or, more specifically as the Chippewas were wont to philosophize, to the will and humor of either Gitchee Manito, the good spirit, or Matchi Manito, the evil spirit. Both spirits, according to the legends, were able to summon the winds at will. Gitchee Manito preferred Jawaninodin, the gentle South Wind or Ningabian-inodin, the steady West Wind. Matchie Manito always seemed to favor Kiwedininodin, the terrible North Wind, or Wabaninodin, the weather-breeding East Wind. When the wind varied between specific quadrants, the Chippewas believed that it was merely an exuberant test of strength and power between the two spirits—a friendly tussle such as often was resolved ere the day was over, when one, in high good humor, surrendered to the other.

Saturday, November 8, began exactly as every other day,

at 12:01 A.M., with Gitchee Manito and Matchi Manito still somewhat at odds over their wind-summoning superiority. Aboard a quintet of harassed vessels in upper Lake Michigan were an equal number of shipmasters who knew nothing, and cared less, about the legendary wind gods who were giving them a damned nasty time. They knew only that strong winds from the southwest, after giving them fits all day Friday with a choppy, quartering bit of slop, had swung into the northwest late that night with brief flights of fancy into the north and northeast before settling down from the northwest to build up some really significant seas.

Beating her way up Little Bay de Noc, heading for Gladstone, Michigan, was the steamer *James H. Prentice,* towing her consort, the barge *Halstead,* an aged one-hundred-and-seventy-one-foot schooner fallen upon evil days. Both were in the lumber trade for the Soper Lumber Company of Chicago, carrying modest burdens at modest speed. Some distance behind them was the twenty-six-year-old wooden steamer *Louisiana,* upbound to Escanaba for ore after delivering a load of coal to Milwaukee. The *Louisiana* had been making fair weather of it as long as she had remained in the lee of the Wisconsin mainland, but after hauling to port on the Porte Des Morts Passage into Green Bay and turning north on the Escanaba course, the going had been decidedly grim. Over to the east, at anchor behind the sheltering bulk of St. Martin's Island, lay the fifty-nine-year-old barge *Plymouth.* The *Plymouth,* like the *Halstead,* had once been a sleek schooner but was long past the day when she would ever again spread her own canvas to the winds. Near her was her motive power, the tug *James H. Martin,* a veteran of forty-four years on the Great Lakes and recently beginning to develop symptoms of grave infirmities. The strong southwest winds of Friday had persisted in blowing the *Plymouth* off to starboard. In deference to the tug's modest horsepower

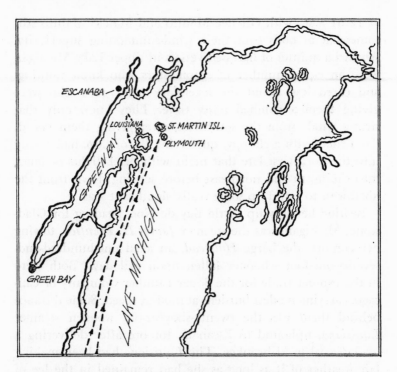

her skipper, Captain Louis Setunsky, had decided to seek shelter in the lee of St. Martin's Island. The tug and barge were both out of Menominee, bound for Search Bay for a load of cedar posts for the Huebel Company.

The *Louisiana*, meanwhile, after plugging into discouraging head seas for some time, gave up the fight. She could make absolutely no headway once the wind had shifted to northwest, and Captain Fred McDonald regretfully hauled around to retreat in the direction of the nearest shelter, which chanced to be Washington Harbor, on the northwest corner of Washington Island. She made the harbor in good shape and quickly dropped both anchors. But the wind had reached such a frightening velocity that observers noted that

she was dragging steadily toward the beach. Word was sent
to the Plum Island lifesavers, who responded by sending their
beach gear to Washington Island by boat and hauling it
overland by wagon to the scene. The *Louisiana,* in the in-
terim, had conveniently caught fire and was successfully
abandoned by her crew of seventeen. The lifesavers lingered
on the site, however, because two schooners were still at
anchor outside the harbor and in imminent peril. For nearly
forty-eight hours they stood by as the *J. M. Stevens* and the
Minerva fought it out with the towering seas, at one moment
on the crest of an enormous billow and the next moment
dropping out of sight in a smother of foam. The lifesavers
were not to be idle in any event. While they were standing
by to aid the schooners should their anchors drag or the
chains part, another emergency presented itself. The barge
Halstead, also blowing off to starboard from the steamer
Prentice, suddenly found itself free when the towline to the
Prentice parted. There was no point in attempting to reconnect under the existing conditions, and aware that the
barge had its own big anchors, the master of the *Prentice*
continued on, assuming that once the weather took a turn
for the better, he could venture out to reacquire his consort.

The northwest wind and good fortune brought the *Halstead* into Washington Harbor, too, dragging her anchors,
flying distress signals and fetching up on rocks some distance
off the beach. The lifesavers, under Captain William Robinson, made valiant efforts to succor the imperiled *Halstead*
crewmen. A line was shot over the vessel, but before a
breeches buoy could be rigged and sent aboard, a tremendous
sea picked the barge up bodily and carried it right up on
the beach. During their long hours at Washington Harbor,
the snow had been driven in so furiously that Captain Robinson's men were sometimes working in drifts up to their
waists.

Meanwhile, over in the lee of St. Martin's Island, things had gone from bad to worse on the tug *Martin* and her tow barge, particularly on the tug. The managing owner of the tug, and also its engineer, was Donald McKinnon of Menominee. Its captain, Louis Setunsky, newly hired, was finding that the tug's condition was not all that McKinnon had represented it to be. Once at sea and with a strain on the towline, the *Martin* did not have the power to manage her tow, particularly if the wind and sea were kicking up. The barge continually sheered to one side or the other, frequently putting the tug "in irons" and in danger of capsizing. Then, too, the engine turned out to be cranky and unpredictable, requiring frequent repairs. The hull also leaked consistently, and the tug's low freeboard caused her to make water constantly in anything but calm seas. Mr. Setunsky was very unhappy with his charge and made that point painfully clear to his employer.

Things were not much better on the aged *Plymouth*. Her captain, Axel Larsen, was an experienced, capable seaman, but the other six crewmen scarcely knew fore from aft. One of the six, Chris Keenan, a Deputy United States Marshal, was assigned to the barge merely as a custodian. The *Plymouth,* however old and bedraggled, was the subject of court litigation and until the question of ownership or claims against her were resolved, he was to guard her against harm or piracy while she continued to earn her keep. And Mr. Keenan was finding life aboard a barge in a storm very distressing.

When the wind shifted from southwest to northwest and finally north, Captain Setunsky had started out again, figuring that he could make progress without that nagging southwest wind dragging the barge off on a tangent. But the *Martin* was simply incapable of making headway against any kind of wind as fast as she made water below decks. With the wind and sea continuing to rise, Captain Setunsky, in desperation, decided to leave the *Plymouth* at anchor in the lee of little Gull Island, in St. Martin's Passage, while the *Martin* ran for shelter at Summer Island to pump out and make repairs. After blowing the agreed-upon signals, the crew of the barge dropped its anchor and hauled in the towline. The *Martin* then beat a hasty retreat, frequently out of sight from those on the barge as she dropped into the valleys between the snow-dusted seas, now great graybeards marching down from Manistique and Seul Choix Point.

Gathering strength as it swept down Lake Michigan, a malevolent Kiwedininodin, the North Wind, was accompanied by rapidly falling temperatures and heavy snow. For the first time within memory the car-ferry sailings across the lake were canceled. At Muskegon the wind velocity hit eighty miles per hour, tumbling smokestacks at several factories, breaking in store windows and filling the air with debris from broken signs, dismembering fences, disintegrating chimneys and flapping strips of roofing. At Holland dozens of pleasure launches were sunk, boathouses blown down and shoreline interurban tracks washed away. The steamer *D. C. Perry* was blown from her moorings and swept up on the beach. Across the lake, at Milwaukee, hundreds of citizens braved the cold early on Sunday to watch the seas destroy fifteen hundred feet of a new breakwater project and demolish two floating pile drivers. The wind reached its shrill crescendo in Chicago, where miles of trolley, light and telephone cables came down. Two men were literally picked up and hurled into the Chicago River to their death. Like their counterparts in Milwaukee, thousands of Chicagoans braved the wind and flying debris to watch and murmur in awe at the sight of seas cresting over the breakwaters. An added attraction was the lumber-laden schooner *C. D. Buys*, flying distress signals a mile off Van Buren Street. Fortunately, the record snows that hit Cleveland did not reach Chicago, although in nearby Indiana drifts had brought all interurban traffic to a halt. Chicago's big loss, estimated at $200,000, was the complete destruction of an extension of Lincoln Park, eight years' work wiped out in as many hours. Among the unhappy spectators who groaned as the undertow of each wave took a ton or two of earth away with it, was Daniel F. Rice, chairman of the park extension committee of the Lincoln Park Board.

Said the Chicago *Tribune:* "It was the biggest job of groaning he has done in years."

In nearby Gary, Indiana, the big steamer *Clarence A. Black* was reduced almost to a wreck while moored at her dock. The wind was so fierce that it blew in all her deck windows, snapped her mooring cables and bashed her repeatedly against the concrete dock wall, crushing in her heavy shell plating.

At Michigan City, Indiana, over two hundred feet of the pier and elevated walk were carried away, necessitating the use of the breeches buoy for the transfer of the lightkeeper across the gap. In Gary, too, sand from the beaches was driven in with such force and in such quantity as to make some streets impassable and confine most residents to their homes all day Sunday.

Lake Michigan was the last great arena for the fresh-water sailing vessels, the nature of its commerce was such that it was still possible for the plodding old "wind ships" to eke out an existence when their usefulness on the other lakes waned. Being wind sailors, the skippers were a shrewd, weather-wise lot who placed great faith and trust in their barometers. Few, therefore, were caught out on the lake during the worst of the storm, although even holed-up in some snug harbor they got a good mauling by the wind. They were slow boats that carried commodities scarcely affected by a day or two of delay. Lumber, cedar fence posts, barrel staves, shingles, salt, pulpwood, saw logs and coal were durable products not expected at their destinations at specifically scheduled times. The fast steamers had long since stolen the perishable fruit trade from the fabulously productive east shore of the lake— peaches, cherries, apples and grapes that were rushed overnight to markets in Chicago and Milwaukee. But potatoes were another matter. The old schooners, because their rates were understandably lower, still carried their share.

The schooner *Cora,* Captain John Locklund master, was loading potatoes at Egg Harbor, in Green Bay, when the great winds struck. She had already taken aboard about five hundred bushels at the John Bertschinger dock but had to suspend loading while all hands rigged extra lines to keep her off the beach. The steamer *Christie* with her consort, the barge *Interlaken,* both heavily loaded with hardwood lumber, ducked into Sturgeon Bay for the duration of the blow, but like the *Cora,* had to keep all hands up through the night securing new mooring cables as others parted. Elsewhere, all along the Lake Michigan shores, in Benton Harbor, Grand Haven, Manistee, Frankfort, Kewaunee, Manitowoc and Sheboygan, scores of venerable sailing craft stayed snugly moored wherever they happened to be, unmindful of the lost time and grateful for the shelter.

The *Illinois,* a passenger and freight steamer skippered by Captain John H. Stufflebeam, happened to be starting down Lake Michigan from the Straits of Mackinac when conditions quickly became intolerable. The *Illinois* had been to Mackinac Island and was returning to Chicago after making stops at Petoskey, Charlevoix and Traverse City. She was still scheduled to touch at Frankfort and Ludington after leaving the somewhat protected waters of Grand Traverse Bay, but once out in the open lake, with the seas building up and the wind increasing, Captain Stufflebeam began to yearn mightily for some place to hide. The state of the sea ruled out any dash to Frankfort. Nearby Sleeping Bear Point offered no protection at all in a northerly gale. So Captain Stufflebeam decided on a course of action that would have been foolhardy for a shipmaster without his intimate knowledge of the lake and all its waters. He headed for South Manitou Island, where the outlying shoals were already studded with the bones of other vessels who encountered them under similar circumstances. There was no dock at hand, and holding ground for anchorage was poor, to say the least. But the canny Captain Stufflebeam knew of one approach free of shoals and a nearby sandy shingle of beach. So that's where he took the *Illinois*, driving her bow right up on the beach. Even so the wind, hammering at her hull and strumming through her rigging, threatened to tear her away from her temporary home on the beach. Captain Stufflebeam kept the engine "full ahead" for forty-nine hours, the propeller thrashing steadily as the bow groaned and grated on the sand and gravel. Finally two of the crew were able to get ashore with a hawser which they secured to a large tree. The engine was then stopped, but the *Illinois* had to stay on the beach for another twenty-four hours before it was safe to back off. The vessel did enjoy the luxury of wireless, however, and was able to communicate with several ports, including Frankfort, thus relieving her owners of undue concern. It was a weary crew that took the *Illinois* back to Chicago, three days behind in her schedule. There the Chicago River docks offered mute witness to the perils of Lake Michigan. Various long overdue vessels wandered in, battered, with deckloads washed away. Three tardy arrivals, at first presumed lost, were the steamers *Sidney O. Neff, Wotan* and *Peters.*

The gale had practically blown itself out before Captain Setunsky felt justified in taking the tug *Martin*, still leaking and cranky, out to reconnect with his tow, the barge *Plymouth,* supposedly bobbing at anchor these many long hours off Gull Island. But the *Plymouth* was gone! The supposition was that the anchor chain had parted under the stress of the gale, and that the old schooner had been carried far to the south, possibly to fetch up somewhere down the lake. But though the *Martin* and other vessels scoured the beaches and probed the shores of every island, the *Plymouth* and her crew of seven had vanished! There was much speculation and bitterness in Menominee, the tug's port of registry and the home town of most of the *Plymouth*'s crew. Many people felt that if it had been necessary to abandon the barge in the face of rising seas, her crew should have been taken off by the tug at once. Public indignaton rose to a fever pitch with the discovery of a bottle, a week later, cast up on the beach near Pentwater, Michigan. It contained a note, written on a billhead of a Menominee firm. It was from Chris Keenan, the unlucky Deputy United States Marshal:

Dear Wife and Children:
    We were left up here in Lake Michigan by McKinnon, captain of the *James H. Martin;* tug at anchor. He went away and never said goodbye or anything to us. Lost one man yesterday. We have been out in the storm forty hours. Goodbye dear ones. Might see you in heaven. Pray for me.

                                                    Chris K.

They found Chris Keenan a few days later near Onekama, Michigan, about eight miles north of Manistee and eighty-three miles from Gull Island. It was almost a month later when Captain Axel Larsen made his final rendezvous with land, north of Muskegon and one hundred and twenty miles from where the *Plymouth* was last seen afloat as the *Martin* ran for shelter. The other five members of the crew—James Sabota, Henry Kossak, Peter Johnson, Clifford Duchaine and Clyde Jessup—were never found.

Strangely, the policy of leaving a barge to her own devices was not an unusual procedure. It was actually considered the lesser of two evils when extremes of weather dictated. Most barges with proper ground tackle were well able to take care of themselves. The classic example was in the great November storm of 1905. The steamer *Mataafa* had departed Duluth harbor towing the barge *Nasmyth*, both vessels loaded with iron ore. A few hours later a great gale swept down on the lake, sending every vessel scurrying for shelter. The *Mataafa* fled back to Duluth, but her captain, realizing that he could not possibly get the barge into the ship canal and harbor, ordered the *Nasmyth* cut loose several miles outside the harbor. The *Mataafa* herself was wrecked and broken in two on the canal piers, and the gale sank or wrecked many large and sturdy vessels. The *Nasmyth*, however, was still afloat and her people safe when tugs came out looking for her. Not being a sailor, Chris Keenan would not have been aware of this practice and must have been bewildered and appalled when the *Martin* went snorting off into the snow, seas and scud.

Captain Setunsky fell heir to much of the blame and lashed out at McKinnon, charging that the condition of the *Martin*'s engine was badly misrepresented to him by McKinnon. "A rescue was out of the question," said Captain Setunsky with some heat; "the tug was taking water badly and was in no condition to aid the barge. Had I realized the actual condition of the *Martin*'s engine, I would never have taken her out of the harbor."

The Menominee newspaper, in an editorial, demanded a federal investigation into the seaworthiness of the *Martin* and *Plymouth*, the qualifications of the men navigating each and the merits of the assertion of Captain Setunsky and owner McKinnon that rescue of the men on the barge was impossible because of high weather. Local mariners were free in their claims that had the tug been in proper condition, as required by the government steamboat inspectors, she should have experienced little difficulty in taking off the luckless crew of the *Plymouth.* Up in Marquette, Michigan, the steamboat inspectors then preferred charges for alleged misconduct and set a date for hearings.

It is a rare occasion when knowledgeable marine experts, sitting in judgment in a warm courtroom, condemn a vessel's officers for lack of action under conditions they did not witness, and where every bit of evidence pointed out that the instance under investigation took place in the worst storm within memory. The inspectors at Marquette were not exceptions. After a decision to revoke McKinnon's license, a finding he appealed, the inspectors came to the conclusion that the loss of the *Plymouth* involved no criminal liability on the part of Captain Setunsky or owner-engineer McKinnon.

The ancient tug had already proven the point of her seaworthiness. Almost as if she was ashamed of her role in the affair, apologetic for her infirmities and sorry for her inability to weather the storm long enough to rescue the *Plymouth*'s people, the *James H. Martin* sank to the bottom of Menominee harbor on the last day of November.

The findings of the steamboat inspectors notwithstanding, the atmosphere in and around Menominee must have been decidedly unpleasant for Captain Louis Setunsky and Donald McKinnon. Those poignant few words of Deputy United States Marshal Chris Keenan could be difficult to forget, and probably were: "He went away and never said goodbye . . ."

10

The Last Laugh of Jimmy Owen

Beyond the fact that the month began with the mildest seasonal temperatures mariners could recall, Friday, November 7, 1913, could well be described as typical of any early November. The exigencies of Great Lakes commerce being what they were, a great many vessels found themselves on Lake Superior, the world's largest body of fresh water, in plodding pursuit of cargoes or already burdened with them. Downbound from Duluth, Two Harbors, Superior, Ashland and Marquette were the full-bellied iron ore carriers with loads destined to top off the winter stockpiles of lower lakes' mills and furnaces. From Duluth and Superior, too, others set courses for the Soo filled to the hatch coamings with wheat, barley or oats. Departing from Thunder Bay, the common harbor for the Canadian Lakehead ports of Fort William and Port Arthur, came another straggling procession of long ships, their funnels vomiting dark streamers of smoke, the wind dragging them across a making sea, caressing the pines of Trowbridge Island and sullying the bleak face of the Sleeping Giant. A few carried iron ore, but most of them were laden with newly harvested and graded grain from the bulging elevators that lined the bay. Once through the Soo locks and the serpentine lower St. Marys River, they would take divergent courses for Georgian Bay, Lake Huron or Lake Erie, converting centers where their cargoes would be processed into countless bags of flour, later to be converted into incalculable thousands of loaves of bread.

Upbound on November 7 were a variety of big boats, from the conventional ore carriers to package freighters, canallers and the big Canadian passenger and freight vessels, among them the *Sarnian, Huronic* and *Hamonic.* Some of the bulk carriers were light, sacrificing upbound cargoes for speed in transit and faster turn-around time to concentrate on iron ore tonnage. Others, with coal cargoes based on seasonal contractural commitments, slogged northward at a reduced pace, accepting their lot as the inevitable consequences of shore-side business arrangements that provided two-way-pay compensation for their owners. Many vessels would, as a matter of course, return with ore, but some, again at the whims of the mercantile gods ashore, would be shunted under the spouts of the big gray elevators to load grain. With luck, there was the possibility of three or four more trips before the inevitable fall gales disrupted schedules, freezing temperatures froze the ore in the hopper cars and, finally, ice forced the closing of the locks at the Soo.

Lake Superior is typical of all the Great Lakes in that it covers such a large geographic area that weather conditions in one locale do not necessarily prevail in others. At Duluth on Thursday small-craft warnings had been flying since early morning, the result of brisk, cool winds from the southwest. Once beyond the blunting effect of the steep hills behind the city, however, the winds had built up considerable seas that marched up the "gut" between Isle Royale and the mainland and grew in stature with the passing hours. At the other end of Lake Superior, the St. Marys River country, the weather was sublime and entirely unseasonable as Jawanin-odin, the South Wind of the Chippewas, reigned supreme. All the way up the winding channels from DeTour the steamer *E. H. Utley* and her crew had enjoyed bright sunshine and eighty degree temperatures. "It was just like summer," recalls William M. Ward,[1] one of her wheelsmen. "We had loaded coal at Lorain and were headed for Superior. The weather was splendid all the way up Lake Huron. Some of the lads even took off their shirts to get one more good dose of sunshine."

Late on Thursday afternoon the *Utley,* operated by the Franklin Steam Ship Company, locked through the Soo and steamed into the broadening upbound track. At eight o'clock in a flat calm, she was abreast of Point Iroquois with Gros Cap Light winking at her from starboard. At eight o'clock, too, a pair of shipmasters, quite by happenstance, chanced to be in the office of a grain elevator complex in Fort William. Both, in making the trek from their vessels to the dock office in cool and gusty winds, had accumulated considerable grain dust and chaff on their uniform jackets. One was Captain S. A. Lyons of the steamer *J. H. Sheadle* of the Cleveland-Cliffs Iron Company. The other was Captain William H. Wright, skipper of the spanking-new Canadian steamer *James Carruthers* which, on the previous trip, had set a new cargo record for carrying flax. The *Carruthers,* launched in May and thereafter subject to fitting-out and sea trials, was on her third trip, loading 375,000 bushels of wheat. Captain Wright, obviously proud of commanding the newest and largest Canadian vessel, accepted Captain Lyons' congratulations, commenting: "We've still to learn all of her tricks, and the

[1] Captain William M. Ward, the *E. H. Utley*'s wheelsman during those terrifying hours on Lake Superior, got his mate's license in 1914, became a captain in 1926 and sailed until 1955, his last assignment being that of skipper of the big *Arthur M. Anderson* of the Pittsburgh Steamship Division of United States Steel.

lads in the fo'c'sle are complaining that the paint in their rooms is still a little sticky."

Although both skippers had planned to leave their docks about the same time, the *Carruthers* was apparently delayed for an hour or two. When Captain Lyons got the *Sheadle* outside Thunder Cape, he found that the southwest wind had kicked up quite a sea—a bit more, in fact, than he expected or cared for. He turned his boat and steamed back to the shelter of Pie Island, dropping his starboard anchor at ten o'clock. A 3:30 A.M. on Friday, the 7th, after the wind had modified somewhat, the *Sheadle* hove anchor and proceeded on her way. The *Carruthers*, meanwhile, had departed her elevator berth, clearing Thunder Bay on the Passage Island course even as the *Sheadle* was hoisting her anchor to do likewise.

At ten o'clock on the morning of Friday, November 7, upon telegraphic orders from Washington, H. W. Richardson of the Duluth office of the United States Weather Bureau sent storm signals fluttering aloft. Elsewhere, at the Soo, Whitefish Point and at harbors along the south shore—Grand Marais, Munising, Marquette, Houghton and Ashland—the same, ominous precursors of a southwest storm were sent upward into a gray tattered sky—a square red flag with a black center over a white pennant. But the warning was too late for many vessels already at sea in diligent pursuit of their commercial duties. Indeed, it is questionable whether or not many shipmasters would have paid heed. Storm warnings in November were not a rarity and the Weather Bureau people were frequently critical of the seemingly casual, even hostile disregard of their warnings. Nevertheless, a few cautious mariners, still in port or where the signals were visible, did give credence to the grim advice and either stayed in port or sought the nearest sheltered anchorage.

The steamer *L. C. Waldo,* John Duddleson master, had

departed Two Harbors with a cargo of iron ore two hours before the storm signal was raised. Downbound, too, was the whaleback steamer *Alexander McDougall*, with Captain F. D. Selee in command. Ahead of them the grain-laden *William Nottingham*, angling down from Fort William, was making good time in what was still relatively normal weather for the season. At the opposite end of Lake Superior, most of them unaware of what was in the offing, ships and their crews were savoring what the old-timers would call "most unusual weather." The *E. H. Utley*, Captain Edward Fitch master, found Lake Superior still in a benevolent mood early Friday—warm and misty with mild temperatures and light winds still prevailing.

When the *Alva C. Dinkey* passed upbound through the Soo locks at 11:00 A.M. on Friday, the southwest storm warnings had been hoisted by the Weather Bureau man, Alexander G. Burns. They were still there at two-thirty that afternoon when the *Cornell* passed up. Both were Pittsburgh Steamship Company boats, upbound light for iron ore. The same southwest storm warnings were visible when they crawled past Whitefish Point some hours later. But again, storm signals in November were pretty much routine and were customarily given little notice other than a notation in the ship's log.

Late in the afternoon the advance of the storm made itself felt in areas previously free of disagreeable conditions. By six o'clock the *Utley* was rolling so heavily that the crew ate standing up after the weather racks on the mess table failed to contain the dishes. At midnight Captain Fitch, watching his steering pole repeatedly dipping into the crest of oncoming seas, ordered all hands out to tighten and check hatch clamps. The captain himself took the wheel, sending wheelsman Ward and the mates down on deck to help. He found, too, that he had to keep the telegraph "full ahead" to maintain steerageway and keep his boat from falling off into the troughs of the seas.

Wheelsman Ward still remembers those hours spent tightening hatch clamps with painful clarity. "The seas came aboard, every one of them, soaking us good and so powerful that one of the lads was detailed to watch for them and sound a warning so we could find something to grab. It had begun to snow and such snow as we had never experienced, so heavy and thick that if you opened your mouth, it was like getting a big bite of cold mush. The noise was something terrible as the seas climbed right over us. And the effect of the seas and driving snow was such that although our whistle was sounding continuously, we couldn't hear it on deck."

Although Captain Fitch did not mention the fact until later, while he was alone at the wheel about midnight, a long vessel slid silently across the *Utley's* bow. He could see her lights faintly through the fitful, driving snow and could see the steam blasts from her whistle although the sound was inaudible. The two boats missed a fatal collision only by a few yards. "There just wasn't anything I could do but watch," Captain Fitch told Ward later. "Never did find out who she was, or if she sighted us. All I could do was stand there, hang onto the wheel and pray that we'd miss."

But as bad as the deteriorating situation was, the worst was still to come. It happened about three o'clock on the morning of Saturday, November 8. The southwest storm, furious as it was, swung quickly to northwest, blew with extreme intensity for a couple of hours, and then, with diabolical swiftness, veered directly into the north and with such ferocity that it made winds in the earlier hours of the storm seem like tropical zephyrs. And with the shift of wind and seas that rolled like black mountains came the snow—snow like no shipmaster could ever recall. It came driving like a blanket of cotton with such force that a sailor venturing out on the bridge wing could not open his eyes or mouth. With stinging force it quickly built up to four or five inches on pilothouse windows, hardened there by the freezing spray booming up over the bow. For with the abrupt change in weather had come an ominous, paralyzing drop in temperature. Railings and grab rails quickly grew foot-long whiskers of ice as masts, shrouds, ventilators, lifeboats, davits and all deck fixtures assumed grotesque and unreal shapes beneath the coating of ice that grew with every sea and spray that shot as high as the mast tops. Under such conditions the *Utley, Turret Chief, George Stephenson, F. G. Hartwell, Cornell, J. T. Hutchinson, Peter White, A. E. Stewart, Hydrus, Maricopa, Huronic, Saronic, Sarnian, B. G. Berry* and the *Henry Cort* struggled on, along with the two vessels whose masters had exchanged greetings and small talk in the Fort William elevator office, the *James Carruthers* and the *J. H. Sheadle.* Many boats, large and small, light or loaded, were caught unprepared when the storm shifted rapidly from southwest to northwest and finally to the north. Those that could alter course beat a frantic retreat for shelter—behind Whitefish Point, the Lily Pond in Portage Bay or around the hook of Keweenaw Point where Bête Grise Bay offered protected anchorage and good holding ground. But these havens of refuge were denied to many shipmasters because of distance and the fact that the seas were of such malignant proportions that a loaded vessel would have been quickly overwhelmed had she attempted to turn and thus necessarily expose herself to the trough of the seas. So, having really no alternative, they plugged on, along the north shore and the south shore, with many masters, and for good reason, not quite sure just where they were. For shipmasters of that era, without the miracles of radar, automatic direction finders or ship-to-shore radio-telephone, had the barest necessities to guide them. They had only the glimpses of buoys or beacons to identify landmarks, the taffrail logs to register distance, clocks to tell them steaming time and magnetic compasses to steer by. The savage snow, in unremitting violence, had long since rendered beacons or buoys useless; the taffrail logs had been early victims as the lines that trailed them astern grew to the thickness of a man's leg before snapping under the weight of ice; magnetic compasses were somewhat unreliable in a country where fantastic iron deposits along the shore caused needles to vary and waver spasmodically. The ship-master, then, had only his own familiarity with the lake and an intuitive sense of direction and superb seamanship to bring his vessel home safely. But the malevolent forces afoot on Lake Superior that night were of such magnitude that most captains could not judge the distance they were being driven off course, could only wait until some visual evidence presented itself, hopefully at daylight. But dawn brought no relief to most of them. The snow came driving on as relentlessly as ever, limiting visibility to an arm's length, while the ice kept building and the gray seas heaved like mountains and came in dark packs, only the advance guard visible through the snow. For another twenty-four hours many vessels could do naught but roughly calculate how far off course they had been driven, and when they instinctively felt an unfriendly shore was near, haul around again and head into the driving seas and snow. In their zigzag maneuvering some actually steamed the equivalent of two trips the length of the lake!

Out there somewhere near the *Utley* was the black-hulled steamer *Peter White,* another Cleveland Cliffs Iron Company boat, without cargo and en route to Marquette for ore, clearing the Soo at 5:00 P.M. on Friday. In command was Captain James Kennedy, who registered extreme displeasure when the wind shifted to the north at 3:00 A.M. and blew like the furies of hell. With it came the same smothering, all-encompassing snow, driven in impenetrable and lashing curtains. Captain Kennedy could do little but head his vessel north, watching the steering pole vanish into something dark and emerge a-lather, meeting the enemy head on. But the seas became so high that the propeller broke water as each one slipped astern, causing the engine to race. This required the chief engineer to stand his post at the throttle, slowing down the propeller as the valleys between the seas swept under the fantail. This maneuver, while highly successful in saving the engine undue strain, so slowed the speed of the *Peter White* that the next sea would throw her bow five or six compass points off the course. Then Captain Kennedy would order "hard starboard" to bring the steamer completely around to again meet the asault head on. During the turning periods, the seas struck so heavily and the vessel's hull worked so excessively that many of the heavy wooden hatch covers dropped into the cargo hold. For nearly thirty hours, her crew sleepless, the *Peter White* took the worst of what Lake Superior had to dish out, rolling and pitching outrageously as she turned time and again to face the seas. When the snowstorm appeared to be ending at six o'clock Sunday morning, Captain Kennedy, with some skepticism but at the repeated suggestion of second mate Milton J. Brown, headed his boat for the narrow passage between the Pictured Rocks and Grand Island, there, hopefully, to anchor in safety in the lee of Trout Point until the storm had blown itself out. But just as the steamer approached the narrowest, most dangerous phase of the passage and too late to retreat, the snow came again with a venegeance, thick and blinding. Exhausted, hollow-eyed and overwrought from the ordeal, the captain, in utter frustration, threw his hat on the pilothouse floor and jumped up and down on it, expressing vexation at second mate Brown for urging the Grand Island course. "Now," he roared, "you've made me lose my boat."

Seconds later, as suddenly as it began, the snow stopped. The *Peter White*, miraculously, was still headed in on the range lights, in perfect alignment.

Very late that afternoon while the steamer lay at rest in quiet waters, the now contrite captain summoned Brown, who had gone aft for coffee. "See if you can hear it too," said Kennedy. "I'm sure I heard a vessel blowing distress signals."

"You must be hearing things," Brown replied. "Nobody in their right mind would go out in this weather."

The steamer *George Stephenson,* upbound, light, had been caught in the same shift of wind to the north that had given Captain Kennedy many anxious and vexatious hours. The *Stephenson,* although she had full ballast tanks and some water in her cargo holds, continually fell off into the trough of the seas. Her captain, A. C. Mosher, finally turned and headed east again. He was most fervent in his desire to reach the shelter of Keweenaw Point, but he wanted to do so in daylight, and the retracing of his course for a couple of hours would kill time until dawn, and hopefully a cessation of the heavy snow. At eight o'clock on the morning of the 8th a moderation in the seas seemed to indicate that the full force of the gale was being blunted by long-sought Keweenaw Point, although the snow prevented Captain Mosher from seeing anything beyond the steering pole. Continued moderation of the seas and a sounding that showed forty-two fathoms with clay bottom convinced him that they were safely behind the Point. Thankfully he ordered the anchors dropped at 10:00 A.M. in twelve fathoms of smooth water. The driving snow continued the balance of the day and some concern was expressed about the possibility of another storm-driven vessel charging into the sheltered anchorage and cutting them down. It was nearly midnight when Captain Mosher lay down to catch forty winks. At daylight he was awakened by the mate, who reported a steamer ashore on nearby Gull Rock, on the westerly tip of Manitou Island. She appeared to be abandoned, since she was showing no lights and no smoke came from her stack. The absence of smoke became understandable as the light improved. The wrecked vessel's hull was broken, the after end angling downward so that the thirty-foot seas that murderously mauled her had left only shells of her after cabins. The bow and forward houses looked like an iceberg. But there was life aboard her! At 7:00 A.M. the men on the *Stephenson* saw a distress signal crawl upward on her foremast. They hoisted one in response.

To take his own vessel to the assistance of the unknown steamer was a course Captain Mosher could not consider. The exposed area where the wreck lay, relentlessly combed by thundering big seas, would mean the certain loss of the *Stephenson,* without cargo, high out of the water and thus easy prey of the winds. Captain Mosher, therefore, hove anchor and steamed into Bete Grise where the mate went ashore in a lifeboat with instructions to send word to the Eagle Harbor Life Saving Station, on the far side of Keweenaw Point, over thirty miles from the wreck site. It blew hard and snowed again all the afternoon and evening of Sunday, November 9, with the *Stephenson,* of necessity, keeping to her snug anchorage in Bete Grise Bay. On Monday morning Captain Mosher sent the second mate ashore in the boat to get definite word on whether or not the stranded sailors had been rescued and, if not, to notify the Portage Lake Ship Canal Life Saving Station. The Eagle Harbor lifesavers, the mate reported, had made an attempt to round Keweenaw Point but had been driven back. The Portage Lake Ship Canal Station, eighty miles away, he learned, had not been notified of the wreck but would start out immediately. The snow came again, however, and Captain Mosher was never

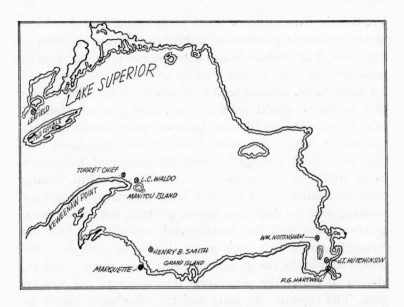

quite sure whether the lifesavers had reached the wreck.
That night, when the wind and seas went down and the
snow was succeeded by a clear sky and bright moon, he
ordered the anchors hove up and continued his voyage. At
eleven o'clock, as the *Stephenson* steamed out between Keweenaw Point and Manitou Island, he could see the battered steamer, a ghostly, white-rimed outline against the
rocks and trees.

The hulk that lay awash in the moonlight was the *L. C.
Waldo*, which Captain John Duddleson had taken so con-
fidently out of Two Harbors on Friday morning. By ten
o'clock that night his boat was being swept from astern by
the biggest seas Captain Duddleson had ever encountered.
They stripped tarpaulins from the hatch covers, battered in
the fo'c'sle bulkheads and climbed over the after cabins with
fearful regularity. Captain Duddleson was trying desperately
to find his way around Keweenaw Point to take shelter in its

lee. But the heaviest snow in his memory and hail that hammered against the pilothouse like buckshot limited visibility to a few feet. The landmarks and lights that would guide him in good weather were lost in a white wilderness that stretched for many miles. Instinct kept him plotting a wavering course that he knew would have to carry him around Manitou Island before he could turn into the quiet waters that lay temptingly behind the point. Under the circumstances, narrow Gull Rock Passage between Manitou and Keweenaw Point would be out of the question. The dreadful, hissing combers a-building all the way from the north shore kept running over the ship from astern, pillaging her after cabins, playing havoc with her hatches and exploding against the forward houses with such gusto that spray shot over the masthead. Finally the grandfather of all seas came rollicking aboard to batter the pilothouse into splinters and broken glass. The captain, the mate and the wheelsman barely escaped with their lives by diving down the companionway into the captain's bedroom, already partially demolished by previous seas. Then, in what must have been one of the most terrible journeys in Great Lakes history, the captain and mate battled their way aft to the emergency steering apparatus, the mate holding a small compass and lantern while Captain Duddleson fought the wheel, still navigating mostly by instinct.

Down in the engine room the men were sore beset with problems of their own. The propeller was out of the water as often as it was buried under the overtaking seas and had to be throttled down after the crest of each sea climbed over the fantail. At 3:00 A.M. the rudder was torn away and there was nothing more they could do. Completely at the mercy of the gale now, the *Waldo* was driven on in darkness and the merciless snow. An hour later it came, first a sudden jolt and then, successively, several others as the following seas lifted the hull and drove her further on Gull Rock. Now the after cabins, battered and plundered by every sea, were untenable. The men began their perilous march to the forward cabins, carrying the two women in the galley crew, Mrs. Rice and Mrs. Mackie, both of whom were paralyzed by fear. To release one's grasp on the wire cable railings would have meant certain death. Slowly, smothered every minute by the icy seas, they inched their way forward. Finally the entire crew of twenty-nine were safe in the only dry place on the *Waldo*, the windlass room, but the entire bow was being pounded heavily and they fully expected this lone haven of refuge to disintegrate at any moment. The hull had already broken in two and the after end sagged lower and lower, the break also precluding any possibility of obtaining food from the galley, providing the seas had left any. On his way forward as the engine room flooded and sank deeper, engineer Al Hacke passed through the ravaged galley, scooping up two one-gallons cans of what he assumed to be vegetables.

In the frigid tomb of the windlass room the people of *Waldo* huddled, cold and wet. The forward crew's bathtub was finally wrenched from its moorings and in this they built a small fire. And to keep it burning they sacked the forward end of everything combustible, paneling from the captain's quarters, furniture from his office, bunks from the crew's rooms, even the wooden frames from around the station-bill instruction sheet. The fire kept them alive, but the smoke almost blinded them. And still the cold persisted, frost building up on the bulkheads, and outside the ice grew a foot thick. All the while it was like living in a bass drum as the seas hammered away like an insane musician pounding out a macabre and never-ending dirge. The two tins of what the engineer had assumed to be vegetables were opened by the famished sailors. The first can did indeed prove to be green peas, but the second yielded peaches in heavy syrup. Half starved, chilled to the bone, their eyes red and sore from the smoke, the *Waldo's* people lived in their ghastly metal tomb for nearly ninety hours before both the Eagle Harbor and Portage Ship Canal lifesavers arrived, under the escort of the tug *Daniel L. Hebard*. The *Hebard* could not approach the wreck, but stood off while the lifesavers ran in close to pluck the grateful crew from the wreck.

Miraculously, plotting by dead reckoning, pure instinct, experience and courage, Captain Duddleson had come within a couple of hundred yards of reaching and passing through Gull Rock Passage into the safe waters in the lee of Keweenaw Point!

Unknown to the wretched souls marooned in the *Waldo's* windlass room, they had company nearby on Keweenaw Point. But under the circumstances, they were not likely to come calling.

The *Turret Chief,* owned by the Canadian Lake and Ocean Navigation Company, and managed by the Merchants' Mutual Line, rammed ashore on Keweenaw Point five miles east of Copper Harbor, not far from the *L. C. Waldo's* bed of rocks.

Her arrival there, unlike the superior seamanship that brought Captain Duddleson almost to his goal, was the result of an atrocious bit of navigation, so inept that the *Turret Chief's* skipper, Tom Paddington, was later severely censured for his lack of seamanship by the Dominion Wreck Commissioner. There were no storm signals flying from Whitefish Point when the *Turret Chief* passed at 10:00 A.M. on Friday morning, nor had there been any exhibited at the Soo, according to Captain Paddington and second mate William Bowman. All the ship's officers were in agreement that the abrupt change in weather came at nine o'clock that night as the boat was on her normal course for Passage Island and Fort William, shifting rapidly from southwest to north. The barometer, according to the captain, gave no indication of a change. The *Turret Chief* was being steered by compass although her master admitted that they had not been adjusted during the current year and were out about one-half point. Built in England, the *Turret Chief* was 257 feet long and was in all respects in good order at the time she departed her dock at Midland, Ontario, after unloading grain.

The seas, testified Captain Paddington, were of such a nature that they broke open the door of the lower pilothouse and burst the steam pipes. With them came the terrible snow—so heavy that the vessel's own stern lights could not be seen. Nor, over the tumult of the gale, could any signals or bells be heard. The wind literally spun the *Turret Chief* around several times while frozen scud hammered for attention against the cabins. From her normal speed of ten miles per hour the boat was practically stopped in her tracks by the monstrous seas she attempted to meet head-on.

Captain Paddington, by his own admission, hadn't the slightest idea where his vessel was after being in the storm for a couple of hours. He knew only that the wind and seas were taking him south. When asked why they didn't put the vessel on an easterly course, where plenty of water prevailed and where there would be little danger of running ashore, both Captain Paddington and first mate Joseph Phillips merely shrugged their shoulders.

As it chanced, the *Turret Chief* had been carried by the force of the wind and the driving seas about a hundred miles from the captain's estimate of his probable position. And when she "went on" at 4:00 A.M. on Saturday, rumbling over two reefs and sticking her bow practically out of the water into a nest of boulders, it was no problem at all to put a line over the bow and step over the rocks to dry land, which the crew hastily did. Once ashore in a grim and inhospitable wilderness, they built a shelter of tree limbs. But unlike the unfortunate souls nearby on the *L. C. Waldo*, there was no shortage of food, for the *Turret Chief*'s galley was nearby and readily accessible. For three days they lived in their makeshift shelter as the interminable snow blew and drifted. The *Turret Chief* was burdened by an estimated fifteen hundred tons of ice by Monday when the crew left to walk to Copper Harbor.

Far to the east, only an hour's steaming time from safety behind the sheltering hook of Whitefish Point, the *William Nottingham*, with 300,000 bushels of grain in her holds, had come a cropper. Within a couple of hours after her departure from Fort William the *Nottingham* had been hammered, first by the strong southwest winds and later, when they shifted to northerly, she had been boarded rudely and regularly by overtaking seas from astern—a merciless picket line of advancing hordes. Several times the long boat had been hauled around to face the gale, barely maintaining steerageway although her engine was at full throttle ahead. For seemingly endless hours she remained at bay, laboring mightily but going nowhere. Probably she would have continued to face the enemy had circumstances permitted. However, the long struggle had made outrageous inroads on her fuel supply, the last few tons of coal scarcely covering the bottom of her bunkers. Her captain, obviously alarmed, hauled around again and fled before the tempest, hopeful of getting in the lee of Whitefish Point. But the coal situation was even more serious than he had anticipated or understood. In what could only be a decision born of utter desperation, he ordered the crew to strip off the tarpaulins and open the aftermost hatch. Then, forming a bucket brigade, they began shuttling the wheat cargo into the fuel bunkers. Wheat burns briskly, the captain knew, and a few hundred bushels might mean the difference between shipwreck and a sheltered anchorage. The wheat did indeed inspire the steam gauge dials to register approval, but it was too late. Shortly after 7:00 A.M. she bumped hard on rocky bottom and fetched up on Parisienne Shoal, there to be assaulted relentlessly by each smoking sea that came romping down from the north, each booming over her fantail and spar deck. Both lifeboats were splintered and carried away within minutes of the grounding. The life expectancy of the *William Nottingham*, being exposed to wind and sea from every direction, was not great. This fact inspired three of the crew—watchman John Karp, oiler William Best, and deck hand J. F. Thorburn—to launch a yawl boat in an attempt to reach the mainland and summon help. But the yawl boat was quickly smashed against the steamer's hull and the three volunteers were lost. Not until the weather moderated several days later were wrecking tugs and lighter able to moor alongside. So badly was the *Nottingham* mauled, her side tanks and holds open to the sea, that speed was of the essence in refloating her before bad weather struck again. Most of the grain was dumped overboard. Even so, the weather deteriorated again. In the face of rising wind and seas the revenue service steamer *Tuscarora* went alongside at considerable peril to herself to take off fourteen men and a woman cook. The captain, two engineers and one fireman stuck to the *Nottingham* until she was later released.

Two shipmasters, concurring in the old adage that caution is the better part of valor, anchored at Point Iroquois, near the junction of the upper St. Marys River and Whitefish Bay. The *Fred G. Hartwell* of the Tomlinson fleet dropped her hooks one mile east of the point; the *John T. Hutchinson* of the Pioneer Steamship Company did likewise one mile west of the Point. Neither master could have anticipated the shift of wind from southwest to north, nor could they have predicted the unprecedented force of the gale that soon after reached a shrieking crescendo. Both vessels dragged anchor, struck the rocky bottom and sank in shallow water, there to lie helpless while being punished by the seas.

In Whitefish Bay itself the Northern Navigation Company's passenger vessel *Huronic* was aground on a sandbar, one of the few soft spots in Lake Superior. Near her was the big *A. E. Stewart,* "on the ground" but resting easily. At the Soo, Captain Frank Root of the Great Lakes Towing Company went aboard the revenue cutter *Mackinac* to visit the *Hartwell* and *Hutchinson,* salvage work on both of which would accrue to his company. Outbound the *Mackinac* encountered a tug that had spoken both vessels, ascertaining that all hands were safe, but that the *Hutchinson* was short of food. The cutter turned at once to return to the Soo for one thousand pounds of supplies, a task much simpler than transferring them to the stranded steamer, still being swept regularly by the big graybeards a-building all the way from Michipicoten Harbor. Finally the *Hutchinson*'s hungry crew steamed tons of ice from a lifeboat, lowered it and, in the modest lee offered by their vessel's stern, took aboard the food.

The cutter *Tuscarora,* meanwhile, had received word that the wooden steamer *Major* had been so badly abused by the storm that her crew had abandoned her thirty miles from Whitefish Point, preferring to take their chances with the giant seas rather than stay aboard the badly leaking ship.

The whaleback steamer *Alexander McDougall* of the Pittsburgh Steamship Company, with precious little freeboard when she was loaded, had come almost the length of Lake Superior practically submerged with the big, billowing hills stalking her. Each and every sea climbed aboard from astern, sweeping the length of the hull and engulfing the turrets that supported her accommodations above water. Captain F. D. Selee was most anxious to find Whitefish Point and snuggle up to its lee shore. But visibility was never more than a couple of hundred yards, usually only a few feet. The direction of the wind and snow precluded seeing the Point itself or hearing the whistle which sounded in storm and fog. The submarine bell on the buoy anchored offshore was another matter. While the first mate tied himself to the starboard bridge wing and kept the deep sea sounding lead going, the second mate and a wheelsman were concentrating on picking up the sound of the bell. They heard it, finally, and when it came abreast of them, Captain Selee swung the *Mc-Dougall* around the rocky point and into quiet waters without ever having a glimpse of land.

Another Pittsburgh Steamship Company whaleback, the *Henry Cort*, had her own troubles coming down Lake Superior with a cargo of iron ore. Like the *McDougall,* she was practically submerged with each overtaking sea. They plucked away her running lights, stripped off her port rail and even claimed her headlight, mounted high on the foremast. She finally staggered into temporary anchorage at the Soo so badly iced up that she appeared to be an apparition vaguely resembling a confection made to look like a vessel but with an overabundance of meringue. Her first assistant engineer, Gordon Rattray, was so pleased by the *Cort's* behavior under extreme duress that he wrote home to his mother, humorously chiding his brother Earl, second assistant engineer on the *Cornell,* another Pittsburgh Steamship boat that had started up Lake Superior, light, on Friday afternoon. The catastrophic shift of wind from southwest to north, accompained by the wind and snow of incredible force, had struck the *Cornell* at 2:00 A.M. on Saturday, when she was ninety miles above Whitefish Point. The first mate, in the pilothouse with Captain John Noble, suddenly became ill. To ease the task of getting the mate down to his cabin and to bed, Captain Noble turned the *Cornell* before the wind. But when the emergency was over, he could not get her turned around again. She wallowed in the troughs of thirty-foot seas for thirteen agonizing hours, rolling outrageously and setting everything in the galley and her cabins adrift. By late Saturday the *Cornell* had been driven broadside to within a mile and a half of the beach, near the Deer Park Life Saving Station. To get around and head-to in the seas, both anchors were dropped and the engine worked full speed ahead, while crewmen poured oil out of her hawsepipes. When they finally got her turned, she was even closer to the beach, with only eight fathoms of water under the keel. For another twenty-four hours the *Cornell* lay tethered to the bottom, every minute of it with her engine still working full ahead. Late Sunday, Captain Noble seemed to detect a moderation in the weather, at which time he ordered the anchors hove up and steamed away from the beach, steering north by east. At 10:00 P.M. the gale returned with renewed fury, once more trapping the vessel in the troughs of the seas. Somewhere east and south of Caribou Island, Captain Noble had an anchor dropped again and once more got her headed into the seas. At five o'clock Monday morning a monstrous sea thundered aboard over the fantail, breaking off all the overhang of her after cabin, smashing all the doors and flooding the dining room, galley and crew's quarters. Now, once more, the *Cornell* wallowed in the troughs. The other anchor was dropped and held long enough to get the vessel heading back into the seas before the "wildcat" on the windlass broke, dropping the chain into the lake. But again the *Cornell* was perilously near the beach, this time off Crisp Point, where she lay pounding until Monday afternoon, when the remaining anchor was hove and a new course set. Again she quickly fell off into the terrible valleys between the seas, and the anchor went down in ten fathoms of water, the engine once more working full ahead to bring her around and into the marching seas. Finally, at 10:00 P.M. on Monday the wind subsided enough for a grateful Captain Noble to steam seaward, away from that clawing, threatening shore.

Earl Rattray, brother of the *Henry Cort*'s Gordon, also wrote his mother:

We were seventy-two hours without sleep, expecting each hour to be her last. Toward the last we were so tired we began to feel as though we wished she would go . . . everything is a wreck . . . when the house went in Jack Kittell, the first assistant, said "goodbye, kiddies," . . . he has a boy 10 and a girl 6. . . . He was thinking of them . . . We've got our smokestack but that's about all.

Broken and beaten, the *Cornell*, still without cargo, returned to Lake Erie for extensive repairs.

At the Soo and Fort William considerable apprehension was being expressed over the whereabouts of the sturdy steamer *Leafield*, a fear heightened by the fact that two of her sister ships of the Algoma Central Steamship fleet had already experienced disaster on the same routine course to Fort William from the Canadian Soo. The *Leafield*, the superstitious concluded, was predestined to follow them in calamity. Only the previous summer the *Leafield* had ripped her belly open on a shoal in Georgian Bay, putting her out of commission for two months and sticking her owners for heavy salvage and repair costs. "Sandy" McIntyre was her captain at the time, and since the stranding was considered a blundering bit of seamanship, he was not in command when she fitted out for the 1913 season. The owners, probably on the theory that a change would bring better luck to both vessel and skipper, transferred McIntyre to another boat, the *Thomas J. Drummond*. The *Leafield* was one of four vessels, three of them built in England, purchased by F. H. Clergue and brought to the Great Lakes to serve the needs of the Algoma Steel Corporation. The others were the *Theano, Paliki* and *Monkshaven*. Like the *Leafield*, they were originally built for salt-water tramp or coasting operations. On the lakes they carried iron ore to the Algoma Steel Corporation's mill at the Canadian Soo and the furnaces of the Canada Iron Corporation at Midland, Ontario. Often they loaded coal at Toledo for the Soo, and between coal and iron ore cargoes frequently carried grain from Fort William to Midland. Upbound from the Algoma mills, they usually hauled finished steel railroad rails. All were typical salt-water well-deck vessels that kept their cargoes low and in good order.

Strangely, however, the Algoma Central boats seemed to have developed an unhappy affinity for the islands that flank the entrance to Thunder Bay. First to go was the *Monkshaven*, upbound with railroad rails when she impaled herself and sank among the rocks of Pie Island in the wild late November storm of 1905. A year later it was the *Theano*, also with a cargo of rails, striking one of the reefs at Trowbridge Island, again in November. The *Paliki* still steamed on, but now it was November again and, God forbid, was the *Leafield* gone, too?

The *Leafield* had departed the Algoma Steel dock on Friday evening with her usual heavy cargo of railroad rails. The dock was above the Soo locks where storm warnings were flying, but it is doubtful whether Captain Charles Baker would have paid much heed in any event. Storm signals were the lot of the mariner late in the fall. If a master lingered in the shelter of a bay or in the lee of an island every time he observed such warnings, his record of tonnage carried for the year would not be conducive to employment the next season.

When she departed her dock, the *Leafield* had on board her usual crew of eighteen, including chief engineer Andy Kerr. The make-up of her crew graphically pointed up how a whole community can be affected by a vessel's fate through its officers' natural inclination to hire friends and fellow townspeople. By tradition the captain hires the navigational and deck people, the engineer assumes responsibility for employing his assistants and the black gang. Captain Baker had chosen Captain Alfred Northcott as first mate, Fred Begley as second mate and Eddie Whitesides as one of the wheels-

men. He had also hired Paul and Richard Sheffield as
stewards. Andy Kerr had taken on Tom Bowie as his first
assistant, and another friend, Charlie Brown, as one of the
firemen. All were from Collingwood, Ontario.

But where was the *Leafield?* The first word of her possible
fate was brought into Port Arthur on Monday afternoon
when the Northern Navigation Company's big passenger ship
Hamonic, sheathed in ice, made her dock. Captain R. D.
Foote reported to authorities that he had spotted the wreck
of a vessel he believed to be the *Leafield* up on the bluff face
of Angus Island, not far from Pie Island, where the *Monkshaven's* hull still hung awash. The second reported sighting
was by Captain W. C. Jordan of the steamer *Franz,* also of
the Algoma Central fleet. Captain Jordan, brother-in-law of
Fred Begley, the *Leafield's* second mate, said that the rail-laden
Leafield was about twenty miles ahead of him, upbound
on Sunday, but that the driving gale of snow had prevented a further sighting. The *Franz* had docked at Fort William, loaded grain and departed for the Soo without further
visual contact. It wasn't until his boat locked through at the
Soo, headed for Port McNicoll, Georgian Bay, that Captain
Jordan was informed by the marine manager of the Algoma
Central fleet of the probable loss of the *Leafield.* Captain
Foote's earlier report, as confirmed by his officers, inspired a
quick visit to Angus Island by a tug. It found nothing. The
wreck, as viewed from the *Hamonic,* was in a precarious position because of the steep bluff face of the rock island. It was
unanimously agreed that the seas that still roared over the
hulk when seen from the passenger ship, had swept the *Leafield* off the rock and that she had gone straight down. Captain
W. O. Zealand of the steamer *Plummer,* recalling a survey of the area he made prior to 1912, reported that the bottom, off Angus Island, was in one hundred and fifty-five
fathoms of water. Nevertheless, the Dominion authorities

sent Captain Marin and his tug *Arbutus* out to search for the *Leafield,* her people or her wreckage, with orders to cover thoroughly the areas around Angus Island, Pie Island, Thunder Cape and Isle Royale. Other tugs, out of Houghton, Michigan, cruised the south shore and Keweenaw Point for signs of wreckage, but without success. The *Arbutus* did recover and bring to port a broken uppermast with no identifying marks. In Fort William quite by chance, was the skipper of the *Thomas J. Drummond,* doughty Sandy McIntyre, the *Leafield*'s unlucky master of the previous season. After examining the mast section carefully, he stated flatly that it hadn't come from the missing steamer. Now, of the four vessels Mr. Clergue had brought from England, only the *Paliki* was left!

There was another mystery of Lake Superior in that terrible November of 1913, but the mystery was not in the loss of the big ore carrier *Henry B. Smith,* but rather why her master would take her out in that maelstrom of wind, snow and wracking big graybeards before she was made ready for sea. Many who saw her depart concluded almost at once that she would be lost. Even before she was out of sight, dark and ugly rumors began making the rounds of docks and waterfront sailors' haunts—that the captain had suffered a mental breakdown, that he had been ordered by the owners to sail "or else," that he had been drinking heavily all day. Another tale in rapid circulation was that he was so helpless from drink that he required help from two dark, swarthy men to board his vessel, and this even as the last "pocket" of ore went rumbling into the *Smith*'s holds.

But perhaps the true answer to the mystery was reflected in the insidious pressures brought to bear by owners to whom only cargoes and their sum total at the end of the season justified the existence of the boats, the captains and the crews. Many owners piously issued orders to take no chances, but still judged the man and his opportunity for advancement on the basis of trips completed and tonnage carried. Long after the season was finished and the storms forgotten, the judgment was made, too often by men who had never sailed but spent their days in warm, safe buildings where the weather was always good and statistics prevailed. It was this lack of personal experience, many skippers hotly contended, that led to so many losses. Bonuses for skippers making the most trips was another incentive for taking chances, even during hazardous periods of the season.

What pressures, real or imagined, or what orders, real or unspoken, inspired Captain Jimmy Owen to take his big 565-foot steamer out of Marquette harbor when every other shipmaster on the lake was either in a harbor or steaming frantically for shelter?

Captain Owen had brought the *Henry B. Smith* into Marquette on Friday morning on a trip from Milwaukee where he had unloaded a cargo of coal taken on at Lorain. The *Smith* was actually under the loading chutes of the Duluth, South Shore & Atlantic Railroad dock Friday evening, but the extremely cold weather had resulted in frozen ore in the hopper cars, greatly slowing the process of dumping them. Storm warnings had been posted Friday afternoon. The Marquette *Daily Mining Journal* gave some indication of what was to be expected in its Saturday edition:

> Sou'wester Coming! Marquette and the entire Upper Peninsula will today be swept by one of the most severe storms expected this year, according to the weather bureau. Storm warnings were displayed yesterday afternoon. The wind is to come from the southwest accompanied by rain and followed with snow.

When the storm struck, earlier than expected on Saturday morning, its intensity was such that all loading was suspended and the dock men sent home. To Captain Owen the turn of events was viewed as just another in a long and unfortunate series of troubles that had plagued him all season—things for which, since they affected the efficiency of his boat, his owners had chided him repeatedly. He had frequently had the ill luck to arrive at lower lake ports when three or four other boats were ahead of him at the unloading rigs, resulting in delays of three or four days. On other occasions there had been mechanical breakdowns at the docks. Then, too, through no fault of his own, he had frequently had the misfortune to arrive at or be in congested passageways when fog compelled the *Smith* and other vessels to anchor for many hours. None of these quirks of fate were the fault of the captain personally, but the fact remained that the total time lost was the equivalent of several more trips. The *Smith* was far behind in the tonnage commitments her owners had contracted for and assigned to her, and since Jimmy Owen was captain, he got all the flak from the front office. Past performance obviously meant little, since Captain Owen had commanded the *Smith* from the day she was launched in 1906, and the fact that he was still her master indicated perfect satisfaction. Nevertheless, it had been a long, unlucky season and Jimmy Owen was worried. He had protested bitterly when the loading had been stopped on Saturday. That night, obviously under duress and in desperation, he had appealed personally to the Duluth, South Shore & Atlantic dock officials to put aside dock tradition and complete the loading of his vessel. The urgency of his manner and some knowledge of the pressures Captain Owen was under apparently moved the officials, for dock superintendent Harland was ordered to finish loading the *Smith* on Sunday.

In a brief visit to the dock office on Sunday morning, the captain told a dispatcher: "I will clear as soon as the ore is aboard. Wire the owners that I am coming!"

The *Henry B. Smith*'s owners were William A. and Arthur Harrison Hawgood of Cleveland, owners and operators of eight vessels, of which the *Smith* was the largest. It was no secret at any of the docks the *Smith* touched, or in any of the other boats in the fleet, that the Hawgoods were less than pleased with the *Smith*'s performance during the current season. And from some of the messages he had received when he arrived hours or days late, it was also abundantly apparent to Jimmy Owen.

Captain Owen's anticipation of an early departure was somewhat premature, however. The bitterly cold weather had caused much of the Cambria grade ore to freeze in the hopper cars, and each had to be thawed by small coal fires built beneath them along the dock approach. The slow pace did nothing for the captain's disposition. Nor did the fact that his second mate, James Burke, decided to call it a season, right there in Marquette. Mate Burke had not been well for several days, suffering from a heavy chest cold he feared was turning into pneumonia. He wanted nothing more than to be home under his wife's care as soon as possible. Early on Sunday afternoon he caught a train to the Soo, where he would make connections with other trains that would eventually take him to Cleveland.

It was just before five o'clock that Sunday afternoon when the *Smith* took aboard her last car of ore, an event signaled by first mate John Tait waving his arms vigorously to the crew high up on the dock. It was a time, too, for brisk work on the part of the deck crew. The *Smith* had thirty-two hatches to be closed, covered with tarpaulins and thoroughly battened down with locking bars and clamps, a couple of hours' work for even the most diligent crew. It was with amazement then that the dock people and others heard Captain Owen, just as he had earlier predicted in the dock office, give orders to cast off the lines. There was a muffled ringing of the telegraph, and, sure enough, the *Smith* backed away from the dock to get some clearance forward and then steamed slowly ahead, circling in the harbor. Captain Owen obviously intended to sail right out through the breakwater opening into the teeth of the worst gale the Marquette area had experienced within memory. And this with most of his vessel's hatches still open, the rest insecure, and under conditions that would surely make the deck untenable for any of the crew who sought to finish the task.

Sailors on the *Denmark* and *Choctaw*, moored nearby, watched without envy as they saw the *Smith*'s deck crew frantically trying to close hatches. Captain Charles Fox of the *Choctaw*, standing on the bridge of his boat, stared in disbelief when the outward-bound *Smith* passed by. He watched the first great seas break over her bow and cream up over the pilothouse, spewing tons of water aft where the luckless deck hands were trying valiantly to close the hatches. The *Smith* continued to steam directly out to sea for perhaps twenty minutes. Then suddenly, and Captain Fox could well understand the reason, instead of hauling to starboard on the course for the Soo, the *Smith* turned to port, rolling horribly as she fell into the troughs of the seas which romped ten feet over her spar deck. It had taken Captain Jimmy Owen only a few moments to become aware of his folly, and now he was steering what had to be a most desperate track for the shelter of Keweenaw Point, where a half dozen more prudent shipmasters were already at anchor, and where, nearby on Gull Rock, the people of the *L. C. Waldo* still despaired of rescue.

Other than second mate James Burke, there were two other people in Marquette who, by a twist of fate, were not aboard the rolling and pitching *Henry B. Smith*. They were Mr. and Mrs. F. O. Brown, former residents who had been visiting in Marquette for some time. They had hoped to return to Cleveland on the *Smith*, being friends of Captain Owen, but through negligence or design he had neglected to invite them. Despite the bravado he exhibited to the dock people, did Jimmy Owen have a premonition of disaster?

Another witness as the *Smith* swung to the west instead of taking the Soo track to the east was William Armstrong, a clerk at the D. S. S. & A. dock. After the paper work on the *Smith* had been completed, Armstrong and a friend took a trolley car to Presque Isle, drawn there along with other Marquette citizens to watch the tremendous seas explode over the breakwater. It was a spectacular sight. The most furious seas many of the witnesses could recall. Armstrong and his friend started home and got off the car at Baraga Avenue, end of the line, to walk up the short hill to Lakeside Park, overlooking the lake and harbor. The *Smith*, almost lost in the spray and spume, was still plugging into head seas. "We watched her turn," Armstrong recalls, "but it was getting dark, and since boats frequently turned north or west for a time to keep out of the trough of the seas, we thought nothing of it and went home."

The crew of the steamer *Frontenac*, two days later, were subjected to the grim sight of a dead sailor, supported by a life preserver, being driven shoreward from a point eleven miles east of Marquette. About the same time wreckage, apparently cabin finishings of a large steamer, began to drift ashore near the Lake Superior & Ishpeming dock at Marquette's Presque Isle. Fears for the *Smith*'s safety had already been freely expressed, since she had not yet locked down at the Soo nor had she been sighted by other vessels arriving from that direction. Captain Murphy of the *Frontenac* was quite eloquent in his assessment of Captain Owen. "If Captain Owen, after seeing that the sea was too strong for him, endeavored to seek shelter, he could turn to ports along the Keweenaw shore, which furnish perfect protection," said Murphy. "But then, a man who would have left port in a storm like that would do anything."

Even before the grim evidence began to drift ashore at Presque Isle and although they had no knowledge of events at Marquette or of Captain Owen's foolish decision, the men of the steamer *Peter White* were given a few clues. It was Captain Kennedy of the storm-racked *White,* now safely and thankfully anchored in the lee of Grand Island's Trout Point, who first spotted it—the same Captain Kennedy who had earlier querulously inquired of second mate Milton J. Brown if he, too, could hear a vessel's distress whistle, the sound of which Kennedy asserted he had heard several times. "No," Brown had replied. "You must be hearing things. Nobody in their right mind would go out in this weather."

There it was, however, all about them—bits of wreckage, odd pieces of wood painted white, cabins doors and a half dozen oars and pike poles. Later, Dan Johnson, brother of William Johnson, secretary of Marquette's City Water Board, while beachcombing along Chocolay Bay, Shot Point and Laughing Fish Point, east of the city, found considerable wreckage on the beach—part of a deckhouse painted white and four oars, three of which bore the stenciled name *"Henry B. Smith."*

In Cleveland, on Monday morning, Arthur Harrison Hawgood departed his Belleflower Road home as was his custom to take a streetcar to his office in the Perry Payne Building. The first indication that a major storm was upon the city was revealed when he looked out his bedroom window and became more apparent long before he reached his office. He immediately telephoned home to tell his daughter Aldythe not to attempt to go to school that day. Earlier, at breakfast, he had scoffed humorously when his wife Belle told him of a dream she had experienced during the night—a dream about a terrible storm in which a ship was lifted on the crest of a great wave and then disappeared. Arthur Harrison Hawgood was about to become a firm believer in dreams. At his desk

he went about the daily ritual of determining the whereabouts of all the Hawgood vessels, although he suspected
that the weather conditions, if they prevailed on the upper
lakes, would drastically alter the situation. The *H. B. Hawgood* was supposedly upbound light in Lake Huron. The
J. M. Jenks, downbound with grain, should be approaching
her destination of Midland, in Georgian Bay; the *Edwin F.
Holmes,* if all was well, was upbound light in the lower St.
Marys, probably near the Soo locks; the *Henry B. Smith,*
according to the telegram from Captain Owen, was loaded
with ore and downbound in Lake Superior. The others, the
S.S. Curry, Wisconsin, Umbria and *Bransford,* were elsewhere
on the lakes, each on a mission from which, God grant, they
would return safely with some margin of profit to William A.
Hawgood, Arthur Harrison Hawgood and other Hawgoods
associated with the firm.

Conditions in Cleveland, by noon on Monday, were most
deplorable. The heavy wet snow had brought down all lines
of communication and the city was an isolated, wintery oasis
in which each of its thousands of citizens waged his own
personal war with the elements. Streetcars were overwhelmed
by six-foot drifts and abandoned; inbound trains stalled
miles from the city, and in outlying areas interurban cars
bogged down, their passengers rescued by impromptu ex-
peditions utilizing skis and toboggans.

It was not until late Tuesday, when partial communication service, mostly wireless, was restored, that Mr. Hawgood was able to determine the whereabouts of some of his
vessels. The situation was exceedingly grim. The telegram
sent from the Marquette dock announcing the impending
departure of the *Henry B. Smith* was almost a mockery. Further communication with the ship reporters at the Soo confirmed the fact that the *Smith* had not yet put in an appearance. Later wires dispatched at once to north shore Lake

Superior ports seeking word of her brought only negative replies. Beyond that two other Hawgood boats were in trouble. The *H. B. Hawgood* was ashore at Weis Beach in lower Lake Huron and the grain-laden *J. M. Jenks* was on the beach near Midland, Ontario. The rest were as yet unreported, and Mr. Hawgood could only hope that they had found shelter or anchorage in a safe place. By now shipping men were becoming aware that the lakes had been visited by a storm of monumental proportions. Wires to shipping offices began to resemble the casualty tolls posted after a major naval engagement. Mr. Arthur Harrison Hawgood departed hastily for Sarnia, Ontario, to marshal salvage forces to free the *H. B. Hawgood* and the *J. M. Jenks*. But in another office William A. Hawgood and his staff began to receive word of wreckage of the *Henry B. Smith* drifting ashore. Captain Jimmy Owen's streak of bad luck had come to a cataclysmic and final end. From crew rosters and records of the Lake Carriers' Association hiring halls the list of those aboard the *Henry B. Smith* when she departed Marquette breakwall was published:

> James Owen, master, Geneva, Ohio
> John Tait, first mate, Kingston, Ontario
> James Burke, second mate, Cleveland, Ohio
> Ed Shipley, wheelsman, Deckerville, Michigan
> Charles Cattanach, wheelsman, Marine City, Michigan
> John Peterson, watchman, New York City
> William Shotwell, watchman, AuGres, Michigan
> Edward Whelan, deck hand, Duluth, Minnesota
> James McGee, deck hand, Cleveland, Ohio
> John Shire, deck hand, Lorain, Ohio
> John Cousins, deck hand, Cleveland, Ohio
> Joe Zink, boatswain, Corruna, Ontario
> Charles E. Rayburn, engineer, Eldred, Pa.
> John Gallagher, third engineer, Escanaba, Michigan
> John H. Olsen, oiler, Brooklyn, N.Y.

Christ Loefen, oiler, Cleveland, Ohio
Carl Hoppel, fireman, South Chicago, Ill.
Charles J. Nilsen, fireman, Cleveland, Ohio
Peter Costandakis, fireman, Cleveland, Ohio
Matt Maralick, fireman, Lorain, Ohio
Roy Kelly, fireman, Smithport, Pa.
Otto Becker, fireman, Buffalo, N.Y.
Rufus Judson, steward, Toledo, Ohio
H. R. Haskin, second cook, Sandusky, Ohio
Lawrence Perry, porter, Duluth, Minnesota
George Carey, second engineer

Word of second mate Burke's sudden decision to leave the vessel and return home to the care of his wife had obviously not been transmitted to the office of the owners, accounting for the discrepancy in including his name among those lost. Mr. Burke, delayed overly long in reaching his destination because the snow had disrupted all rail traffic, arrived home in Cleveland to find that his wife, overcome with grief after reading the list published in the Cleveland papers, had fled to her brother's home in Ashtabula for comfort and consolation.

The captain's wife, after spending long hours in the Hawgood offices waiting for word, finally returned to her home in Geneva when it became obvious that no hope remained.

In a bakery shop on Cleveland's Detroit Avenue, Mrs. Margaret Doran, sister of Captain Owen, had to go on selling fancy little coconut cookies while reiterating her praises for her lost brother.

"My brother laughed at danger," she sighed. "He laughed when he went into a storm and he laughed when he came out of it. Nothing was big enough to break down his great good nature and power to joke away difficulties. He was perfectly fearless. They say he went into this storm as he did into others, and I'm sure he was never frightened a moment at the end."

While it may be true that Captain Owen was indeed fearless, marine men doubted that he was doing much laughing after he left the shelter of Marquette harbor. More likely the last laugh was enjoyed by Kiwedininodin, the merciless Chippewa north wind that ruled Lake Superior that dreadful afternoon.

The inevitable message in a bottle that seems to be part and parcel of every sea disaster was found by a fisherman about a mile south of Coppermine Point Light, thirty-five miles above the Soo. He entrusted it to the master of the Dominion Line steamer *Caribou* who in turn gave it to the company's agent at the Soo. In substance the message said that the *Henry B. Smith* had broken in two at number five hatch, about twelve miles east of Marquette. The general feeling among marine authorities, despite the stated location which was contrary to the course the *Smith* was steering when last sighted, was that the message was authentic and that the *Smith* had broken up—the same theory that most of them had held from the moment the first wreckage came ashore.

Earlier in the storm, before the *Henry B. Smith* departed Marquette and before the weather gods had unleashed their full fury, a host of battered and iced-up vessels steamed thankfully into lakehead ports or the relatively safe sanctuary of the St. Marys River, near the Soo locks. The *Saronic* eased into the Canadian lock looking more like an iceberg than a boat. Behind her but in an American lock was the Pittsburgh Steamship Company's *Maricopa*, with Captain William Storey telling the lockmaster how the wind blew sixty miles an hour all the way down Lake Superior from Duluth, and how the pilothouse iced up so quickly and frequently that he had detailed a crew to steam away the accumulation so he

could see where he was going. Captain C. C. Balfour of the
B. F. Berry had to return to the Soo for anchors after losing
both while at anchor in Whitefish Bay. "We were laying under Whitefish Point when the wind took a turn to the northeast so quickly that before we could meet it, our chains
snapped," he related. Altogether, five other steamers lost
anchors while supposedly sheltered at Whitefish. The *James
A. Farrell* lost both anchors in spite of the fact that she was
steaming ahead to ease the strain. So did the *Sheldon Parks*
and Captain O. J. Soleau had no choice but to go aground,
or charge out into the lake and meet the wind and seas head
on. He chose the latter course. To entranced listeners as the
Sarnian was steaming off some of her one thousand tons of
ice, Captain Neil Campbell told about his five-day trip from
Port Arthur. "We left at midnight. My barometer was falling, but the wind had not sprung up yet. When I got around
Thunder Bay Cape, it began to blow from the southwest. I
saw my boat could not make it with the wind from that direction, so I went back behind the Cape. Five times I made the
effort to get out, but it took twenty-four hours before we
could make it. Then we got only as far as Jackfish, where we
laid under the bluffs until Friday night. I saw the lights of
Mission Point Saturday night, but was forced to find shelter
behind Michipicoten Island until Sunday morning."

The *Tagona* of the Merchants' Mutual Line staggered into
Fort William so heavily iced that the official ship reporter
was unable to identify her for some time. The *Assiniboia*,
sleek flagship of the Canadian Pacific Railway passenger fleet,
was nearly as bad with ice as high as her mast tops.

The *Alva C. Dinkey*, which had locked through at the Soo
two and one-half hours before the *Cornell*, also upbound
light, had easier going of it. Captain William J. Hunt had
just taken a bearing off Stannard Rock when the wind veered
suddenly to the north and began blowing a gale. Captain

Hunt turned his vessel into the wind, filled all her ballast tanks and pumped four feet of water into her cargo holds. He ran the *Dinkey* directly into the wind for twenty-three hours and then, fearing he was too close to the north shore, turned and ran before the wind for several hours before coming about once more. And by now, the wind having shifted again, he was steering north by east. The *Dinkey's* whistle was blowing continuously for twenty-five hours, but because of the wind and snow Captain Hunt did not hear it once. The *Dinkey*, as she ran back and forth, into and before the wind, may have been the vessel that steamed across the bows of the *E. H. Utley* before the startled eyes of Captain Edward Fitch.

Early on Saturday evening three vessels with relieved ship-masters snored single file down the narrowing St. Marys River to the Soo locks. Hugging the north shore and passing north of the Slate Islands and Michipicoten, they had ex-perienced a terrifying passage but were unaware that they were ahead of the worst phase of the great gale which reached its peak late Sunday, about the time foolhardy Captain Jimmy Owen took the doomed *Henry B. Smith* out of Marquette harbor. Two of the vessels were the spanking-new *James Car-ruthers* and the *J. H. Sheadle*, whose masters, Captain S. A. Lyons and Captain William W. Wright, had chatted briefly at the Fort William Elevator office as they cleared their grain-laden vessels for passage down Lake Superior. As their labor-ing vessels were pounding along the north shore in high seas, building ice and gale winds, Captain Lyons might have been recalling, and for good reason, a November of eight years before when he had skippered the steamer *Angeline* un-der very similar circumstances. Captain Lyons had been forced by wind and sea to abandon the normal steamer tracks and steam into the tempest for forty-eight hours, as a result of which the *Angeline* was overdue two days and reported lost. The third vessel in the trio approaching the Soo locks was the ore-carrying *Hydrus* of the Interlake Steamship Company, falling in behind the *Sheadle,* which was preceded by the *James Carruthers.* A phenomenon of nature decreed that all three would join an anchored armada just above the locks. The sudden low pressure from the north with its accompanying frigid temperatures, in conflict with the mild, almost summerlike weather on Lake Huron and the St. Marys River, resulted in fog or "sea smoke" which, mingled with the snow flurries, had reduced visibility to a few feet. When clearance was given to proceed, they left their anchorage in an orderly fashion and rightful sequence.

The *J. H. Sheadle* locked down at 8:30 P.M. Saturday, moments after the *Carruthers* cleared and shortly before the *Hydrus* left an adjoining lock. Still but a short distance apart, they steamed down the serpentine and narrow lower St. Marys River, whistles hooting passing signals to upbound vessels.

Far behind them now, but beginning to experience the full fury of the merged low fronts, the comforting lee of Whitefish Point was fast becoming a crowded refuge. Over fifty long boats lay at anchor, facing the wind like a flight of resting ducks, a thousand lights flickering in the gloom of night and the fleeing pall of smoke from their funnels darkening the fresh snow on the gaunt hills of the Tahquamenon country, the legendary habitat of Hiawatha.

In one of the narrow passages of the lower St. Marys the *Carruthers* met the upbound *Midland Prince,* James Tindall master. Fireman Jack Daley of the *Midland Prince* was standing near the galley door as the vessels came abreast. Wheelsman Angus "Ray" McMillan of the *Carruthers* spotted his friend Daley and shouted over: "We're going to Midland this time, Jack. I'll tell your father we passed you." Daley, who was once a fireman on the *Leafield,* waved his acknowledgment and disappeared through the galley door.

Captain Tindall had planned to wait out the bad weather

behind Whitefish Point, but when he arrived there, he found so many other vessels at anchor that he deemed it unwise to enter the bay. There was no choice then but to follow his usual Passage Island course to Thunder Bay, where he was to load grain. So severe was the sea and wind that the men on duty at the moment could not be relieved. Jack Daley spent thirty-six straight back-breaking hours firing the boilers. A survey of the *Midland Prince* at Fort William revealed that nearly a thousand rivets had been sheared off by the plates working as the boat rolled and pitched.

The three steamers, each with a souvenir rime of ice from Lake Superior and down to their winter marks with cargo, slogged down the winding St. Marys River, a difficult course at best, a sailor's horror at night with high, gusting winds and heavy, intermittent snow flurries. Methodically they plodded past long familiar landmarks now unseen in the snow—Stribling Point, Johnson Point, Sailors Encampment, Lime Island and Round Island, as the double watch on the bows called out the channel buoys and spars. In their respective pilothouses Captain Lyons of the *Sheadle,* Captain Wright of the *Carruthers* and Captain John H. Lowe of the *Hydrus,* hollow-eyed from lack of sleep, nerves taut from trying to interpret whistle signals distorted by the wind, peered hopefully ahead for the broadening reaches of DeTour Passage and Lake Huron. Judging from what they had been through for several days, it would have been completely human and understandable to assume that conditions simply had to be better on Lake Huron. But if, indeed, they harbored such assumptions, they were delusions born of utter exhaustion and desperation, entirely inconsistent with the stew the weather gods were still brewing.

For them the main event was still to come.

⚓

11

The Devil's Wind and
Dancing Chauncey Ney

Night warnings for a northwest storm, two lanterns, white above red, routine, all according to regulation, were hoisted and clearly visible at the Pickands, Mather & Company fuel dock at DeTour when the *James Carruthers,* at 12:53 A.M. on Sunday, hauled to starboard to take on coal bunkers. And just as routinely they were ignored by the masters of a long procession of storm-weary vessels that plodded the winding downbound track from the Soo. They were disregarded earlier by the *Matthew Andrews,* among others, and later by the *Wexford* which followed a few miles behind the *Carruthers,* the *J. H. Sheadle* and the ore-laden *Hydrus.* Nor did the masters of other vessels downbound in the early hours of Sunday pay heed to the ominous signals. Such warnings were pretty much to be expected in November and the skipper who was thus inspired to seek shelter could usually expect a sharp note from his owners regarding time lost when other steamers made their ports of discharge without incident. It was as simple as that.

Similarly, at the far end of Lake Huron where, after long and demanding passages on the St. Clair River, another straggling line of long boats found open water, the same storm signals greeted them at both the American and Canadian weather station towers and were just as blithely unheeded. The *Matoa* slipped by between Port Huron and Sarnia a few minutes after midnight, followed shortly, almost furtively, by the *H. W. Smith*. The *John A. McGean* was only minutes ahead of the *George C. Crawford,* officially reported upbound at 3:00 A.M. Then, around five o'clock on that blustery Sunday morning, almost as if in close-order drill, came the *Isaac M. Scott,* the *Howard M. Hanna Jr.* and the *Charles S. Price.* At 6:10 A.M. the *Senator* snored by, followed forty-five minutes later by the *Manola.*

Far to the north the *Carruthers,* approximately an hour ahead of the *Sheadle,* took on her coal bunkers at DeTour with promptness and dispatch, the task supervised by first mate William "Bill" Lediard. If the dock crew had not immediately recognized the forty-four-year-old mate, it was because something was missing—his mustache, gone now for exactly a week. Its disappearance was probably the result of some subconscious, psychological reasoning. For one thing it was distinctly inferior to the magnificent specimen worn proudly by Captain Wright. Secondly, since he was an experienced and qualified master in his own right, Lediard had every reason to believe that he would get command of the new steamer that the owners, the St. Lawrence & Chicago Navigation Company, had already commissioned from the Collingwood Shipbuilding Company. Her keel had been laid immediately after the *Carruthers* had been launched. She was to be an exact sister ship. It made sense for the owners to assign him to the *Carruthers* as first mate to give him experience on an identical boat. What other reason could there be? And Bill Lediard did not want to take command, assuming that he got it, as a carbon copy of Captain Wright. Without the mustache he would still appear to be a mature but vigorous man.

The *Carruthers* had departed the fuel dock and started down the lake by the time the *Sheadle* came abreast of De-Tour. Both would steer the same course for a short time. The *Carruthers* would then haul to port on a course that would keep her well south of Great Duck Island and on a straight line for Georgian Bay and the grain elevators at Midland. The *Sheadle*, fifteen miles off Middle Island Light, would alter her course twenty-four degrees, steering S by E, ¾ E, for one hundred and five miles when, twelve miles off Harbor Beach, another alteration of nineteen degrees would put her on a 180° heading for Port Huron and the St. Clair River channel. The lights of the *Carruthers* could be seen briefly between snow flurries but faded away almost as soon as she hauled on the Georgian Bay course. The *Hydrus* was lost in the snow astern as Captain Lyons of the *Sheadle* resigned himself to a rather unpleasant voyage down Lake Huron.

Three to four hours behind the *Sheadle* was the *Wexford*, laden with 96,000 bushels of grain from Fort William. A typical British tramp steamer, she had been built by William Doxford & Sons in Sunderland. Operated by the Western Steamship Company, Limited, of Toronto, she carried whatever was offered in the way of cargoes upbound—general freight, railroad iron, coal or salt. Downbound, especially in the fall, she concentrated on grain. Compared to the large bulk freighters, her capacity was limited, and she plugged along at a more sedate pace. Like many vessels of her time and trade the *Wexford*'s crew, below the men of officer status, were a restless lot. The company officials would be hard pressed to come up with an accurate crew roster for any trip, or month, for that matter. On this particular voyage she was short one navigation officer and had aboard two men who were not members of the crew in any sense. On the previous trip down first mate James McCutcheon had left the boat at Windsor to visit friends in Detroit, intending to take a train to Port Huron and get aboard the *Wexford* when she docked across the river at Sarnia. But McCutcheon had dallied too long in Detroit, missed his train by ten minutes and the *Wexford* by several hours. The two added starters at Fort William were Murdoch and Donald McDonald, twenty-four-year-old cousins from Goderich, Ontario. Murdoch had been wheelsman on the *Turret Court* but fell ill and decided to return home on the *Wexford*. Donald McDonald, on vacation, had gone north as a passenger on the *Turret Cape,* but when the vessel faced a long delay at Fort William, Donald, fearing he would not get back to his job on time, requested and got passage as far as Goderich from young Captain Bruce Cameron. The officers of the *Wexford* were a steady enough lot, first mate McCutcheon, second mate Archie Brooks, chief engineer James Scott and assistant engineer Richard Lougheed. Even wheelsman Orrin Gordon and watchman Allan Dodson had put in considerable time on the job. Among the newcomers was young and homesick James Glenn, who had arrived from Scotland in May and had been saving most of his pay to bring his wife to Canada. The present trip was to be his last before returning to Scotland for her. A friend of Glenn's was George Wilmott, the vessel's cook, an older and somewhat dyspeptic gentleman who prided himself on his collection of patent medicine literature while assuring others that it was no reflection on his culinary skills. Captain Cameron, since his destination was Goderich, hauled to port on the same course the *Carruthers* took, but instead of turning on the Main Channel course into Georgian Bay, north of Cove Island, would continue down the lake, well off shore of the Bruce Peninsula.

Shortly before the *Manola* steamed out of the St. Clair River and into Lake Huron at seven o'clock on Sunday morning, the *Regina* departed Sarnia, oblivious of the same storm warnings that had been up for hours. Another British-built boat, the *Regina*, had a keel length of just over two hundred and forty-nine feet and was in the package freight fleet of the Merchants' Mutual Line. Partially loaded when she docked at Sarnia, the six-year-old *Regina*, under direction of Benjamin Shultis of the dock crew, took on eight railroad cars of canned goods from Leamington and a variety of merchandise from Dresden, Chatham and Sarnia manufacturers. Aboard the *Regina* the stowage was supervised by first mate Wesley Adams. Topping off the cargo offering was a shipment of one hundred and forty tons of baled hay, most of which had to be accommodated somewhere on the deck, covered with tarpaulins and lashed down. With her considerable deckload, the *Regina* was probably as ill-equipped to begin a voyage under the threat of bad weather as any vessel on Lake Huron that morning. But if there was any doubt about her seaworthiness, no indication of it was apparent in the actions of Captain Ed McConkey when he signed the cargo manifest presented by Shultis. Twenty-two-year-old Robert Stalker was at the helm when Captain McConkey ordered the bow lines cast off, thus permitting the swift current in the river to work the *Regina*'s bow away from the dock. Then the stern lines were taken in and the *Regina* started out on a voyage that would require stops at several north shore ports. Busy in the engine room was oiler Dave Lawson, who had signed on only for the previous trip, intending to go only as far as Fort William, from which port he intended to work his way north and west to Winnipeg. But for some reason, and it may have been the meals prepared by steward Alfred Clark, he elected to stay on for another trip or two. Missing and feeling very sorry for himself, was watchman George Gosby of Toronto. Three weeks earlier he had stumbled over a hatch cover and had fallen into a hold as the *Regina* was loading, suffering a broken leg. "Just my luck," he had groaned to shipmates as he was lifted out. "My luck every time. Here I break a leg and miss the rest of the season."

Some distance up Lake Huron when the *Regina* steamed away from the Sarnia freight warehouse was the big bulk steamer *John A. McGean* with dapper, peppery "Dancing Chauncey" Ney in command. Chauncey Ney, who loved to dance, was probably grumbling because his coal cargo had been loaded and he had been compelled to leave port early Saturday morning, thus missing another Saturday night dance. If there was anything Chauncey Ney relished, it was being in port, loading or unloading, on Friday or Saturday night. Then, apprised of the location of the festivities by understanding dock superintendents, Dancing Chauncey Ney tripped the light fantastic until the orchestra wearily played "Good Night, Ladies."

In addition to its light-footed skipper who once piloted a Detroit fireboat, the *McGean* was somewhat unusual in that two of its wheelsmen, Thomas Stone and George Smith, were full-blooded Indians from the reservation near Sarnia where members of both the Ojibway and Chippewa tribes lived.

Among the other long boats beating their way northward up Lake Huron on that particular Sunday morning were the *Argus,* with Captain Paul Gutch; the *Northern Queen* with Captain Crawford in command; the *Isaac M. Scott* with coal for Milwaukee and Captain Archie McArthur in charge; and the *Charles S. Price,* William A. Black, master, also burdened with coal. Plugging along a couple of hours behind the *Price* was the *Senator,* coal from Ashtabula to Escanaba. Second mate Henry F. Wiersch [1] was in the upper or "fresh air" pilothouse, his overcoat collar pulled up as high as he could get it, the ear lugs of his cap down as far as he could manage,

1 Henry F. Wiersch, the *Senator*'s second mate during the "Big Blow," had a long career as a shipmaster, retiring in 1958 as marine superintendent for the Columbia Transportation Division of Oglebay, Norton & Co.

and the two wedded and secured by a big red handkerchief. It had begun to snow and blow not long after the *Senator* left the shelter of the St. Clair River. Captain Ernest, warm and comfortable in the lower pilothouse, shouted up through the gruff box for Wiersch to "keep her headed into the seas and keep the whistle blowing."

After loading 9120 tons of soft coal at Lorain, the *Howard M. Hanna Jr.* began her voyage to Fort William with all hatches battened down, tarpaulins in place and hatch bars properly wedged. The weather after entering Lake Huron at 5:12 A.M. on Sunday was fair and clear with a westerly wind until the *Hanna* passed Harbor Beach. At this time Captain William Hagan noticed that the wind had shifted to SE for a few moments before swinging to NE and then NNE, from which direction it continued to blow with increasing velocity. That afternoon, with the wind still a-building, it began to snow heavily and by dusk the *Hanna* was burying her steering pole in huge gray seas that came mounting the bow rail. Captain Hagan could see only the advance guard, the rest of the endless marching legions of rolling dark mountains mercifully hidden beyond the swirling and lashing curtains of snow. By eight o'clock the *Hanna* could no longer make headway and began falling off her course to lie helplessly in the deadly troughs while the dark monsters out of the night mauled her. One had already torn off the top of the pilothouse. Another, climbing over the stern, carried Sadie Black, wife of steward Clarence Black,[2] through an interior bulkhead and dropped her, along with the furnishings of her room, down the engine room ladder before the startled eyes

---

2 When salvagers arrived at the wreck of the *Howard M. Hanna Jr.* in the spring of 1914, they found it unnecessary to remove her cargo. Shoreside residents and commercial fishermen had already relieved them of that chore, crossing out on the ice to "liberate" the cargo of over nine thousand tons of coal. When steward Clarence Black visited the area on vacation ten years later, they were still burning it.

of chief engineer Charles Mayberry. The *Hanna* never got out of that fatal trap in the valleys between the seas. After rolling and tumbling for what seemed like an eternity, she fetched up broadside on Port Austin Reef at ten o'clock Sunday night, broken in two at number seven hatch. Like the *L. C. Waldo,* up on Lake Superior, the *Hanna* was to have midnight callers, too, on nearby Point aux Barques, but there was little liklihood of the crews fraternizing.

Northwest warnings were up, and the wind was from that direction when the *Manola* was logged upbound at Port Huron. Off Sanilac she passed the *Regina.* Captain F. W. Light had already concluded that if the weather got too bad, he could easily make the shelter of Harbor Beach, there to lie behind the breakwater until the situation bettered. Shortly, however, the wind died completely for about five minutes and then began to blow a gale from the Northeast, rapidly building up a tremendous sea. At noon Captain Light spotted the Harbor Beach Light and ran for it, the *Manola* rolling so outrageously when she entered the anchorage that both bilges touched bottom. With the help of a tug Captain Light did succeed in getting his vessel tied up to the breakwater, using three lines forward and five aft. All eight lines snapped under the pressure of the wind against the *Manola*'s hull, and the captain was then forced to drop both anchors. Even so, protected as he was from the seas, he had to keep his vessel headed into the wind and keep the engine running full ahead to keep from being driven ashore. The seas exploding over the *Manola* had broken windows and damaged the engine room skylight in the brief period it had been moored near the breakwater. The *Manola*'s officers watched incredulously as the seas peeled off sections of the cement breakwater itself.

Four hours ahead of the *Manola* and thus fifty miles farther up the lake, Captain Hugh McLeod of the *Matoa* was far above the harbor of refuge and could do little but take conditions as he found them. Off Sturgeon Point the *Matoa* began to take aboard very heavy seas, each of which strode the length of the deck, spewing upward in a scene of awesome turmoil when they encountered the after mooring winches, but quickly regrouping forces to batter away at the boiler room bulkheads and bunker hatch. One romped the length of the spar deck and stove in a section of the after cabin, flooding the mess room, galley and spurting into the engine room. At this point Captain McLeod elected to turn and run before the wind and seas, taking the calculated risk of being overwhelmed in the troughs of the seas as he turned. The turn was completed although it took about four minutes to get the *Matoa* around and headed south by east. Now the following seas piled in over the fantail to systematically dismember the after cabins and gush down into the engine room. The luckless engineers, already working in clouds of steam created by boarding seas finding the boilers, were now further endangered by debris dropping down from the demolished after cabins—the steward's icebox, chairs, tables, beds and dressers. Shortly after midnight, with the snow so heavy he could not see the bow of his boat, Captain McLeod felt the first grinding jolts as the *Matoa* went ashore, rumbling another one thousand feet over the rocks at Point aux Barques, a scant couple of miles from where the crew of the *Howard M. Hanna Jr.* huddled in their wrecked and broken steamer.

The violent winds, shifting suddenly to varied and unexpected quadrants as the day progressed, produced the most disastrous twenty-four hours the Great Lakes had ever experienced. Strangely, at least one shipmaster had a grim foreboding of what was to come, although he would have had little chance of convincing others—particularly those who consistently ignored the official storm warnings. He was Captain George Holdridge of the steamer *Robert W. Bunsen*. Two days earlier, on Friday, as the *Bunsen* was downbound on Lake Huron under what everyone else thought were ideal weather conditions, he had made his prediction. The weather was unusually warm, about eighty degrees as the *Bunsen* slogged along on glassy seas and under a singularly weird, copper-colored sky.

"The sun was out, but you couldn't see it," recalls Captain Arthur W. Dana,[3] then the *Bunsen*'s second mate. "The sky had an odd, coppery hue that reflected on the water and

[3] Captain Arthur W. Dana, the *Robert W. Bunsen*'s second mate in 1913, started sailing in 1903, got his first captain's assignment in 1923 and retired in 1953, after a half century of service on the Great Lakes, all with the Pittsburgh Steamship Division of United States Steel.

gave everything an unreal appearance." But Captain Holdridge was an old salt-water sailor with years of experience on
the China Sea where a shipmaster learned to know his barometer and know it well. Captain Holdridge had been peering at and tapping the pilothouse barometer all morning.
At noon, when the *Bunsen* was off Harbor Beach, he shook
his head and said to Dana, "Boy, you're going to see a storm
such as you never saw before!" The captain knew, too, that
while a barometer gives an accurate indication of bad weather
to come, it cannot predict when. It might be in thirty minutes or thirty hours. Taking no chances, Captain Holdridge
called down to the engine room and asked the chief to give
the engine all the revolutions he could get out of her.

There had been higher winds on Lake Huron than those
that howled and hammered all day Sunday and most of Monday, but none that persisted for as many hours, building up
seas of such stature that even grizzled old skippers watched
in awe. Strangely, too, the forces of nature were so malevolent in character that the chivvied and harassed mariners
often found monster seas assaulting their vessels from one
direction, the eighty- to ninety-miles-per-hour winds from
another. And all the while the tempertaure continued to
drop, each boarding sea adding to the accumulation of ice
on the laboring steamers. By noon on Sunday what had been
an orderly procession of many vessels following the approved
Lake Carriers' Association's upbound and downbound courses
turned into a shipmaster's nightmare. It was no longer a
matter of following a prescribed course, but one of staying
afloat, turning, steaming frantically in any and every direction, like chickens who flee before the shadow of a hawk, to
ease the strain on tortured hulls and imperiled cabins. But
worst of all was the furious, unrelenting snow, lasting for
twenty-four hours, often limiting visibility to a few feet and
vastly increasing the probability of collisions.

On land, along the pleasant shore of the Bruce Peninsula and farther down on the Canadian coast of Lake Huron, there had been no warning of a storm of such intensity. The early hours of Sunday morning were calm with seasonable temperatures. Churchgoers were somewhat startled when the temperature dropped spectacularly within minutes and the storm came in off the lake, rain at first, then sleet and snow, driven like buckshot. South of Kincardine, William Emmerton had driven his wife to the Bethel United Church as usual, leaving his horse at the hitching rail. Midway during the service the storm hit with such swiftness and fury that the rattling windows drowned out the words of the minister. Going home, Emmerton had to lower the top of the buggy to keep it from blowing away and borrow a scarf from his wife to keep his hat on. All the way home the horse kept his head down between his knees to make any progress against the wind, stopping frequently to stick his head straight up in the air to get his breath. Once home, Emmerton did not dare open the barn doors. The wind was so strong that it would have filled the building and demolished it.

In Kincardine, Lucy Ann Campbell, homeward bound from church with her daughter and small nephew, stopped to view the lake from the town bridge. A brutal gust of wind literally pulled the nephew from her grasp and rolled him helter-skelter up the street. At Kincardine, too, the first indication that a major disaster was in the making out on the lake was apparent just before noon. Clarence Allen and a few friends were on the hill overlooking the lake and watching the storm when they saw the first distress rockets far out on the horizon. With the aid of binoculars they could make out two vessels, neither of which could be identified, in obvious trouble and in dire need of help. Despite the seas which were now cresting at twenty-five feet and creaming unchecked over the modest Kincardine breakwater, the tug *Onward*,

"June" McGaw in command, made an attempt to go out. But the violence of the seas drove the *Onward* back even before it came abreast of Hurdon's warehouse. It had been a frantic, very human attempt to help, doomed from the start, but it was an effort that had to be made.

Shortly after noon the sleet had turned to snow, driven in off the lake with such fury that few householders ventured outdoors. By dusk drifts had stopped all traffic and the wind had blown down all the phone and telegraph lines. Out in the farming areas hundreds of chickens and sheep died in the fields and were soon covered by the drifting snow. All along the Ontario shore towns and hamlets were completely isolated, the connecting roads impassable and the community streets littered with sheets of tin roofing, broken fences, the wreckage of chimneys, signs and tangled wires.

Across the lake, on the American side, similar conditions prevailed. At Harbor Beach the commercial fishing docks disappeared in a lather of timbers and white water, wiping out the life work of Alfred and George Roberts. Houses along the shore that had never been endangered in the past were swept from their foundations and scattered pell-mell along the beach. At Port Sanilac the entire community dock was demolished and carried away, destroying one thousand barrels of apples and twenty-five tons of hay awaiting shipment. A similar disaster at nearby Lexington washed away two carloads of apples and a big shipment of fish.

The effect of the prolonged north wind was that of raising the water level at the lower end of the lake, thus permitting the towering breakers to run far ashore, destroying everything in their path. In Port Huron, Captain George Plough of the lifesaving station watched in horor as the seas undermined the station's boathouse, the sides hammered outward and the roof tumbling in on top of the rescue craft. All the bathhouses and the pavilion at Lakeside Park were under·

mined and wrecked. On the Canadian side the granolithic sidewalk that extended along the beach at Lake Huron Park was destroyed, the seas heaving the huge blocks of concrete around like dominoes. Rows of cottages were driven far up on the beach, most of them battered beyond repair.

Far up and off the tip of the Bruce Peninsula two lonely lighthouse keepers spent a fearful night and day, beset by both sea and ice. In both cases the lighthouses guard the rocky passage between Lake Huron and Georgian Bay. In fog or snow they send out their growling fog signals to warn mariners. At the Cove Island lighthouse, keeper William Simpson was besieged by the rapidly forming ice. Although it was fifty yards from the lake and ninety feet above the rock on which it was built, and the rock ten feet above the surface of the lake, ice formed continually on the glass at the top of the tower. The building that housed the coal-burning steam boiler which turned the generators and supplied air pressure for the fog signal was nearby. But because the wind would have blown him away had he attempted to leave the tower door, Simpson had to chop out a window on the lee side of the tower and then hack his way through the frozen underbrush to keep the boiler fired and the steam pressure up. Over on Flower Pot Island, keeper William Spears had to fire a boiler, too, and it was in a building sixty feet above the lake level. The hissing black seas ran right over the island and he had to time his dashes to the fog alarm building between them. Ice built up over the Light and fog alarm building until both looked like freshly created confections. Along the Lake Huron side of the Bruce Peninsula the entire coast from Cape Hurd to Purgatory Cove and Chiefs Point was raked by rampaging seas. Farther south, at Southampton, Port Elgin, Inverhuron, Kincardine, Goderich, Bayfield and Port Franks waves charged over the beaches, demolished scores of small craft and swept away docks, boat houses and cottages. At Tiverton, near Inverhuron, acres of pines, over-burdened by snow and hammered by the wind, came crashing down to furnish a full winter of work for the Donnelly family sawmill. A peculiarity of the storm as noted by William Emmerton and others was that while the seas were higher than anyone could recall, the surface was a frothing white, almost as if the water were boiling. That night Harry Stowe, night engineer at the Goderich Electric Light and Power Plant, was certain he heard the *Wexford's* whistle blowing distress signals at midnight, when the storm was at its worst. Others claimed to have heard the whistle earlier, but Stowe did not start the foghorn until eleven o'colck.

What happened aboard the stricken vessels out on Lake Huron that dreadful afternoon and night was, and is, largely conjecture. Only one boat went down before the eyes of a witness late on Sunday afternoon. Captain Walter C. Iler of the steamer *George G. Crawford* saw the *Argus* go down, but he was so preoccupied with saving his own boat that his account was necessarily terse. Upbound without cargo, but in ballast, the *Crawford* was having great difficulty staying head to wind. Early on Sunday afternoon she blew off into the troughs and Captain Iler could not bring her around. So he put her before the wind, steering south by east for three hours until he felt that he was getting too close to land in the "pocket" at the lower end of the lake. He was unable to turn the *Crawford*, however, and she again lay in the troughs of the seas, so he ordered both anchors dropped, feeding the chain out gradually to ease the strain. Both chains parted in less than five minutes. But a fortunate and very temporary lull in the wind helped him get his boat turned into the wind and headed up the lake once more. When running before the wind the *Crawford*, light and therefore high out of the water, was several times flooded by seas coming over the stern, washing out the dining room, galley and crew's quarters. Sometime late Sunday, between the intermittent curtains of snow, Captain Iler saw the coal-laden *Argus* laboring mightily and trying to get out of the trough of the seas. Then, what every lake shipmaster dreads became a fatal reality—the bow and stern suspended by different seas with the cargo-heavy midships virtually unsupported in the valley between them.

In Toledo, where the *Crawford* retreated to have hundreds of rivets replaced in her storm-racked hull, Captain Iler said simply, "The *Argus* just appeared to crumple like an eggshell and then disappeared!"

Captain A. C. May of the *H. B. Hawgood* had proceeded some distance up the lake when the growing seas and fierce wind compelled him to haul around and start back for the St. Clair River and a safe anchorage. Just north of Harbor Beach the *Hawgood* met the *Charles S. Price*. "She was headed into it and making bad weather of it," he reported later. "We met the *Regina* about fifteen miles south of Harbor Beach, and she, too, was making very bad weather and burying herself in the seas. The *Isaac M. Scott* we met about three-thirty Sunday afternoon about five or six miles north of Port Huron Light with the seas breaking over her. I thought the captain was a fool to leave the river. I would have given my head to have been inside, at anchor."

Captain May was of the opinion that after he saw the *Price* "making bad weather of it," Captain William A. Black may have tried to turn the *Price* around to run for shelter, thereby putting her into the troughs of the seas where she could be overwhelmed. This was considered likely because residents of Lexington, twenty-two miles north of Port Huron, heard distress signals out on the lake Sunday afternoon.

At the foot of the lake Captain May concluded that the blinding snow would make it impossible to enter the river, so he hauled to port and dropped his anchors. The *Hawgood* was rolling so badly that in order to get from one side of the pilothouse to the other he had to get down on his hands and knees and crawl. The anchors proved to be only a temporary gambit, however, for shortly thereafter the *Hawgood* rammed ashore near Port Edward with such force that Captain May was almost thrown through a pilothouse window. Stranded and temporarily safe, the *Hawgood* was shortly joined by two other compatriots of the storm, their fate determined by an outrageous bit of blundering, a comic-opera degree of devotion to official red tape.

The mariner's guide to the narrow channel leading from Lake Huron into the St. Clair River was the government lightship, stationed offshore, its light and fog signal acccepted as the absolute beacon for shipmasters to avoid Corsica Shoal and Harlem Reef. At midafternoon on Sunday the seventy-five-mile-per-hour winds had dragged the lightship and her anchors two miles east and two miles south, fetching her up on the Canadian shore. Unexplainably, her light and fog signal continued to operate, thus serving as a trap to lure downbound vessels into shoal waters. The first victim was the *Northern Queen*. Steering on the fog signal, she drove hard on at Weis Beach, six miles above Sarnia, while her master, Captain Crawford, had every audible assurance that he was in safe waters. On Monday morning the lightship, still flashing her light and sounding her fog signal, claimed the *Matthew Andrews*. Captain Joseph Lampoh had successfully brought his boat down the length of Lake Huron although it had been a terrible voyage. Nearing Port Huron and unable to see because of the snow, the fog signal inaudible over the tumult of the storm, he had turned the *Andrews* into the wind and dropped both anchors. At nine o'clock Monday morning, after a most difficult night spent at anchor while the seas continued to run over the spar deck, Captain Lampoh ordered the anchors hove and the *Andrews* was headed for the river with conditions of limited visibility still existing but still accepting the lightship as prescribing the correct course. An hour later the *Andrews,* loaded with iron ore, was hard up on Corsica Shoal, the tantalizing gleam of the lightship still piercing the gloom!

The lightship fiasco could be credited only to its captain, a hardheaded man who religiously "went by the book," and who, for an expenditure of only twenty-five dollars, could have saved the *Northern Queen* and the *Matthew Andrews* from heavy damages. When he was notified by observers on the American side of the river that the lightship was adrift and flying distress signals, Captain Tom Reid of Sarnia, owner of the Reid Wrecking Company, immediately dispatched the tug *Sarnia City,* which offered to tow the lightship back to its assigned station. But the captain of the government vessel would not accept the offer of a tow, even though the estimated cost would be only twenty-five dollars, until he had received proper authorization from Washington. Nor could he be induced to extinguish the vessel's beacon light or shut off the booming fog signal without official orders. Red tape had triumphed over common sense.

The storm continued to rage most of Monday with but little abatement, but when the wind did subside, the lake, due to the marked difference in the air and water temperatures, was mercifully hidden in a heavy fog for some hours.

The first indication of disaster was discovered by farmer Robert Turnbull, who was walking along the shore of his modest farm near St. Joseph to appraise the erosion damage done to his property. There, in the wraiths of the fog a quarter mile offshore, he perceived the hair-raising sight of a man beckoning to him. It was James Glenn, the homesick Scot from the *Wexford,* his upraised arms frozen stiff and seemingly waving, as his body, supported by a life preserver, bobbed up and down in the surf. It was almost as if he had at

long last found a friendly shore and was motioning his shipmates to follow. And follow him they did—cook Wilmott
who had thoughtfully brought along his collection of patent
medicine brochures; wheelsman Gordon; chief engineer
Scott; second mate Brooks; assistant engineer Lougheed;
watchman Allan Dodson and cousins Murdoch and Donald
McDonald, all wandering ashore there on the Turnbull farm
where the beach was white with the *Wexford's* grain. One
of the vessel's lifeboats drifted in, too, but it had obviously
not been used by the crew.

About the same time another gruesome find was made at
Port Franks, several miles to the south. Perhaps drawn together by the comradeship that is inspired by working and
living together, ten of the *Regina's* crew rendezvoused on
shore and in the heaving surf. Those still in the water were
surrounded by acres of debris—thousands of cans from the
eight railroad cars loaded at Sarnia, boxes, barrels, drums,
crates and great quantities of baled hay. On the beach was a
lifeboat clearly stenciled *"Regina,"* and in it were the bodies
of fireman Gustave Oleson and Dave Lawson, the restless
oiler who had originally planned to leave the boat the previous trip. Wheelsman Stalker was up on the beach, too,
along with deck hand François LeBreton and first mate
Wesley Adams.

With the entire area still literally without communications,
news was slow in coming out of the little Canadian lake-shore
communities that were now reaping the awful harvest of the
worst storm in history. The return of seasonal temperatures
quickly melted much of the snow, and the dirt roads were
impassable except by horse and buggy. At Port Huron early
on Monday, disconsolate because the storm had demolished
his life-saving station, Captain George Plough made out a
"dark object, about one hundred feet long and quite wide"
floating about three miles out in Lake Huron. Unable to

investigate himself, Captain Plough called Captain Reid in Sarnia. Once more the tug *Sarnia City*, still bucking high seas, steamed out on an errand for which there would be no pay. Captain Reid found the object to be what Captain Plough thought it was—the overturned hull of a big vessel, about one hundred feet of her forward end out of the water, the stern underwater and probably "anchored" there by her after spar. It was impossible in the prevailing conditions to send a diver down to ascertain the victim's name, but Captain Reid offered the opinion that it was "one of the big fellows—possibly the *E. A. S. Clarke*." But there were many marine men, judging from the proximity of the wreckage at Port Franks, who felt that the upside-down boat was the *Regina*. There was considerable debate based upon the color of the visible portion of the hull, which appeared to be black. But there was some indication that rust that had developed during the season or after the disaster was camouflaging the true color, which could have been red. The *Regina*, claimed Captain Reid, was painted green on the bottom.

The owners of the *Regina* were somewhat positive that the floating hull was not that of their vessel, since it lacked a kink in the lower stem, the result of some misadventure with a concrete dock Captain McConkey had experienced earlier in the season. Fog and gusty weather frustrated several attempts to put a diver over to positively identify the wreck while rumors circulated briskly on both shores. On Sunday night the hulk, obviously a major hazard to navigation, had been passed in the snow by a mere one thousand feet by the *J. H. Sheadle*, the only survivor of that trio of vessels that had locked down at the Soo early Saturday evening. Captain Lyons had experienced a most fearful passage down the lake and at the lower end had twice been forced to turn and run north because of poor visibility in the snow and flying scud. The *Sheadle* had flexed so much that the wires connecting the pilothouse telegraph to the engine room instrument were one moment so tight that the telegraph was inoperable, the next moment the slack so pronounced that the result was the same. The *Sheadle*'s after cabins had been rudely mauled by seas boarding over the fantail, gutting the dining room and the cook's big walk-in refrigerator. Both times when the vessel was hauled around to avoid going ashore, she rolled so alarmingly that Captain Lyons, hanging onto the small hand-steering wheel, was literally suspended in a horizontal position. He estimated the seas at about thirty-five feet and, along with other skippers that survived, noted that they seemed to come in series of three and did not lengthen out as they usually did when the wind increased in a normal fashion.

From the fantail of the steamer *Panay* cook Walter Vizneau saw the upside-down boat when he stepped from the galley to dump potato peelings overside for the gulls. The *Panay* had left a lower lakes dock with coal for Milwaukee some eight hours behind the *Charles S. Price*.

Now the hazardous hull, lying directly in the shipping lanes, was being watched over by the revenue cutter *Morrell* and word of the obstacle and the *Morrell*'s role as a tempoary warning buoy was passed to shipmasters at the Soo and Port Huron. Then came another classic example of official stupidity. The *Morrell* was detached from her wreck-guarding duty to stand by the *G. J. Grammer*, a steamer ashore near Lorain, on Lake Erie. The *Grammer* had fetched up on sand bottom, had suffered no damage, nor were crewmen in any danger. Yet Washington, in a move that dramatically illustrated its utter ignorance of the Great Lakes and their commerce, had arbitrarily ordered the *Morrell* to aid a vessel that was in no trouble while leaving the mystery hull, a frightful hazard to the many vessels still plying the lakes, awash in Lake Huron. A fuming William Livingston, president of the Lake Carriers' Association, quickly advised Washington officials of their mental shortcomings and hired a tug to stand guard over the wreck in Lake Huron.

Although several attempts were made to determine the identity of the turned-turtle hull, it wasn't until late Friday that diver William H. Baker was able to descend to the submerged bow and carefully examine the upside-down lettering, checking twice to make sure. As soon as his helmet was taken off and as a battery of marine men and reporters waited with bated breath, Baker said, "It's the *Charles S. Price!*"

This word, carried in the largest type the Port Huron *Times-Herald* afforded, electrified the Great Lakes marine world. It was a Great Lakes phenomenon. Never before had a long boat loaded with coal or ore capsized!

The fact that something had happened to the *Price* was no longer news over along the Canadian shore where rumor was reduced to fact by the findings along the beach while the upside-down hull was still being labeled in the papers as a mystery ship. Men of the *Price* and *Regina* came ashore together, sometimes entwined in each other's arms. A day or two later the body of John Groundwater of Cleveland, chief engineer of the *Price*, was quickly and positively identified by Milton Smith, the *Price*'s assistant engineer until he had quit the boat just before she left Lorain.

"Are you sure?" ask the coroner.

"As sure as I know my own name is Smith," was the reply.

"Well, this man had on one of the *Regina*'s life preservers!"

This episode furnished good copy for newspapers in all the Great Lakes cities and precipitated many fresh-water mystery yarns in the years to come. But chief engineer Groundwater was but a single example. Altogether, twelve other *Price* crewmen wore life preservers from the *Regina!* Obviously, in the most likely explanation offered by marine men, the two vessels had met in collision during the frightful hours of wind and snow and, while they were temporarily locked together, crewmen from one boat, believing theirs doomed, jumped across to the other. In the mad and desperate scene that inevitably followed, whatever life preservers were available would hastily be put to use, regardless of the name stenciled on them. It was the only explanation that made sense despite the fact that when last sighted, and apparently not long before they went down, the two vessels were at least fifteen miles apart!

Some seventy-five miles to the north of the stricken *Price*, another upside-down derelict, a hull with a red bottom, was sighted and reported by the steamer *William H. Gratwick*. The *Gratwick*'s skipper, despite foul weather, had deliberately passed quite close to the wreck but could not locate any wreckage by which it could be identified. By the time the wind and seas had moderated enough to send out a tug, the hull had gone to the bottom.

The almost complete absence of long-distance communications that existed for several days had led many shipping executives to hope that their vessels, long overdue at scheduled ports of call, had been driven ashore or wrecked in isolated spots and that their crews might still be safe. But such supreme confidence in the ability of their boats to survive the weather that reigned on Lake Huron that wild weekend proved unwarranted. As the week went on, the regiments of lost sailors who wandered sluggishly ashore along with broken lifeboats, cabin doors, chairs, tables, shattered paneling and hatch covers grew with each passing hour. A telegram to the Pioneer Steamship Company in Cleveland from Coroner A. C. Hunter of Goderich confirmed beyond a doubt that the *John A. McGean*, Dancing Chaucey Ney's command, had gone down with all hands. Coroner Hunter reported that one of the *McGean*'s life rafts had drifted to shore with the bodies of three men lashed to it. Two of them were wheelsmen George Smith and Thomas Stone, the two Indians from the Sarnia reservation. The other was watchman John Olsen. Another raft from the *McGean* carried a single sailor. But the rest of the crew were nearby, some of them high on the beach and frozen, others still wallowing bashfully offshore, as if reluctant to admit defeat. Chauncey Ney was not among them.

Among the small army of shipping people and relatives of missing sailors who had rushed to the area to assist with identification problems was James McCutcheon, the tardy first mate of the *Wexford*, the man who missed his train and consequently his vessel when she departed Sarnia. In a trembling voice as he named the *Wexford*'s cold and silent crewmen, he confessed that this was the third time in his career that he had missed the boat, and in each instance the craft had met with disaster. The first time the boat caught fire and burned with a heavy loss of life, and in the second instance there had been a shipwreck with similar unpleasant consequences. As he looked over his dead shipmates of the *Wexford*, he could only shake his head and mumble, "I'm the luckiest guy alive!"

With McCutcheon was Captain W. J. Bassett, managing director for the owners of the *Wexford*. Appearing at an inquest held by Dr. Campbell of Zurich at the Turnbull farm where the *Wexford*'s people made their final landfall, Bassett stated positively: "Captain Bruce Cameron's body will never be found. I am convinced he would stay with the boat." Captain Bassett was also certain that the *Wexford* had been anchored off Goderich late Sunday afternoon, blowing distress signals. He expressed some bitterness because the Goderich fog signal had not been blowing.

"The boat could not have been saved," he grumbled. "But if they had known where they were, some of the crew might have saved themselves."

Back in Toronto, where his tumble into the *Regina's* hold three weeks earlier had ended his sailing for the year, George Gosby had grown very introspective in a remarkably short time.

The week was a grim one all along the Canadian shore, as nearly every hour brought word from volunteer beach patrols that "we found more of 'em." It became apparent that some of the finest products of British, American and Canadian shipyards had been unequal to the strains, stresses and seas found that cataclysmic weekend. Horses, knee-deep in the mud left from melting snow, shuttled bodies from the beaches to temporary morgues set up in empty stores, barns and furniture emporiums in Port Franks, Goderich, Kincardine and Inverhuron. It was shortly obvious that the *James Carruthers,* Canada's newest and largest lake steamer, making only her third voyage, was lost beyond a doubt. Evidence came in slowly at first—a lonely life preserver or two, an oar, and small pieces of wood that could or could not have been part of her cabin paneling. The tug *Logie,* working between Kincardine and Goderich, passed through miles of wreckage that included more life preservers from the *Carruthers,* a dozen oars, rudders from two lifeboats, window frames, screens, new oak furniture and quantities of woodwork from a steamer's cabins. Canadian marine men simply found it difficult to believe that such a new, large and powerful vessel could be so completely overwhelmed. The *Carruthers,* because the Captain was William H. Wright and A. A. Wright was the manager of marine affairs for the owners, was jocularly called "the all-Wright boat."

When the loss was confirmed beyond a doubt by the finding of some of her crew, most around Point Clark, south of Kincardine, Captain Wright was easy to identify by virtue of his splendid red mustache and a ring with the initials "W.H.W." Chief engineer Edward O'Dell was nearby, as was Mrs. Mary Agnes Heary, the boat's cook, who celebrated her thirty-ninth birthday in Brophy's mortuary in Goderich. Mrs. Heary, widowed shortly after her marriage, was in her thirteenth year of service under Captain Wright. A stroke of fate kept the three Wright children from becoming orphans. Mrs. Wright customarily took the early November trip with her husband, but had postponed it for a week, planning to meet the *Carruthers* at Port Colborne.

Captain William C. Lediard, the *Carruthers'* first mate, sans his mustache, presented somewhat of a problem. Several thought they recognized the silent victim and yet there was something different, something wrong. Then they brought in his father Edgar from Toronto.

"Boys," said Edgar Lediard in a trembling voice, "that's Bill. Bill shaved off his mustache when he was home at Midland a week ago last Sunday, and until now I have not seen him clean-shaven for ten years. But this is poor old Bill. I am sure of the identification." All in all it had been a distressingly bad year for the Lediards. Bill's death was the third in the family since January.

Up in Owen Sound Mrs. William Buckley had hurried to the home of Mrs. Richard Lougheed to offer consolation and sympathy for the loss of her husband, second engineer of the *Wexford*. Shortly it became a case of mutual consolation, for Mrs. Buckley also received a telegram from Toronto with the news that the *Carruthers* had foundered with all hands, including her husband, second engineer William Buckley.

There was more to come. Both north and south of Kincardine more wreckage and bodies came ashore, drifting down from Inverhuron, where residents had reported distress flares and whistles from three vessels late Sunday afternoon and Sunday night. They wore life jackets from two Interlake Steamship Company vessels, the *Argus* and the *Hydrus*. The *Hydrus* was the last in line of the three boats that steamed down the St. Marys River the previous Saturday night, following in the wake of the *J. H. Sheadle* and the *Carruthers*. Captain Paul Gutch of the *Argus* was found without a life preserver, but one marked "captain" was found on the body of second cook Mrs. William Walker, whose husband was the boat's steward. Rank meant little in the order in which the people of the *Argus* made their final approach to land. Boatswain Thomas Nelson, handyman George Hayes, oiler William LaMere, porter Leo Gardner, wheelsman John McDonald and first mate Van B. Young were found close together. Farther down the beach, and it was a sad, eerie homecoming, they found second mate Robert Rowan. Son of a captain, Robert had left Kincardine, where the family had always enjoyed prominence, to take up residence in the United States. Strangely, he was found only a short distance from the family property on the lake shore. And almost as if he knew he was doomed but wanted his former townspeople to know that he had enjoyed a fair measure of prosperity and prestige, Robert Rowan came ashore without a life jacket but togged out in overcoat, gloves and new overshoes.

The people of the *Hydrus* were making their way ashore, too, singly and in groups. Unfortunately, some were lost forever because they wandered in on the rocky shores of the Saugeen Indian reservation and went unrecovered because the Indians were superstitious about touching the dead. But when they were made aware that the Lake Carriers' Association was offering twenty-five dollars for every recovery, the promise of cash quickly overcame the teachings and beliefs of centuries. But by then, in most cases, it was too late. Shifting winds and currents had carried away many of the *Hydrus* crew forever. Five, however, came ashore in one of the vessel's lifeboats. A volunteer beach patrol made up of William Allen, his son Clarence, Billy Cobean and Joe McGuiness, along with several members of the Ever Alert Fire Brigade, watched the lifeboat drift slowly in to the beach. There were five men in the boat, all securely lashed to the seats and all dead. Clarence Allen was one of the men who saw the distress rockets far offshore late Sunday and later concluded that they had originated on the *Carruthers*. Another lifeboat from the *Hydrus* came ashore at Kincardine and was later drawn up in front of the power house, where superintendent Andy Ingram maintained it as a memorial for many years. Far away from the lonely shore near Inverhuron a man named Allen McRae was congratulating himself for his shrewd judgment. He had quit the *Hydrus* only days before she was lost.

But what of the *Isaac M. Scott*? She was missing, too, yet apparently foundered farther up the lake and perhaps so suddenly that few if any of her crew were able to leave her. One of her lifeboats, the canvas covering still intact, eventually drifted in to shore but precious little else in the way of wreckage. This would indicate that the *Scott*, like the *Price*, but with less or no warning to her people, had capsized instantly, the lifeboat breaking free as the steamer rolled over. Was the *Scott* the big, red-bottomed hull the steamer *Gratwick* had reported floating upside-down off Point aux Barques, about seventy-five miles up the lake?

Only four years old, the ill-fated *Scott* was skippered by a peppery Caledonian named Archie McArthur, of Owen Sound, Ontario. On its maiden voyage, in 1909, the *Scott* collided with the *John B. Cowle* in fog-shrouded Whitefish Bay. The *Cowle* had gone to the bottom almost immediately, taking most of her crew down with her. The *Scott* had limped into the Soo with a huge hole in her starboard bow. After the usual official investigation, charges, countercharges and endless debate over who had the right of way in this particular situation, Archie McArthur had been exonerated of all blame. Now it was his turn to meet disaster, and he would not be around to answer questions.

Of the grief-stricken families and relatives of sailors who had come to the east shore of Lake Huron to identify their loved ones, Thomas Thompson of Hamilton, Ontario, was typical—exhausted, nervous and overwrought. He had come in response to a wire from Mrs. Edward Ward, of Sarnia, a daughter: "John has been drowned. Come at once."

Mrs. Ward was sure that her brother, John Thompson, a somewhat itinerant marine fireman, had been on the *Carruthers* and was one of the seven crew members the newspapers said were still unidentified.

At Goderich late on Tuesday night an utterly weary Thomas Thompson peered at one body that looked familiar. Yes, there on the left forearm were the two tattooed initials, "J. T.," that the son had carried for years. The expected scars on the nose and leg were clearly visible and so were the dental peculiarities and the two deformed toes. "Yes, yes, that is my boy John," sighed Thompson.

On Wednesday, John Thompson, idly perusing a Toronto newspaper, was surprised to find that he was supposed to be dead, lost with the *Carruthers*. Rather than wire his family, which would have been the sensible course of action, he decided to take the train to Hamilton and explain in person, thus unduly delaying the reunion for several hours. Meanwhile, the harried and sleepless Thomas Thompson had purchased a cemetery lot, had witnessed the grave being dug, ordered mourning clothes for the family, flowers for the casket, and had arranged for the Rev. Father J. F. Hinchey to read the funeral mass. Floral arangements from friends were already arriving at the Thompson home with some frequency when John arrived back in Hamilton. Foolishly, instead of hurrying right home, he dallied about town for some time, even dropping in at the Northern Hotel to see a friend, proprietor Edward Duffy. Duffy, a devout man and considerably shaken by the "resurrection," advised him to hurry home without wasting another moment.

The wake was well under way when the inconsiderate wretch walked in the front door to witness the casket bedecked with floral offerings, candles burning at its head and the house full of grieving relatives and friends. Mrs. Thompson, after the first terrible shock, was almost overcome with joy at the miraculous reappearance. But poor tired old Thomas Thompson, the full meaning of the dreadful wrong identification, the embarrassment and the unnecessary family debts incurred because of it finally striking home, roundly scored the rascal. "It's just like you to come back to attend your own wake," he thundered, "and you can get right out of the house until this thing blows over!"

It took a full week for shipowners to assess the awful toll of that single disastrous weekend on Lake Huron. When they finished counting boats and noses, the Lake Carriers' Association announced that the *Charles S. Price, Isaac M. Scott, James Carruthers, Argus, Wexford, Hydrus, Regina* and *John A. McGean* had been lost with all hands, a total of 178 sailors. Stranded and damaged were the *Rhoda Emily* and the *D. O. Mills* at Harbor Beach, the *Northern Queen* at Kettle Point, the *Acadian* on Sulphur Island, Thunder Bay, the *J. M. Jenks* at Midland, in Georgian Bay, the *H. B. Hawgood* at Weis Beach, the *Matthew Andrews* on Corsica Shoal, the *Howard M. Hanna Jr.* on Port Austin Reef, and the *Matoa* ashore at Point aux Barques. The *Acadian*, high on the rocks at Sulphur Island, had to jettison seven hundred tons of her cement cargo before she could be pulled off. Both the *Howard M. Hanna Jr.* and the *Matoa* were declared total constructive losses, although they were sold to salvagers, later released and lived to sail for many years under new names. Strangely, two pairs of identical sister ships were among those lost, the *Charles S. Price* and the *Isaac M. Scott*, and the *Argus* and the *Hydrus*, the latter two both former Gilchrist vessels recently absorbed into the Interlake fleet.

Two old mysteries came to light as a result of the waters of Lake Huron being churned up as they had never been before. On the beach near Harbor Beach, fishermen found a body and wreckage from the tug *Searchlight*, lost with all hands in 1908. At Point Edward, near Sarnia, the pilothouse and Texas deck of a steamer drifted in. The wreckage, however, was from a wooden vessel and had probably been on the bottom for many years.

Human nature being what it is, there were deplorable instances of the pillaging of cargo and, in some instances, items that could possibly have helped in the perplexing identification problems. Few of the looters, if any, were people from the lake-shore communities, most of which had men sailing in the Great Lakes fleets. But word of the immensity of the tragedy quickly spread to inland towns and villages where there was no spiritual tie with the sailors. Near Port Franks men were encountered carrying away galley supplies and clothing. One had twelve boxes of cigars and a life preserver; another was conveying a wagonload of canned tomatoes, peas and corn, flotsam from the *Regina*. Another toted a wooden case which, on examination, was found to contain several thousand lead pencils. One ghoul is reported to have removed a money belt containing eight hundred dollars from the body of a sailor. Detective Thomas Acton of Sarnia, along with W. A. Wiggins, Government Inspector of Wreckage, and County Constables Patterson and Pitsfield, spent several busy days tracking down loot and apprehending the culprits.

The practice of vessel captains and engineers hiring friends and fellow townspeople as crewmen, a happy arrangement when all goes well but a monstrous blow to the community when tragedy strikes, was put to its severest test in Collingwood. Lost from friends and neighbors forever were oiler Leo Doyle of the *Regina* and wheelsman Joseph Simpson and fireman Ernest Hughes of the *Carruthers*. Gone with the *Leafield* were Captain Charles Baker, first mate Alfred Northcott, second mate Fred Begley, first engineer Andy Kerr, second engineer Tom Bowie, wheelsman Eddie Whitesides, fireman Charlie Brown and cooks Paul and Richard Sheffield. The *Wexford* took down newly married Captain Bruce Cameron, second mate Archibald Brooks, chief engineer James Scott, watchman Allan Dodson, deck hand George Peere and cooks Mr. and Mrs. George Wilmott.

Collingwood was plunged into gloom. On the Saturday following the great storm all business was suspended and flags drooped at half-mast. A public service honoring all the lost sailors was considered and plans regretfully canceled as a smallpox epidemic closed all churches, schools and theaters. Even private parties or gatherings were prohibited. Dignified services for individuals were held, with the processions to the cemetery including many who were mourning for those who had not yet been found. Saddest of all were the rites for Orrin Gordon, the *Wexford*'s young wheelsman. His mother, Mrs. Charles Gordon, was in quarantine in the local hospital and unable to attend. The pallbearers, however, carried the casket past her hospital window where she waved a tearful last good-by.

More impressive were the services held in Toronto for Captain William H. Wright of the *Carruthers*. Hundreds of friends and associates in the shipping industry gathered to pay their last respects to the master of Canada's largest lake freighter. The eulogies, long and many, were duly reported in Toronto's newspapers the next day. In the same editions, however, were stories more likely to be pertinent to mourners all over the lakes area—"NO COMPENSATION FOR LOSS OF SAILORS"—"AN ACT OF GOD WILL BE DEFENSE OF SHIPOWNERS."

Perhaps the most poignant services of all were not in the big church in Toronto or in any of the simple churches or neighborhood homes in a score of Great Lakes communities. Very probably they took place in a little cemetery on the

Indian reservation near Sarnia, along a muddy road a half
mile from the St. Clair River. They were burying George
Smith and Thomas Stone, the wheelsmen of the *John A.
McGean*. The mourners stood there, all three hundred of
them, and for the first time in the memory of the few whites
in attendance, the stoic Indians wept, not furtively, but
loudly and openly, for one of their own. Nicholas Plain, was
preaching the eulogies. Standing between the two graves
with head bared and hands outspread, this man with the
lean, aquiline face exhorted his brothers in the Ojibway
tongue. He began softly and mild at first, smooth as the
treacherous water which robbed the tribes of two of their
best. What he said the few whites grouped at the back could
not know, but perhaps he was telling them how Matchi
Manito, the evil spirit, had brought down the wrath of Kiwedininodin, the dreadful north wind, to harass and smash
the great long boats of the white men. But they did know
that his voice grew louder, and that as his big hands raised
higher there seemed to be a queer pleading in his tones.
Punctuating this were swift, dramatic pauses. Then the
Indians wept. Pathetic, listless squaws hugged their children
tighter; men shuffled restlessly. While their eyes were still
wet, the Indian choir broke into a slow chant. "Dust to dust"
must have been the words of Nicholas Plain as the heavy clods
of earth began to fall back into the graves. At last the graves
were filled. Out in the west the sun suddenly broke through
a bank of tattered, wind-torn clouds to smile down upon
them. And then, suddenly, as if an unknown force had decreed it, wheelsmen George Smith and Thomas Stone received their final eulogy, and perhaps one they could best
understand. Out on the river the sonorous whistle of a long
steamer, upbound and heavy with coal, sounded a long,
mournful lament.

12

A Simple Case of Duty, So—
"Good-by, Nellie"

At approximately 9:30 A.M. on Saturday, November 8, forecaster William H. Alexander of Cleveland received word from Washington to display northwest storm signals as of 10:00 A.M., these to supersede the southwest storm warnings in effect since the previous morning. A severe disturbance, according to the Washington dispatch, was then centered on eastern Lake Superior and moving southeast. After relaying the information to the affected substations under his jurisdiction, Mr. Alexander, as a matter of courtesy, telephoned the managers of several vessel fleets, advising them of the change. Aside, to an aide, Alexander voiced his doubts as to the effectiveness of this extra service which was not part of the bureau's required duties, and for which the vessel managers showed little or no appreciation. "The attitude generally," Mr. Alexander subsequently reported to his superiors in the United States Weather Bureau, "has been such that I felt we were bothering the officials of these companies."

By noon on Saturday indications were so ominous that Alexander called the telephone, telegraph, streetcar and gas companies, again a routine, simple courtesy not required of him but typical of the interest of a sincere, dedicated career man. The later advisory predicted northwest winds varying from forty to sixty-five miles per hour, probably prevailing for the next twenty-four hours!

The massive storm front predicted for Saturday was late in arriving, although the speed of the disturbance as it moved southeast was something the Weather Bureau could not foretell with any degree of accuracy. Saturday on Lake Erie then found brisk northwest winds and snow flurries—rather normal conditions which found the usual variety of traffic in and out of lower lake ports. Sixteen vessels entered Cleveland harbor, among them the *Anna C. Minch, L. R. Davidson, A. E. Nettleton* and *W. L. Brown* with iron ore; the *City of Detroit, City of Erie* and the *Tionesta* with general merchandise; the *Wyandotte* with cement, the *Penobscot* with sand and the barge *Teutonia* with lumber. Despite Mr. Alexander's warnings, ten boats departed—four with coal cargoes for Lake Superior ports, one with oil for Montreal and the rest either light or with general merchandise. One of the coal-laden steamers, leaving late that night, was the *G. J. Grammer*, which had delivered a cargo of iron ore to Ashtabula, steaming light and in ballast to Cleveland. Eleven vessels cleared Buffalo in the same period, including the *Cygnus* of the Interlake Steamship Company, heavy with coal for Superior, Wisconsin.

The advancing low front from the northwest dominated the weather scene, but a southern front, moving abnormally from the southern states and across Georgia, the Carolinas, Virginia, West Virginia, western Pennsylvania and eastern Ohio, brought warm air with it. The consequences when the fronts merged over the south shore of Lake Erie were calamitous. The north winds provided the hellish seas on the lake, the southern front was largely responsible for the record snowfall.

The storm, as pinpointed by the infallible records of fore-caster Alexander, began about 4:30 A.M. Sunday, November 9, with light rain mixed with very moist snow. The wind was from the northwest and rising, reaching and blowing rather steadily at a maximum velocity of forty miles per hour un-til early Sunday afternoon, when it accelerated rapidly and thereafter blew from forty-two to seventy-nine miles per hour, all the while accompanied by a remarkably heavy snowfall. Of the total of over twenty-two inches of snow measured officially by Mr. Alexander, over seventeen inches fell between 7:00 P.M. on Sunday and the same hour on Monday. The temperature at the beginning of the storm was within a degree or two of the freezing mark. As the north wind continued, bringing plummeting temperatures, all elec-tric, telegraph, telephone and trolley wires were soon en-cased in ice. The snow that succeeded the rain burdened them further, and the gale winds finished the job. Miles of poles and trees toppled like tenpins, effectively cutting off all communications between cities along the south shore. Highway, streetcar, interurban and train traffic came to a halt, stranding hundreds of travelers. The wind and unceasing snow built up drifts that, for almost a week, isolated com-munities in an area that extended from Buffalo on the east to as far west as the surburbs of Chicago. There were two worlds, really—one on land where food, coal, kerosene, milk and medical supplies grew desperately short, and one on Lake Erie where simple survival was the single motivating purpose in life.

Twenty-seven miles west of Cleveland, at Lorain, the Pitts-burgh Steamship Company's steamer *Princeton* was unloading ore at the National Tube Company, or trying to. The wind on Sunday night raged in so furiously that the snow, mixed with iron ore dust, soon reduced visibility to near zero. The unloading rigs were finally shut down and the workers dis-missed. First mate Ed Male, thankful that he was in port rather than out on the lake, supervised the job of securing additional mooring cables in wind so strong that his men were frequently bowled over. In a very short time all wires in the area were down, the city left in darkness. Still the snow came—two feet of it by dawn and drifts of eight to ten feet on many of Lorain's main streets. The early light also revealed an early victim of the night's winds. Hard up on the sand a quarter mile off shore was the steamer *G. J. Grammer*, whose master, late Saturday, had taken Mr. Alexander's storm warnings with more than a grain of salt. She was head-to in the sand but in no serious danger although the seas that raked her deck caused awed landlubbers to shudder and offer up silent prayers for sailors still out in the storm. The lifesavers were early on the scene, but the captain and crew chose to stay with their grounded boat. Only the wife of chief engineer Tommy Sherdin consented to be taken off the beleaguered vessel, probably bewailing her choice of the date to take her annual trip with her husband.

Upbound on Lake Erie with coal cargoes were two Interlake Steamship Company boats, the *Cygnus* and *Cepheus*, both relatively new and of identical dimensions. The *Cygnus* had been rudely boarded by every sea almost from the moment she left Buffalo and set a course for Bar Point, at the western extremity of the lake. Approaching Pelee Passage, the wreck-studded bottleneck through which all deep draft traffic had to pass, the skipper of the *Cygnus* had to make a fateful decision—to go on in snow that blotted out most of the light buoys on a course flanked by shoals and reefs, to say nothing of meeting storm-tossed boats, or haul off to port in the lee of Pelee Island. He took the latter alternative. "You'd have to see the seas on Lake Erie to believe it," first mate H. C. Inches [1] told friends later. "It was so bad that we

---

[1] First mate H. C. Inches of the *Cygnus* began his sailing career in 1898 as a summer deck hand aboard a vessel his father commanded. Advancing "up the hawsepipe" to master, he skippered fifty-one vessels and had a

literally felt our way into the lee by the sounding line, and we got just as close to land as we could. It was blowing so hard that the wind took the tops right off the seas, the scud mixing with the snow and hammering at you like buckshot. I predicted even then that this storm would be a bell-ringer, that we would hear plenty about it later."

On the same course to Bar Point but shunning the shelter of Pelee Island was the *Cepheus,* her skipper determined to keep on until he reached the quieter waters of the Detroit River before anchoring. If he had any regrets about his decision, he didn't voice them to first mate Alfred C. Drouillard,[2] who kept a close watch on the hatches. "We were pounding pretty hard and water was going over the deck continuously," Drouillard told his family later, "but we didn't get a chance to anchor until we were in the river. Later, when we got going again, we passed the *Price*, upside-down, and saw the wrecked *Hawgood* and the Lake Huron Lightship."

Although most citizens were unaware of the dread potential, an ugly situation developed at Sandusky on Sunday afternoon. Several contruction scows, supposedly securely moored for the weekend off Johnson's Island, were torn loose. Buffeted by the wind and seas, they came romping crazily in toward the city and the shipping channel serving the coal-loading facilities of the Lower Lake Dock Company. The scows were almost upon the dock itself when a couple of tugs, maneuvering frantically, were able to recapture them.

---

long and illustrious record of service with the Interlake Steamship Company before bidding a final adieu to the pilothouse. In 1958 he became curator of the Great Lakes Historical Society's marine museum in Vermilion, Ohio, where he manned the helm until his retirement in November of 1970. Few men can boast of such a long and rewarding voyage as master mariner H. C. Inches.

2 Like his counterpart on the *Cygnus*, first mate Alfred C. Drouillard of the *Cepheus* enjoyed a long and distinguished career, commanding over a period of years many vessels in the Interlake Steamship Company's large fleet.

There was good reason for the desperate charging about of the tugs even though their mission was partially unsuccessful. One of the magazine scows, mauled frightfully by the seas piling over her, had lost her deckload—many wooden cases containing eight thousand pounds of dynamite! Vessels already at the dock were detained, those due in were diverted to other ports, and an emergency call went out to Toledo and Cleveland for divers—brave divers.

In Cleveland, forecaster William H. Alexander must have experienced some understandable gratification at seeing the Weather Bureau's predictions borne out even though he regretted the consequences to those who had paid but little heed. The violent winds, after having already wreaked much havoc on the Ontario mainland, grew in strength as they swept over the open lake, building up gigantic seas that climbed contemptuously over the Cleveland breakwater. At one point during that wild, disastrous Sunday, at 4:40 P.M., the velocity reached seventy-nine miles per hour and thereafter, for nine hours, varied only from sixty to sixty-two miles per hour! The passenger steamer *State of Ohio*, moored in the west slip of the East Ninth Street Pier, parted her lines as if they were shoestrings, rode diagonally across the slip and carried with her a fleet of anchored motorboats which she ground to matchwood on the opposite pier. In the east basin and in the shelter behind the breakwater the Pittsburgh Steamship Company had temporarily moored eleven barges— the *Smeaton, Fritz, Roebling, Manila, Maida, Jenney, Thomas, Corliss, Holly, Martha* and *Marcial*, all anchored bow to stern alternately in broadside fashion with two-inch wire mooring lines running diagonally from barge to barge. So boisterous was the treatment they received from the winds that the wire lines stretched and loosened, the big steel barges banging against each other like monstrous cymbals in a tumult of symphonic discords. In some cases the mooring bitts were pulled right from the decks, freeing the barges

Thomas, Holly and *Jenney,* which came charging up on the beach. Nearby, also behind the breakwater, the steamer *Richard Trimble* was striving mightily to keep off the beach. Although ballasted with eight thousand tons of water and both anchors and forty-five fathoms of chain out in good holding ground, her skipper was compelled to keep her engine working ahead constantly to ease the strain on his sixteen tons of ground tackle. Even so she dragged to within three hundred feet of the beach. Pittsburgh Steamship officials, peering at the buckled hulls of the barges later on, estimated the damage at about $100,000!

East and west from Cleveland all land travel and communication ceased. Between Cleveland and Buffalo the parallel lines of the Lake Shore & Michigan Southern Railroad and the Nickel Plate Road were out of business due to enormous drifts and thousands of poles and trees down across the tracks, the whole tangled mess then encompassed in drifts. Sleighs were utilized to move stranded passengers into towns or private homes along the route. The trains themselves were abandoned. Still the relentless snow came, driving, swirling and drifting as high as porch roofs in many areas. Householders for the most part stayed where they were and did what they could to conserve supplies of food and coal for their stoves and furnaces. Instead of losing its momentum, the storm seemed to marshal renewed energy as it gradually moved to the east. Strangely, too, the wind direction shifted several times without lessening in velocity. Indeed, the speed, if anything, seemed to increase as it changed quadrants to dramatize the cyclonic characteristics experienced earlier on Lake Huron.

Tied up at the No. 4 dock at Conneaut, Captain George Holdridge, the old China Sea skipper and barometer-wise master of the *Robert W. Bunsen,* found his prediction coming true—and with a vengeance. On Friday, while on glassy-smooth Lake Huron, in eighty-degree weather but under a weird coppery-colored sky, he had remarked to second mate Arthur W. Dana: "Boy, you're going to see a storm such as you never saw before!" And now, forty-eight hours later, Dana could gratefully add: "And won't want to see again."

The wind at Conneaut had been brisk enough all day Sunday. Late that afternoon it hauled quickly around to the north and blew with such intensity that second mate Dana could scarcely believe his eyes. It had been snowing steadily with the south and southwest wind, but the snow that came in from the north blasted the dock with such force and density that Dana could barely see a few feet in front of him. The *Bunsen*, in rather an exposed position, began parting her mooring lines with great frequency. But Captain Holdridge was a man of bold decisions, and he made one that Sunday. Ordering full ahead, he took the *Bunsen* up the long slip, above the McMyler "fast plant," where he planted her bow in the mud, dropped both hooks and put out all the lines he had left. Come what may, his boat was now safe!

Along the eastern shores of Lake Erie that Sunday morning and afternoon the winds were only moderate and ranged from northerly to easterly. At 3:30 A.M. on Monday, however, the wind became unusually high from the south and for fifteen hours blew like the demons of hell, accompanied by an amazing snowfall. But Buffalo forecaster David Cuthbertson had experienced much better response to his storm signals than had Mr. Alexander. Over thirty long boats were snugly at anchor behind the breakwater. Like his Cleveland counterpart, Mr. Cuthbertson had phoned vessel companies and docks with his extremely ominous prediction. In many places the word had already been passed, so to speak. Frantic communications, some by phone before the storm felled the poles, and a wireless message relayed from New York City, told of heavy, disruptive damage to unloading facilities at Lakehead ports on Lake Superior. This, for shipping companies involved in scheduling shipments and working for an efficient and fast turnaround for their vessels, posed many problems, complications and changes. During the height of the gale on Lake Superior fire broke out on the Reiss Coal Company's No. 3 machine at Superior, Wisconsin, destroying the engine room and boiler house. At the same time high winds had toppled three of the six unloading rigs at the nearby Boston Dock, cutting in half its unloading capacity. Some dispatching changes were obviously in order and word of them inevitably made the rounds of the docks and ships, inspiring many shipmasters to make anxious phone calls to the Weather Bureau's Buffalo office.

During Monday morning, from his post in the Telephone Building, where his anemometer was two hundred and eighty feet above the street, Mr. Cuthbertson was aghast when the instrument recorded a velocity of eighty miles per hour, this time from the southwest! Unlike Mr. Alexander, Mr. Cuthbertson's sense of personal satisfaction must have come from knowing that the Bureau's timely warnings were heeded, as witness those many long steamers tugging at their anchor chains behind the breakwater while the wind tore the smoke from their funnels and spat it toward the city.

But however efficiently and effectively Mr. Cuthbertson had disseminated his storm warning, there was one captain, one boat and one crew he could not possibly reach. The skipper was Hugh M. Williams, captain of United States *Lightship No. 82,* stationed in Lake Erie some thirteen miles west of Buffalo, on constant guard over the shallows off Point Abino, on the Canadian side of the lake. An added duty of the lightship was keeping watch on the lighted buoy marking Waverly Shoal and the wreck of the steamer *W. C. Richardson.* But Hugh Williams would necessarily have had to disregard the warnings even in the event he had become aware of them. His job was to keep his lightship on station regardless of the weather. In fact, the dirtier the weather, the greater the service to shipping. No, while Captain Williams might have sincerely yearned to slip his moorings and steam into shelter with the rest of the fleet behind the breakwater, his responsibility was to stay right there in the thick of it to warn away any gale-driven mariners who might chance to wander north of the Buffalo course. A calm, dedicated and resourceful man from Manistee, Michigan, he would not have chosen the lighthouse service had he sought easy duty with little in the way of responsibilities.

Lightship No. 82 was really quite a novel vessel despite her relatively modest dimensions. What she lacked in size she made up for in efficiency and services performed. Built the year before in Muskegon, Michigan, by the Rancine-Truscott-Shell Boat Company, she measured only eighty feet in length and had a beam of twenty-one feet and displaced one hundred and eighty-seven tons. Yet she was a coal-fired steamship with quarters for six, had an entirely adequate galley and, in short, was designed as a vessel capable of accommodating her crew for extended periods of time. Her crew on this particular tour of duty, in addition to Captain Williams, consisted of engineer Charles Butler, assistant engineer Cornelius Leahy, mate Andrew Leahy, seaman William Jensen and cook Peter Mackey who, like the skipper, hailed from Manistee, Michigan. A mastlike post jutted up some thirty feet above her deck at midships and on top of this was the all-important light to warn sailors of Point Abino and the surrounding shallows and rock ledges.

A lightship, since she is more or less permanently moored, has long presented unique problems to designers. The perplexing question, from a standpoint of efficiency and safety, was where should her mooring chain or cable be attached to the hull, or, if she had conventional hawsepipes through which her chain ran, where, for maximum stability and safety, should the hawsepipes be located? The matter was most pertinent since, unlike conventional cargo vessels, they could not hoist anchor and maneuver to their best advantage in event of violent weather, but must stay on station and make the best of it. Stability, then, in seas of any stature, was the prime prerequisite. The distinguished naval architect Arthur D. Stevens, commenting on a paper called "Evolution of the Lightship," and presented at a gathering of men of the profession, said: "I will say in connection with this paper that I have had the privilege of visiting *Lightship No. 4* last year, and one of the strong criticisms made was that when she would sheer in a current and bring her cable across the bow, she would list very seriously, lay over and be a long time recovering. I simply mention that as a criticism which the men on the boat made."

The chairman asked: "Was the hawsepipe too low or too high?"

"I am simply giving you the criticisms of the men on board as to the wearing action that happened to be mentioned here, on *Lightship No. 4*. They criticized it as giving her a serious list when she sheered in the current."

If a mere current bringing a mooring cable across the bow caused serious listing on *Lightship No. 4*, one wonders at the state of affairs on *Lightship No. 82* on that indescribably savage day of November 10. As it is comparatively shallow, Lake Erie is quick to produce monstrous seas, and a characteristic of seas spawned over modest depths is that they have the unique quality of being "short," meaning that they come in quick and endless succession, with little or no time for a boat to recover before she is assaulted by another sea, and another, sometimes for endless hours. Picture the luckless Captain Williams, then, unable to maneuver while his vessel was being boarded by every thundering, cresting graybeard built up by seventy- and eighty-mile-per-hour winds. And if a current alone could cause *Lightship No. 4* to list because her mooring cable crossed her bow, what about that cockle-shell off Point Abino, the swirling, shifting winds swinging her about and banging her unmercifully while the seas still came at her from another direction? To say that these conditions gave her serious listing problems would be the understatement of the century. As it transpired, with *Lightship No. 82* the problems were fatal.

Captain Fred A. Dupuie had brought the grain-laden *Champlain* the length of Lake Erie with her deck constantly awash and following seas hounding him all the way. Off Long Point he altered the course slightly, steering NE by E, ½ E with sixty miles to go to the Buffalo pier light. But something was missing over there to portside. There was no familiar light off Point Abino to warn him of shoal waters or confirm the fact that he was exactly thirteen miles from his destination! Captain Dupuie had a feeling that some calamity had befallen the lightship, although he had at first concluded that she had hove anchor and steamed for shelter. In view of the deplorable weather conditions that had existed for a couple of days and despite the traditions of the lighthouse service, he could well understand why.

"The lightship was gone when we passed her anchorage this morning at 3:20 A.M.," Captain Dupuie reported to the harbormaster. "There was no sign of her and we decided that the boat either had gone to the bottom or had run for shelter. The fact that the lightship is not in port strengthens our fear early this morning that she was driven from her anchorage in the gale and went to the bottom."

After telegraphic communications had established that *Lightship No. 82* had not been sighted from ashore at Point Abino, Windmill Point or Port Colborne, where the raging seas and cyclonic winds might have carried her, intact or as a derelict, a worried Roscoe House, inspector for the Tenth District, boarded the lightship tender *Crocus* to search for her. Later in the day orders from Washington diverted a revenue service cutter from Detroit to assist. Masters of vessels arriving in Buffalo after the *Champlain* reported sightings masts and rigging, still apparently fastened to a submerged hull, floating in the lake west of Long Point. But the masts were those of a conventional freighter, not the lightship.

The searchers found plenty of wreckage, some still adrift on the lake and much that had been washed ashore in and around Buffalo. But most of it came from the old wooden steamer *C. W. Eliphicke* which had gone ashore on Long Point with a cargo of wheat late in October. Captain Alonzo Comins and his crew had safely departed the wreck, but the old *Eliphicke*, her back broken and her cargo ruined, had been abandoned. The winds and seas that raked Lake Erie that fateful Sunday and Monday of November 9 and 10 had thoroughly dismembered the wreck, scattering her timbers all over the "pocket" at the eastern end of the lake.

Undeterred by the missing lightship, the parade of commerce continued, long steamers easing in and out of the Buffalo piers night and day as the revenue cutter and lightship tender picked up, sorted out and rendered judgment on the flotsam. The only thing that could be positively identified as coming from the missing boat was a drawer from the galley of cook Peter Mackey. Then Frank Fleisner, walking along the beach at the Idlewood Club, near Buffalo, found a single life preserver bearing the letters U.S.L.V. and the inscription *Lightvessel No. 82*. Almost at the same time, again on the beach, someone else found the most telling and tragic clue of all. It was a piece of wood, possibly from a door or section of cabin paneling. On it was scrawled Captain Hugh Williams' final document of allegiance to the United States Lighthouse Service and a girl back in Manistee: "Good-by, Nellie, the ship is breaking up fast. Williams."

⚓

13

"...Let the Cobbler Stick to His Last!"

The two massive atmospheric disturbances that united over Lake Erie and southern Ontario on Sunday, November 9, resulted in a highly unusual barometric reading of 28.70 in the Toronto office of the Dominion Meteorological Department. Thereafter the coalesced fronts, moving now as one immense low-pressure force, swept northeasterly the length of Lake Ontario, losing strength as it humped down the St. Lawrence River valley. By Wednesday, November 12, it was well over the Labrador coast and dying at sea. On Lake Ontario, where there had been time to warn shipping of the true severity of the storm and most vessels had been held in port or protected anchorages, damage to boats was light. The only vessel to be rudely treated was the Merchants' Mutual Line steamer *A. E. McKinstry*, which went aground on mud bottom near Brighton, suffering considerable embarrassment, but little or no harm. Elsewhere, from Toronto to Kingston, much havoc was wrought to pleasure craft, marine construction floating equipment, docks, boathouses and waterfront cottages.

But even as the fury of the worst Great Lakes storm in half

a century was reluctantly leaving the field of destruction, great verbal paroxysms of anguished protest, all aimed at finding a victim to blame for the disaster, emerged full-blown on both sides of the border.

First to be denounced were the United States and Canadian weather services, allegedly for not advising shipping interests of the true nature of the storm and for failure to display the proper signals. Congressman William Gordon of Ohio's twentieth district, doubtless at the insistence of his shipping executive constituents, went so far as to wire President Wilson, demanding a complete investigation by David F. Houston, Secretary of Agriculture, the department under which the United States Weather Bureau functioned. Mr. Houston obliged and with Assistant Secretary Galloway, Chief Forecaster Harry C. Frankenfield and Professor Charles E. Marvin, chief of the Weather Bureau, went into the matter very thoroughly, examining in detail all the maps, weather reports and evidence of signals displayed before and during the time period in question. With book, verse and chapter Secretary Houston charted the genesis of the storm and the warnings displayed from Thursday, November 6, and throughout the period of violent weather.

"The department will refuse absolutely to take any responsibility for the acts of vessel owners or captains in ignoring the plain warnings shown by the records to have been issued in advance of the storm. We are not going to submit to any effort on the part of vessel owners or other interests to make a 'goat' out of any of the weather forecasters along the Great Lakes!"

The Secretary's records pointed out that the storm signals had been put up at one hundred and thirteen points along the lake shores, including nineteen weather bureau stations, from any one of which special information might have been obtained upon request.

Since Cleveland was the administrational headquarters for

a majority of the Great Lakes fleets, its forecaster, William H. Alexander, came in for more than his share of criticism. But again, the investigation showed that Mr. Alexander had acted with promptness and dispatch in displaying storm signals as soon as they were disseminated from Washington. Mr. Alexander had previously volunteered that his personal attempts to notify shipping managers of weather changes in the past had not evoked enthusiasm on their part, and, as he mentioned to a co-worker, "The attitude of the vessel owners generally has been such that we felt we were bothering the officials of these companies."

When asked by a reporter if the companies ever called him for weather predictions, he said: "Only the passenger lines and the Pennsylvania & Ohio Transportation Company, operators of the car ferry *Ashtabula,* have seemed to appreciate this service and call us daily."

"The history of the Great Lakes," Secretary Houston thundered, "contains many instances of storm warnings having been ignored by vessel owners. And in many cases the vessel owners taking these risks have gotten out without loss. In cases where they take the hazard and lose, they themselves must assume the responsibility!"

Up in Toronto things got even stickier with charges and countercharges being hurled about with reckless abandon, and with various experts, presumably qualified, adding their opinions and conclusions—all being liberally quoted in the city's newspapers, the *Daily Star,* the *Globe* and the *Telegram.*

A petulant Mr. A. A. Wright, manager of the St. Lawrence & Chicago Steam Navigation Company, understandably but perhaps unwisely, rose to the bait when newspapers printed the views of several people, the gist of which was the claim that wealthy owners, making twenty and thirty percent annual profit, had been sending out unseaworthy ships and forcing their captains to ignore weather conditions.

These opinons, in turn, had probably been inspired by a

newspaper statement of Mr. Wright's—his reaction to a suggestion that all vessel sailings should be scheduled in accordance with weather reports.

"In twenty years of conversing with men who have been sailing first-class steel ships, similar to those which were lost, *no master ever paid any attention to the weather reports. If they had, they would never have got anywhere,* and they have always guided their actions by the weather they were experiencing and what they could judge they were likely to encounter."

This was a bold, if incautious statement which, in effect, said that vessel captains customarily paid no heed to the projected weather reports or the appropriate signals. This was a practice of which most marine men were already aware. Mr. Wright's words merely confirmed the fact.

Another critic who had suggested that the decision to sail in bad or threatening weather be left up to the deck hands instead of the master, got a brisk and heated answer from Mr. Wright.

"This would be like putting the office boy in charge of a business ashore."

Mr. Wright, obviously under great pressure due to the loss of his company's new vessel, the *James Carruthers*, had first fired off a barrage of invectives in the direction of R. F. Supart, director of the Dominion Meteorological Department.

"The weather bulletins were all wrong," he fumed, citing the prediction for Lake Huron and Georgian Bay for Saturday, November 8, and Sunday, November 9:

> Gales southwesterly to northwesterly; rain, turning in many localities to snow; Sunday, strong winds and gales, northwesterly, decreasing by night; local snow flurries but mostly fair and cold.

"What was actually experienced on Georgian Bay on Saturday was a strong southwest gale, which continued until about 6:00 A.M. Sunday. At 7:00 A.M. Sunday it was blowing a gale from the north-northeast after a few minutes' calm. This persisted until between 11:00 A.M. and 12:00 A.M., when a furious snowstorm came on, which persevered until sometime on Sunday afternoon, and probably all day Sunday and until Monday morning. The wind continued from the north and north-northeast and blew harder than the captains of two boats which were on Georgian Bay had ever experienced, with the heaviest sea either had ever encountered."

After pointing out other alleged variances between the weather predictions and the actual conditions, he continued: "It should be very evident that in this case the weather probabilities gave not the slightest indication either of the kind of storm or the direction from which the wind would come."

"The wind carried only an eighth of the compass farther than had been predicted," replied director Supart, refusing to get melodramatic. "That is, from north-northwest to north-northeast. It is quite true that had we a hurricane signal it would have been hoisted, but the hurricane signal has not been used for over fifty years, and is now only operated in the south for West Indies hurricanes and tropical tornadoes. We did have up our No. 4 signals, our heavy gale warnings. They were hoisted at 11:00 A.M. on Friday, two days before the storm hit Lake Huron. In November this signal has always meant that any vessel putting out did so at great risk. All we could do was give the warnings."

The position of the weather forecasters in both the United States and Canada was bolstered and graphically illustrated by the fact that heavy gale warnings were flying at Sarnia and Port Huron, facing each other across the St. Clair River, at the foot of Lake Huron. But the ominous warnings had been blithely ignored by shipmasters from both countries, offering further corroboration to Mr. Wright's enlightening statement that *"No master ever paid any attention to the weather reports. If they had, they would never have got anywhere!"*

"Nonsense," is the way Mr. Supart characterized the statement that boats would not get anywhere if they heeded the storm signals. "Only twice on Lake Huron, aggregating three days and four hours, and only five times on Lake Superior for a total period of six days and seventeen hours, have the heavy gale warnings been displayed this year. In 1912 they were hoisted four times on Lake Superior and six times on Lake Huron, but for only one day in each instance."

At one time, immediately after the storm, when Toronto reporters were desperately seeking out marine men for knowledgeable opinions, Mr. W. E. Redway, a naval architect, ventured the opinion that perhaps the lake vessels were not built strongly enough and were getting too long for their beam and molded depth, a subject he should be familiar with since he had been designing and building steel ships for forty years, and twenty-five years earlier had been elected a member of the Institution of Naval Architects in London.

Mr. Redway had enlarged upon the matter of hatches which were built for the convenience of the unloading machines, aft deckhouses which had been damaged so quickly in the storm, ordinary windows instead of portholes and sundry other points of interest.

Mr. Wright, in some heat, countered quickly and with but a single sentence, "Rubbish; he doesn't know it all!"

Now entering the fray with a bit more enthusiasm, Mr. Redway replied in print: "This I cheerfully admit. I am still learning and expect to continue doing so for the rest of my life. I was a member of the Institution of Naval Architects before there were any large steel cargo ships on the lakes, or many small ones either—so that I may be expected to know as much about the design and construction of a steel ship as my critic, who is not an expert in that line—'Ne sutor supra crepidam iudicare.' In other words, 'Let the cobbler stick to his last.' "

In further pursuance of his point, Mr. Redway compared the "girder" strength of two ten-thousand-ton vessels, one built for salt water, the other for the Great Lakes bulk trade.

	Ocean Boat	Lake Boat
Length	460.1	530.0
Beam	58.5	56.0
Depth	41.0	31.0
Indicated horsepower	4000	2000
Watertight bulkheads	6	3
Freeboard, in feet	14	12

"These two boats are constructed within a very small margin of precisely the same weight of metal. Looking upon them roughly as girders of equal weight but different proportions, we have in the ocean boat about 4750 tons of steel in a girder 460 feet long, 41 feet deep. In the lake boat about 4750 tons of steel in a girder 530 feet long and 31 feet deep. It does not take much of a calculation to find out which is the strongest vessel longitudinally. I am not saying that the 530-foot vessel is too weak for her work; that is what we want to find out!

"There are two screen bulkheads in the main hold of the lake boat," Redway continued, "but not watertight. The hold is about 390 feet long, so that in case of collision and serious damage to any part of this space, the pumps cannot keep the vessel free and she must inevitably sink."

While the two adversaries were probably unknown to each other in person, they continued to thrust and parry in the newspaper columns, to the delight of the marine fraternity. In a moment of candor Mr. Redway had suggested to a *Daily Star reporter* that the average lake freighter was little more than an elongated metal box, a tank really designed for moderate weather, that these vessels were frequently, not to say usually, overloaded, that the lives of captains and crews were seemingly not considered in the Canadian shipping laws as compared to the British Board of Trade laws; that the average lake freighter was open to criticism in the matter of freeboard, bow shaping and the construction of the hatches.

The wide-eyed reporter asked, "Is there no regulation to prevent the shipowner's loading a vessel so deeply that even the safe margin of freeboard they may have now is reduced below the danger point?"

"I don't like to say, but I am afraid it is true."

"Is there no law?"

"Not on the lakes."

"What about ocean freighters? How much freeboard do they have?"

"Oh, that is different. It is worked out differently for each ship, taking everything into consideration—length, beam, type of decks, kind of cargo she is intended to carry, engines, and so on. It is an intricate calculation that takes a good draughtsman perhaps half a day to calculate what freeboard a vessel should have under the rules of the British Board of Trade."

"But isn't that done with our lake boats?"

"No, there is no rule."

"What about overloading?"

"There is no rule here. There is on the ocean, of course. The British Government places what is called the Plimsoll mark on the side of every vessel. She must have that mark. It shows her maximum load line for summer and for winter. She must not load deeper than that mark."

"But what is the practice in Canada? On the lakes?"

"There is no rule. They load practically the same in summer and winter. This Plimsoll mark gets its name from a man who introduced the legislation forbidding the overloading of ships. I was in England when it came into force.

In the small town where I was living, eighteen or twenty boats were all condemned under the new law."

Mr. Redway pointed out that unlike the ocean tramp vessels, the large Great Lakes boats were built specifically to carry bulk cargoes—iron ore, coal and grain primarily—and that their unusual profile, pilothouse forward, engines aft, had evolved for the convenience of the mechanical shore gear that unloaded them. This resulted in a long "clean" deck where the dock machines could roam at will, unfettered by cabins, masts, ventilators or rigging. The efficiency of the system was unquestioned. What Redway and others questioned was the necessity of many hatches, again for the convenience of the unloading gear. Each hatch was an opening that was bound to have some bearing, however slight, on the longitudinal strength of the hull girder. Since some of the long new boats had over thirty hatches, it was natural to question the matter of girder strength eroded away by so many hatches. Mr. Redway pointed out that the ratio of length to depth on the ocean freighter was 11.2 on a vessel with perhaps only four hatches. While the ratio on the lake boat, with many hatches, was 17.1!

The *Daily Star* had added fuel to the fire with editorial comment pointing out that most of the losses were among the newer and longer vessels, while many older boats had managed to survive.

Mr. Wright, feeling called upon to refute the suggestion of overloading, fired back another volley. "As to being overloaded, the steamer *Carruthers* had over twelve feet of freeboard when loaded to the greatest depth she could load coming through the Soo, which is more freeboard than Plimsoll's rule would call for."

In another statement, this one to the *Globe,* he remarked: "It has now, of course, been demonstrated to everyone that there must be some weak point on the lake type of ship which was not equal to such a gale as prevailed on November 9 because, while no one knows with absolute certainty, it is quite probable that at least some of these ships were lost by other causes than collision."

"It would be superfluous of me to suggest that Mr. Wright knows it all," the *Globe* quoted Mr. Redway, "but it is a safe prediction that he will know much more by the time a thorough investigation has been held."

The *Daily Star*'s man in Ottawa, apparently testing the prevailing sentiments in the office of the Hon. J. D. Hazen, Minister of Marine, included a significant paragraph in his dispatch of November 16:

> For one thing there is a feeling the time has arrived when there should be a more rigid inspection of marine architecture. It would also appear that much needs to be done to provide safe harbors and get-at-able refuges in times of danger. The inauguration of wireless precautions will also be brought to the attention of the Government.

Meanwhile, if Canadians in general and sailors in particular were gaining an alarming insight into the lack of protection for mariners on the great inland seas, they were still more discomfited by news stories coming out of Goderich, where Coroner A. C. Hunter and Crown Attorney Seager were conducting an official inquest into the death of Thomas Stone, the Indian wheelsman of the *John A. McGean*. The testimony pointed up the fact that on the American side of Lake Huron there was a harbor of refuge, Harbor Beach, for vessels seeking shelter from weather, full-time lifesaving crews and beach patrols and career attendants for lights, foghorns and navigational aids. In contrast, Goderich was the only harbor of note on the Canadian side and it was hopelessly too small for the vessels then plying the lakes. Furthermore, the local lifesaving crew was a volunteer one. The only aid to navigation other than the lighthouse was a foghorn, poorly placed on a dock, practically inaudible in a storm such as that on the previous Sunday, and operated in an intermittent and casual manner.

There was sharp questioning on whether or not the foghorn had indeed been operating in the terrible hours of Sunday afternoon and night. Especially critical of the haphazard management of the foghorn was Captain W. J. Bassett, managing director of the Western Steam Ship Company, owners of the *Wexford*. Captain Bassett had hurried to the lake shore to help identify the bodies of the *Wexford's* crew and had remained to give expert testimony at the inquest. A sailor since 1872 and a former commander of the *Wexford*, he had earlier expressed his opinion that had the foghorn been operating continuously during the snowstorm, some of the men of the *Wexford* might have been saved. His sentiments were strengthened by the word of three townspeople who claimed to have heard the steamer blowing distress signals off the harbor.

An important witness was G. J. Parsons, superintendent of the Goderich Elevator and Transit Company. "We expected the *Wexford* from our information to be here on Sunday morning and the *Empress of Fort William* about the same time. I did not hear signals from the vessels outside, but I have heard it reported that Frank Bingham and Harry Stowe, the latter at the powerhouse after midnight, did hear signals."

Crown Attorney Seager asked Mr. Parsons as to the fog signal and when it was blown.

"It did not blow until ten or eleven o'clock Sunday night, but continuously after that."

Mr. Seager did not concur in this statement, and from very personal knowledge. He had awakened at 3:00 A.M. and had stuck his head out of a window to see if the storm was slackening. It wasn't, and at that time neither was the fog-horn blowing! The testimony made it abundantly clear that all Sunday afternoon, as the snow limited visibility to a few feet, the foghorn had been silent—silent at a time when only sound would have helped a storm-tossed vessel find its way to Goderich. The lighthouse would have been useless.

The foghorn was located on the waterworks pumping house. J. B. Kelly, chief engineer of the waterworks, said that he started the fog signal when he saw a fog on the lake, or when someone told him to start it. He did not start it on the Sunday in question, he told the coroner's jury, because he "just didn't think of it."

Captain Robinson, the Goderich lighthouse keeper, re-marked that if the horn had been sounding between two and three o'clock on Sunday afternoon, it could have been heard out about three miles, which was about the time the *Wexford* would have been due if there was any truth in her being sighted thirty miles northwest in the morning. After three o'clock the storm was such, he estimated, that the horn could not have been heard out past the end of the piers.

Crown Attorney Seager firmly developed evidence of mis-placed trust and inadequate instructions on the blowing of the fog signal, a complete absence of any orderly or official procedure. The waterworks officials at one point contended that they were supposed to be notified by the lighthouse keeper when to start the signal. The lighthouse keeper, on the other hand, had no telephone communication facilities to the waterworks! Even if he had, his entire attention was required to keep the driving, damp snow from obscuring his main light, the only visible guide to the harbor.

Fred Shepard, foreman at the grain elevator, testified that he had telephoned the waterworks at 10:30 P.M. Sunday to start the signal, as he expected some ships in to the elevator. Henry Stowe, assistant at the waterworks pumping station, said he started the signal "when a man comes along and says there is fog on the lake."

Captain Bassett was somewhat contemptuous of the suggestion that Goderich could be considered a harbor of refuge.[1] "Not by any stretch of the imagination. If the weather outside got so rough that a boat could not live in it, then some captain might run his boat in. But he would lose the boat and cargo while saving his crew. Goderich is a $2.50 harbor," he snapped. "Just like a lot of other Canadian harbors—just good enough to keep the vote."

Back in Toronto, despite Mr. Wright's expressed scorn for naval architect Redway and his contention that the esteemed Mr. Redway "didn't know it all," it is significant that as a result of that one calamitous Sunday on Lake Huron, the St. Lawrence & Chicago Steam Navigation Company, of which Mr. Wright was manager, ordered important changes in their vessel then under construction at Collingwood, the same boat the *Carruthers'* first mate, William Lediard, had high hopes of commanding. Orders went out that the cargo hatches, originally specified to be on twelve-foot centers, as on the *Carruthers*, were to be constructed on twenty-four-foot

---

[1] In an atmosphere favorable to change and with unanimous agreement in official quarters that a harbor of refuge was a "must" for the Canadian shore of Lake Huron, a hopeful band of citizens of the Bruce Peninsula took heart and action.

The people of Inverhuron, nine miles north of Kincardine, felt that they had the logical location for such a facility, with relatively deep water and the anchorage already offering protection from northeast to south winds. An adequate breakwater and navigational aids, they felt, would make Inverhuron the ideal location and at minimal costs. A delegation went to Ottawa to be heard by Ministry of Marine officials and Sir Robert Borden, Prime Minister of Canada. They pled their case well and the need of such a harbor was so obvious that Prime Minister Borden promised that they would get it.

But tragic events in other parts of the world spawned World War I and the harbor, of necessity, was delayed to another day. And projects thus tabled, however valid the reason, are rarely resurrected to become reality. Today Inverhuron is just what it was in 1913—a charming village and delightful summer resort with but a limited number of permanent residents. Canada still has no harbor of refuge on Lake Huron.

centers. Further, that the telescoping metal hatch covers, that were features of the lost boat, were to be replaced with four-inch spruce hatch covers fitted (salt-water style) inside of Tyzack's patent hatch rest bars and supported underneath with steel strongbacks fitted fore and aft and athwartships. Heavier construction was also dictated for the after deck house, with internal stiffening. All door openings were ordered with twelve-inch coamings. The doors themselves were to be of solid teak, two and one-quarter inches in thickness. Overhang on the after cabins was eliminated entirely. All deckhouse windows showing in the original plan, as on the *Carruthers,* were to be replaced with fifteen-inch brass side lights. All were points of possible weakness Mr. Redway had enumerated in his informal dissertations on ship construction for the edification of eager Toronto reporters and to the consternation of Mr. Wright.

When the news got around, as it inevitably does, Mr. Redway, snug in his office, could be forgiven a warm feeling of satisfaction and perhaps a smug smile or two.

> Ne sutor supra crepidam iudicare. . . .
> Let the cobbler stick to his last!

Bibliography

Bannister, Dr. John A.—"Long Point and Its Lighthouses." Lawson
    Memorial Library, University of Western Ontario, London, On-
    tario, 1944.
——"Port Dover Harbour."
——"Western Ontario History Nuggets."
Baraga, Rt. Rev. Bishop—"A Dictionary of Otchipwe Langauge." Mon-
    treal, 1878.
Barcus, Jack J.—"Freshwater Fury," Wayne University Press, 1960.
Billow, Jack J.—"The Tragedy of the *Eastland*," *Inland Seas*, Fall,
    1960.
Blue Book of American Shipping, 1913—. Penton Publishing Company.
Bowen, Dana Thomas—"Shipwrecks of the Lakes," 1952.
Chicago, Illinois, *Daily Tribune*—July, 1915.
Chicago, Illinois, *Daily Press Tribune*—Issues of July-December, 1860.
Chicago, Illinois, *Tribune*—July 19, 1953.
Clark, Dwight F.—"The Wreck of the *Lady Elgin*." Illinois State His-
    torical Society Journal, 1945.
Cleveland, Ohio, *Herald*—June 18, 1850.
Cleveland, Ohio, *News*—July 4, 1939.
Cleveland, Ohio, *Plain Dealer*—August 14, 1954.
Collins, Bob, and Bob Mann—"The Night the Whisky Ship Ran
    Aground."
deFord, Miriam Allen—"Stone Walls," Chilton Books, 1962.
Document No. 814—House Document, Vol. 144, 64th Congress, First
    Session, 1915-1916.
Dowling, Rev. Edward J., S.J.—"The Vanishing Fleets," *Inland Seas*.

"*Eastland* Disaster Relief Report of the Chicago Chapter, 1915-1918."

Elliott, James L.—"Red Stacks over the Horizon," William B. Eerdmans Publishing Co., 1967.

——"The *Eastland*—A Half Century Ago," *Inland Seas,* Fairport Harbor Historical Society. Summer, 1965.

Glazer, Sidney—"A Report on the Loss of the *G. P. Griffith,*" *Inland Seas,* Fall, 1960.

Glick, David T.—Letters to the Editor—*Inland Seas,* Winter, 1959.

Gordon, William A.—"Lake Erie's Isle of Romance."

Hamilton, Ontario, *Spectator*—November 15, 16, 17, 1913.

Harlow, Alvin F.—"The Road of the Century," Creative Press, New York, 1947.

Henson, W. R.—"Currents and Water Masses of Lake Huron," in conjunction with Ontario Department of Lands and Forests and the University of Michigan.

Johnson, Robert C.—"Ballads of Disasters on the Great Lakes," *New York Folklore Quarterly,* Spring, 1949.

Kelly, S. J.—"Burning of the Steamer *Griffith,*" *Inland Seas,* Winter, 1959.

Knister, Raymond—"Long Point, Lake Erie."

Lake Carriers' Association—*Annual Report,* 1913.

Lange, Marion Cleaveland—A Letter in *Inland Seas,* Winter, 1960.

Law, Rev. W. H.—"Heroes of the Great Lakes," Detroit, 1906.

Lloyd's Steamboat Directory and Disasters on the Western Waters, Philadelphia, Pa., 1856.

Lyons, Bernard—"November, 1913: The Storm and the Story."

Mahar, Dr. John L.—"September 8, 1860—Milwaukee's Night to Remember," *New Life News,* Northwestern Mutual Life Insurance Company.

Mansfield, J. B.—"History of the Great Lakes," J. H. Beers and Company, Chicago, 1899.

Marine Review—July 16, 1903, October, 1911, March, 1914.

Melton, William—"Burning of the *Steamer Griffith,*" Painesville, Ohio, *Telegraph-Republic;* June 9, 1909. From "History of Willowick," Willowick Kiwanis Club.

Midland, Ontario, *Free Press Herald*—May 8, 1940; May 15, 1940.

Newton, Douglas—"Disaster, Disaster, Disaster," Franklin Watts, Inc., New York, N.Y.

Olin, Saul—"The History of Fairport."

Pearce, Bruce M.—"Historical Highlights of Norfolk County."

Portage County, Ohio, *Whig*—June 26, 1850.

Port Arthur, Ontario, *News-Chronicle*—May 2, 3, 4, 6, 1940.

Port Huron, Michigan, *Times Herald*—November 14, 15, 16, 17, 1913.

Pyle, Ernie—"Home Country," William Sloane Associates, Inc., New York, 1947.

Quaife, Milo M.—"Lake Michigan," Bobbs-Merrill, 1944.

Sarnia, Ontario, *Daily Observer*—November 14, 15, 16, 18, 1913.

Ship-Shore News—July, 1966.

Snider, C. H. J.—"Schooner Days," columns in the Toronto, Ontario, *Telegram*, 1948.

Stein, C. E.—"The Saga of Darius Nelson Malott," *Inland Seas,* Winter, 1969.

Stone, Irving—"Clarence Darrow for the Defense," Garden City Publishing Co., 1941.

Thompson, Capt. Merwin S.—"An Ancient Mariner Recollects."

Toledo, Ohio, *Blade*—June 18, 1946, September 4, 1966.

Toner, Ensign Raymond J.—"The Great Lakes Training Squadron," U.S. Naval Institute *Proceedings.*

Toronto, Ontario, *Globe*—November 15, 16, 17, 18, 19, 1913.

Toronto, Ontario, *Star*—November 15, 17, 18, 20, 1913.

Toronto, Ontario, *Telegram*—November 14, 15, 16, 1913.

U.S. Weather Bureau—*Monthly Weather Review,* November, 1913.

Western Reserve Historical Society—"Lake County (Ohio) History," 1941.

Wheeler, Mrs. Henry—"The Story of Abigail Becker," 1899.

Williams, W. R.—"The *Leafield* Was Unlucky," *Island Seas,* July, 1947.

——"The Midland Blast Furnace," *Inland Seas,* Winter, 1963.

Index